Micro Focus Personal COBOL™ 2.0
for DOS

Programmer's Guide

A Micro Focus Publication

MICRO FOCUS GROUP
Palo Alto/Newbury/Philadelphia/Tokyo/Munich/Paris/Barcelona

Part III   Reference

Table of Contents

Acknowledgements

This Personal COBOL Programmer's Guide contains material based on ANS X3.23-1985, the American National Standard for COBOL. That publication requests that documents using material from it should contain the following acknowledgment.

> COBOL is an industry language and is not the property of any company or group of companies, or of any organization or group of organizations.
>
> No warranty, expressed or implied, is made by any contributor or by the CODASYL Programming Language Committee as to the accuracy and functioning of the programming system and language. Moreover, no responsibility is assumed by any contributor, or by the committee, in connection therewith.
>
> The authors and copyright holders of the copyright material used herein:
>
>> FLOW-MATIC (trademark for Sperry Rand Corporation) Programming the Univac (R) I and II, Data Automation Systems copyrighted 1958, 1959, by Sperry Rand Corporation; IBM Commercial Translator Form No.F28-8013, copyrighted 1959 by IBM; FACT, DSI27A5260-2760, copyrighted 1960 by Minneapolis-Honeywell.
>
> have specifically authorized the use of this material in whole or in part in the COBOL specifications. Such authorization extends to the reproduction and use of COBOL specifications in programming manuals or similar publications.

Preface

Welcome to Personal COBOL

If you are new to COBOL, you are about to learn the most successful programming language of all time. COBOL has been the language of choice for business applications around the world for over 30 years. It has stood the test of time because it is based on sound principles and because it evolves to meet the changing needs of computing. When I learned COBOL 24 years ago, I never could have envisioned how it would evolve. The great thing has been that once I learned the basic principles of COBOL, I had a framework which made it easy to learn new COBOL features and indeed to learn new computing and data processing concepts. Amazingly, more than 95 percent of what I have learned is still of value to me today. Since I fully expect COBOL to be around for at least another 30 years, your investment in COBOL should be just as valuable for you.

COBOL stands for COmmon Business Oriented Language. This name is the key to its success and to understanding what COBOL is all about. So what do "Common", "Business Oriented", and "Language" tell us about COBOL?

COBOL is "Common" in the sense that it is common to all computers. In other words, a COBOL program that you write for one computer can later be run on a different make or model of computer. COBOL code is often a major company asset; worldwide the investment in COBOL programs is valued at trillions of dollars. Because of this, COBOL applications need to continue operating as new generations of computers and operating systems come into use. The code you write on your PC with Personal COBOL will run unchanged on other PC's and Unix machines, and on future machines which are undreamed of today.

COBOL is "Business Oriented" in the sense that it was designed specifically for business applications. Everyday components of office life such as files, customer records and balance sheets are represented in a natural form in COBOL. One example of this is the ability to draw a "Picture" of how you would like a number to appear on a report. For example, you can write:

```
Account-Balance, Picture is $9999.99-
```

to indicate that you want the value to appear as a dollar sign, four digits before the decimal point, and two digits after followed by a minus sign if necessary. All you have to do is move the number to "Account-Balance" and it will automatically be formatted with the decimal point and currency symbol appearing where indicated, and a minus sign appearing if the number is negative. Furthermore, any arithmetic is handled to the precision required by accountants. In addition to its Business Oriented features, COBOL is also a good general purpose language, and Micro Focus has added some extra features to make it a good systems programming language.

The word "Language" in the name of COBOL is appropriate because COBOL is a language rather than a code; it is in fact modeled on the English language. For example, you can write:

```
Multiply hours-worked by rate giving pay
```

This aspect of COBOL has the effect of making it more understandable (or "readable") than most programming languages. It does also mean you have to do more writing than in some programming languages, but the effort is repaid many times over when you or someone else looks at your program in the months and years ahead and tries to work out what it is doing. You might not expect your first programs to have a very long life but many COBOL programs remain in productive use for anywhere from 10 to 20 years.

Micro Focus has set out to build the best tools for developers of business applications. It is the world leader in providing COBOL development environments for DOS, Windows, OS/2 and Unix. Micro Focus has made COBOL programmers more productive by providing tools that are specially tailored to their needs. In fact, Micro Focus Animator was the world's first debugger to work at the source code level. Personal COBOL is a combination of those programmer productivity tools that are particularly well-suited to those who are learning COBOL and writing personal applications.

If you want an example of an application that can be written in COBOL on a PC for use on a PC you need look no further than Personal COBOL itself. The Compiler, Editor, Animator, Screens and Help System are all written in Micro Focus COBOL. These are examples of systems programming rather than typical business applications. They do, however, illustrate COBOL as a common and a readable language. The compiler was written originally in 1976. COBOL's "readability", assisted further by associated tools such as Animator, has permitted many developers over the years to understand, debug and enhance it. This allows it to remain a "living" application on the forefront of technology. The fact that COBOL is "Common" has been used to port the compiler to hundreds of different platforms ranging from 8-bit micros to mainframes.

You might want to start with something less ambitious. But whatever you choose as your first application, I wish you many enjoyable hours with Personal COBOL. Have fun.

John Triance
Group Vice President
Micro Focus

PART I

GETTING STARTED

Chapter 1

Introduction

With Personal COBOL, you have the best software tool available for learning COBOL programming on PCs. You can also use Personal COBOL to develop personal or small business applications for IBM PCs or computers that are compatible with them.

You can develop and run COBOL programs on DOS (3.3 or later), in a Windows (3.0 or later) DOS window, or in an OS/2 (2.0 or later) DOS session.

This Book

This book is for all programmers using Personal COBOL, whether experienced COBOL programmers or beginners. It will enable you to become familiar with the structure and capabilities of Personal COBOL quickly. This book assumes you are familiar with the operating system you will be using.

The parts of this book are as follows:

Part 1. *Getting Started*

describes the Personal COBOL System and how to install it; introduces you to some of the technology used throughout the system; and guides you through a brief session using the software so that you will soon feel at home with it.

Part 2. *Tools*

describes in detail how to use each tool in the Personal COBOL System. The tools are described in the order in which we expect you will want to use them.

Part 3. *Reference*

covers the technical detail of specific aspects of programming with
Personal COBOL.

Glossary of Terms

Here is a brief review of what we mean by some of the technical
terms in this book.

ADIS	the module of the Personal COBOL System which provides advanced screen ACCEPT and DISPLAY facilities. Programming for ADIS is described in the *ADIS* chapter of this book.
Animator	Micro Focus' debugger for COBOL programs. Animator is fully described in the *Animator* chapter of this book.
ANSI	the American National Standards Institute. One of the standards defined by ANSI is for the COBOL language.
ANSI 85 COBOL	the dialect of the COBOL language defined by the ANSI standard; this dialect is also called ANS 85 COBOL or COBOL 85 in some references. The ANSI 85 standard is rapidly becoming the basis for commercial COBOL programming and COBOL education.
Checker	The Micro Focus COBOL compiler which translates COBOL source code to INT code (see below). The Checker is described in the *Checker* chapter of this book.
COBOL	the programming language most widely used in business applications. The term COBOL is sometimes used to describe the entire COBOL language and sometimes just a subset or "dialect" of the language such as ANSI 85 COBOL.

Introduction

INT code
short for 'intermediate code', a compact binary code which is produced by the Checker, and which can be executed by the Personal COBOL System. Micro Focus intermediate code files use the filename extension ".INT".

ISAM
an acronym for 'Indexed Sequential Access Method', the COBOL language which allows a simple program to use advanced file handling. The term ISAM is also sometimes used as the name of the Personal COBOL run-time module that handles creation and manipulation of indexed sequential files.

Micro Focus COBOL
the dialect of the COBOL language used in and supported by Micro Focus' products. It is based on and is a superset of ANSI 85 COBOL. Micro Focus COBOL is the most comprehensive implementation of the COBOL language available for any computer.

Personal COBOL
Micro Focus' integrated programming tool system for learning COBOL programming or developing personal or small business applications.

Pcobrun
the module of Personal COBOL which can be used from DOS to run a Personal COBOL program, after the program has been compiled with the Checker.

Run-time system
the part of Personal COBOL which executes the INT code produced by the Checker. Both Animator and Pcobrun use the run-time system.

Screens
Micro Focus' screen painter for rapid development of interactive screen handling. The Screens tool is described in the *Screens* chapter of this book.

Which Version of COBOL Does Personal COBOL Support?

The COBOL language in this system gives you powerful facilities over and above those usually found in COBOL. Notably, you can write programs to make full use of your personal computer's screen display, and you can access many operating system functions.

Personal COBOL accepts COBOL source programs conforming to both of the following standards and dialects:

■ ANSI 85

■ Micro Focus COBOL

How You Use the Personal COBOL System

Personal COBOL is provided as a set of integrated tools. When you start Personal COBOL you enter the Editor main menu. From here you can edit your source or go to other menus where you can invoke the other tools in the system. From any menu you can access the On-line Help System via the **F1=Help** key.

Chapter 3 guides you through a short Sample Session using the Editor and other tools so you can quickly learn the basic steps with Personal COBOL. The Editor and other tools are fully described in Part 2 of this book, and they are briefly introduced here.

Developing a program (in any language) usually involves repeated steps known as the edit-compile-debug cycle. In Personal COBOL this means that you start in the Editor, next you use the Checker, then you use Animator. Because the Personal COBOL tools are integrated, this development cycle is fast and easy. The order in which we discuss the tools here reflects the development cycle.

COBOL Editor

To create your Personal COBOL application, you write the source code using the COBOL Editor. This Editor is designed to make program creation as easy as possible. To use it, just type; you move the typing position using the arrow keys.

When you start the Editor, press **F1** to enter the On-line Help (see below) for the Editor. If you select "Getting Started" from the On-line Help index, this topic will guide you through the few essential functions you should learn to make effective use of the Editor. The Editor is documented in the *Editor* chapter of this book.

Checker

When you have created your program source code, you save it from the Editor (write it to disk as a source code file) and then start the Checker by selecting the check/animate menu from the Editor's COBOL menu.

The Checker checks that the syntax of your COBOL source program is valid, and compiles it to executable intermediate (INT) code. While compiling your program the Checker also produces information files needed by Animator.

The behavior of the Checker can be altered by using compiler directives. The Checker is documented in the *Checker* chapter and compiler directives are documented in the *Compiler Directives* chapter of this book.

The Checker displays error messages for any invalid COBOL it finds. When it finishes it returns to the Editor, passing back information on all errors so you can fix them easily.

Animator

Animator is a program testing and debugging tool. It shows your source code on the screen and allows you to step through your program or run it at a controlled speed. This makes debugging easy and fast. You can step through the execution of your program statement by statement, set breakpoints, query and change data items, enter extra COBOL statements to execute, and interact with your program in many other ways.

When you start Animator for the first time, press **F1** to enter the On-line Help for Animator. Select "Getting Started" from the index. The topic displayed will help you use Animator effectively. Animator is documented in the *Animator* chapter of this book.

When you have finished animating your program, Personal COBOL returns you to the Editor so you can make any changes required.

Screens

If you wish to have interactive screen displays in your program, you can switch from the Editor to the Screens screen-painter tool to create them. Screens helps you quickly and easily design a user interface for your program. Screens will also generate COBOL source code for your program, and can even generate a complete card-index program from your screen if you wish. Returning from Screens to the Editor will incorporate the generated code in your program. Screens is documented in the *Screens* chapter of this book.

On-line Help

The On-line Help System can be started by pressing **F1=Help** anywhere in the Personal COBOL System, and displays help information for whichever tool you are using. You should take a few minutes to familiarize yourself in using the On-line Help System to navigate around and display the help information available. The On-line Help System is documented in the *On-line Help* chapter of this book.

The help information in Personal COBOL details every function available to you in each tool, and will help you get started quickly. You can find specific information directly or via contents menus, and you can also browse through the information or follow cross-references as you wish.

On-line Reference

While you are using the Editor you can press **Alt+1** to read the On-line Reference. The On-line Reference is displayed by the On-line Help System and contains details of COBOL syntax, the Personal COBOL System Library Routines, and other technical information such as compiler directives, and error messages. The On-line Help System enables you to copy text from the Reference and use it in your program. Again, you should take time to see what is available.

Other Components of Personal COBOL

In addition to the tools used in the edit-compile-debug cycle described above, the Personal COBOL System provides many other useful facilities.

ADIS Screen and Keyboard Handler

The ADIS module provides the support for the enhanced full-screen ACCEPT/DISPLAY syntax available in Personal COBOL. If your program uses full-screen ACCEPT/DISPLAY syntax, such as Screen Section data, then the system will use the ADIS module to provide run-time support; ADIS is not used by a program which uses only ANSI ACCEPT/DISPLAY syntax. Programming with the enhanced ACCEPT/DISPLAY syntax is documented in the *ADIS* chapter of this book.

Library Routines

There are many routines built into the system that you can call from your program. They generally provide operations not available in the COBOL language itself. The *Library Routines* chapter of this book documents them and shows how you use them; they are used in a number of the sample programs.

Pcobrun

When your program has been compiled and is working correctly
you can run it from the DOS command line by entering:

```
pcobrun prog-name <parameters>
```

where prog-name is the name of your program, and <parameters>
are the parameters, if any, you wish to pass to your program.

Pcobrun will only run a program which has been compiled
(Checked) with no errors, and which is available as an
intermediate (INT) code file.

Sample Programs

These programs demonstrate features of the Personal COBOL
System, and uses of the COBOL language and the Library
Routines. The sample programs are supplied as source code files,
and must be compiled before they can be used. When reviewing
these programs we suggest that you use Animator.

The sample programs are listed and briefly described in the on-
disk file SAMPLES.LST in your Personal COBOL System
directory. You may distribute the sample programs as part of your
application provided that you properly acknowledge the
copyright of Micro Focus in the material.

Documentation

■ This *Programmer's Guide* introduces the system, describes
the tools in detail, and contains reference material on many
features of the system.

■ On-line Help on how to use each tool is available by
pressing **F1** from within the tool.

■ The On-line Reference is an on-screen quick reference guide
listing reference information such as Checker directives and
COBOL syntax. It is available from the Editor by pressing
Alt+1.

Chapter 2

Installing

This chapter describes the minimum hardware and software that
you need to run Personal COBOL, and leads you step by step
through installing the system.

Hardware and Software Needed

Personal COBOL runs on the following IBM personal computers
and on computers compatible with them:

- PC/XT

- PC/AT

- PC/XT-286

- PS/1 and PS/2 (all 80286, 80386 and 80486 models)

Your computer must have the following hardware:

- at least 640 kilobytes (640K) of memory, with at least 500K
  of free memory after loading any resident utilities.

- at least 3M of free space on a hard disk.

- a floppy disk drive for installing the system.

- a color or monochrome display with at least 25 lines.

And the following software:

■ DOS Version 3.3 or higher.

Installation

This chapter describes how to prepare for and run the installation program, Setup.

Before You Start

First make sure that your Personal COBOL system package is complete. On-disk document PCOBPAK.LST lists what you should have. Then we recommend that you make back-up copies of the issue disks, using the operating system commands DISKCOPY or COPY. See your operating system manual for details of these commands.

Using Setup

One of the issue disks is the installation disk containing Setup. This is indicated on the label.

Setup gives you step-by-step plain English instructions on the screen. It works out for itself many details about your computer system, such as what kind of disk you have and what operating system you have. This makes it very easy to use by simply following the menus. The steps we recommend are as follows.

1. Put the Setup disk in your floppy disk drive. Make this drive current. For example, if your floppy drive is a:, type:

    a:

and press **Enter**. (From now on in these manuals there will generally be no reminders to press **Enter** after typing something at the operating system prompt.)

2.   Invoke Setup by entering the command:

setup

3.   Read the introductory screen and press **Enter** to move on.

4.   The first time you install your Personal COBOL system, Setup asks you to register the license by entering your name. Type your name. The name you type will be displayed each time you use Personal COBOL and cannot later be changed. When you press **Enter**, Setup asks you to confirm your choice, and gives you the opportunity to correct it at this time if you wish. <u>Once your name has been recorded it is not possible to change it, so please take care to enter your name correctly.</u>

If you are reinstalling Personal COBOL, after having previously installed it, Setup will display your name as the licensed user. Press **Enter** to continue.

5.   You should read the Release Notes before continuing. Press **Enter** to display the Release Notes. Use the **cursor up/down, PgUp, PgDn, Home and End** keys to view all the information.

When you have finished reading, press **Escape** to return to Setup and press **Enter** to move on.

6.   Setup asks you to select which parts of Personal COBOL to install. The default is to install both the System files and the Sample and Tutorial files, or you may choose to install either the System only, or the Samples and Tutorials only. If you choose to install only part of Personal COBOL you can run Setup again later to install the other part.

We suggest you install the Personal COBOL System and the Samples and Tutorial files. Press **Enter** to accept the default, or use the **cursor up/down** keys to select your choice and then press **Enter**.

If you choose to install only the Sample and Tutorial files, the installation procedure continues at step 9.

7.   Setup now asks you for the directory to contain the Personal COBOL System. By default it will use C:\MFCOBOL. Change the default drive and name if you wish.

When you press **Enter,** Setup asks you to confirm your choice, and gives you the opportunity to change it if you wish.

8.   If you have other versions of Micro Focus COBOL installed, Setup will inform you and create a batch file PCOBENV.BAT. You run this batch file whenever you want to run Personal COBOL instead of the other version. The section below, *Using Personal COBOL When Another COBOL System is Installed*, gives more information on operating Personal COBOL with another COBOL system installed. On computers where there is no COBOL system already installed, the PCOBENV.BAT file will not be created.

If you chose to install only the Personal COBOL System and not the Sample and Tutorial files, the installation procedure continues at step 10.

9.   Setup now asks you for the directory to contain the Sample and Tutorial files. By default it will use C:\MFCOBOL\SAMPLES. Change the default drive and name if you wish.

When you press **Enter,** Setup asks you to confirm your choice, and gives you the opportunity to change it if you wish.

10. Setup now checks to ensure there is enough space on the selected drive. If not, you will be given the opportunity of selecting another drive.

If there is enough space, Setup installs the system. At times it displays information or questions and lets you reply before it continues.

Setup asks you to insert disks so that it can copy files onto the hard disk. Some files are supplied compressed ("zipped"), so the messages that Setup displays say it is "unzipping" these rather than copying them.

11.   If changes to the operating system files AUTOEXEC.BAT or
       CONFIG.SYS are needed, Setup asks if it should alter them.
       If you reply "**Y**" it first makes backups (which it leaves
       unchanged) of these files, and then adds and changes lines,
       setting such things as your PATH so that Personal COBOL
       can be loaded. It displays the values that it is setting. If you
       tell Setup not to make these changes, you must make a note
       of them and make them yourself later for Personal COBOL
       to work.

12.   Reboot your computer so that the changed start-up files will
       take effect. Your system is now installed.

Your Personal COBOL system is now ready for use.

Verifying the Installation

As a quick check that you have installed the system correctly,
enter the following at the operating system prompt:

    pcobol

If the system is working it displays the Personal COBOL banner.
Press **Enter** and the COBOL Editor screen and main menu appear.
(See the chapter, *Sample Session* for an example of these screen
displays.) If you have any problems, make the following checks in
the order shown:

1.   Use the operating system command SET to check the
       settings of your path and environment variables. Make sure
       that the following changes have been made to your start-up
       files AUTOEXEC.BAT and CONFIG.SYS, and that the
       machine has been rebooted since.

In AUTOEXEC.BAT:

■   The environment variables COBDIR and COBHNF are both
     set to point to the directory containing Personal COBOL.
     These are described in greater detail below in *Personal
     COBOL Environment Variables.*

■ The directory containing Personal COBOL is added at the start of your PATH.

In CONFIG.SYS:

■ The following parameters are set:

```
FILES=100
BUFFERS=10
```

unless they are already set to greater values.

2. Make sure all the required files are present in the COBOL system directory. File PCOBPAK.LST lists the files that should be there.

3. If you have added the Personal COBOL system directory to your path anywhere other than at the beginning, then check that no directory earlier on your path contains a .BAT, .CMD, .COM, or .EXE file with the name PCOBOL. If you find such a file you must move or delete it, or change the PATH command to put the Personal COBOL system directory earlier on the path.

Personal COBOL Environment Variables

Personal COBOL needs two environment variables to be set to point to the location of the Personal COBOL system files. Environment variables are described in your *DOS User Guide and Reference.*

The Personal COBOL installation process usually adds commands to your computer's AUTOEXEC.BAT file so that the necessary environment variables are set when the computer starts. Alternatively if the installation process found that a COBOL system was already installed, the AUTOEXEC.BAT file would not be changed but a new file called PCOBENV.BAT would be created to set the environment variables.

The environment variables used by Personal COBOL are COBDIR, which is used to find the system programs, and COBHNF, which is used to find the HELP (.HNF) files. Both of these should point to the directory where Personal COBOL is installed (usually C:\MFCOBOL).

If Personal COBOL is started without COBDIR being set, then the program cannot run and one of the following error texts is displayed:

■ Running from outside the Personal COBOL directory:

```
Application did not execute
one or more of the following
reasons may apply :
        tools library not found
        tools library did not contain MFCONFIG.GNT or
        INITAPP.GNT
        initial program not specified
        tag name in configuration file not recognized
        application library/program not found
```

```
Executable Parameters:
        configuration file   = PCOBOL.CFG
        tag prefix           = PCOBOL
        tools library        = $COBDIR\TOOLS.LBR
        application library  = PCOBOL.LBR
```

■ Running from inside the Personal COBOL directory:

```
PCOBOL error: 001
Unable to continue - please set COBDIR environment
variable
```

If you receive one of these errors, you need to set COBDIR (and probably also set COBHNF). If PCOBENV.BAT was created when you installed Personal COBOL, you should run that, otherwise you should type at the DOS prompt:

```
SET COBDIR=C:\MFCOBOL
SET COBHNF=C:\MFCOBOL
```

If you chose a different directory from C:\MFCOBOL when you installed Personal COBOL then use that directory in these commands instead. Make sure that there are no spaces before or after the 'equals' sign when you enter the commands.

More System Details

This covers some points to bear in mind when using the system.

Memory Considerations

On DOS you can only access 640K of memory, even if your machine has more. Some very large applications may need more memory. If when you are running an application you get error message 157, 173 or 198 it means you are short of either available memory or available file handles.

If you are short of memory try splitting your program into smaller parts using COBOL's CALL statement. If you are short of file handles, increase the setting of the FILES parameter in your CONFIG.SYS.

Using Personal COBOL When Another COBOL System is Installed

If your computer has a different Micro Focus COBOL system installed Setup will take special action. If your computer does not already have another COBOL system installed you do not need to read this section.

When SETUP installs Personal COBOL it examines the COBDIR environment variable to see if the system is set up to use another Micro Focus COBOL system. If Setup finds COBDIR to be set to a different directory from the one you have chosen for Personal COBOL, it assumes there is already another COBOL system installed. In this case Setup will create a special batch file which will set your computer's environment for Personal COBOL. The batch file is called PCOBENV.BAT, and Setup will notify you if it is created.

If Setup creates PCOBENV.BAT, the file will be in your Personal COBOL system directory (C:\MFCOBOL unless you choose a different directory). After turning on your computer you will need to run PCOBENV.BAT before starting Personal COBOL. When you want to use the other COBOL system on your computer after using Personal COBOL, you will first need to reboot to remove the environment settings made by PCOBENV.

Environment Variables

You can put components of the Personal COBOL system in different directories. To ensure that the system will operate, you must ensure that the following environment variables are correctly set.

COBDIR

tells Personal COBOL where to find the .DLE, .LBR and .CFG files. You must put the path of the directory containing the Personal COBOL system files in COBDIR.

For example, if the files of your Personal COBOL system are in C:\MFCOBOL you set COBDIR as follows:

```
set cobdir=c:\mfcobol
```

COBHNF

tells the COBOL system where to look for the On-line Help System files (.HNF) supplied with Personal COBOL.

COBCPY

tells the COBOL system where to look for COBOL COPY-files if they are not found in the same directory as the main source file.

TMP

tells the run-time system where to put paging files.

Chapter 3

Sample Session

This sample session will familiarize you with the components of Personal COBOL. Using the sample program TICTAC (a Tic-Tac-Toe game, also known as Noughts and Crosses), you will learn the basic steps to compile, animate and run a program.

You will also be shown how to use the On-line Help System to obtain help, the Editor for the creation of programs, and Screens to create interactive forms.

Note: The samples explained here assume you are working with a 25 line screen. If your screen displays more or less than 25 lines, your screen displays will differ from those presented here, and some of the instructions may differ. We recommend that you switch to a 25 line display when trying these samples and switch back when you have finished. You can use Personal COBOL with any number of lines on your screen.

Starting Personal COBOL

To start Personal COBOL, at the DOS command prompt type:

```
pcobol
```

and press **Enter**. The Welcome banner for Personal COBOL is displayed, as shown in Figure 3-1.

If the banner does not appear, refer to the chapter *Installing* to confirm that you have installed Personal COBOL correctly.

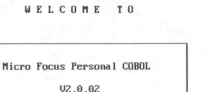

```
              W E L C O M E   T O


         ┌─────────────────────────────────┐
         │                                 │
         │   Micro Focus Personal COBOL    │
         │                                 │
         │            V2.0.02              │
         │                                 │
         └─────────────────────────────────┘



         Personal Programming System for COBOL

         Copyright (c) Micro Focus Ltd 1985-1993


              this copy licensed to

                 A. Programmer

            press any key to continue

                                    issued Jan 1 1993
```

Figure 3-1: Personal COBOL Banner

The banner will display the name which was entered when
Personal COBOL was installed. If this is not your name or the
name of your organization, you may be operating an illegal copy
of Personal COBOL. Please inform Micro Focus of this by
contacting Micro Focus Publishing at 1-800-551-5269 or in writing
at P.O. Box 52160, Palo Alto, California 94303, U.S.A.

Press **Enter** to clear the banner and start the Personal COBOL
Editor. The Editor main menu is displayed as shown in Figure 3-2.

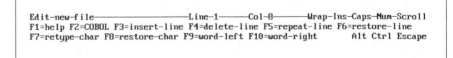

```
Edit-new-file─────────────────Line-1────Col-8──────Wrap-Ins-Caps-Num-Scroll
F1=help F2=COBOL F3=insert-line F4=delete-line F5=repeat-line F6=restore-line
F7=retype-char F8=restore-char F9=word-left F10=word-right      Alt Ctrl Escape
```

Figure 3-2 Editor Main Menu

From here you can edit your source files, or go to other menus to
use the other tools of the system.

In all tools, pressing **F1=Help** from any menu takes you into the
On-line Help System, and displays the appropriate help for the
tool you are using.

On-line Help System

On-line help is available from every menu simply by pressing **F1**. The On-line Help System enables you to view and navigate around the on-line help information.

The On-line Help System is also used from the Editor to view the On-line Reference, by pressing **Alt+1**. If the cursor is on a COBOL word when you press **Alt+1** then the topic of the On-line Reference displayed will give details of the syntax required by that word. To get the most from Personal COBOL, you should make full use of the On-line Reference.

1.   Press **F1=Help** to enter the On-line Help System

The help topic for the Editor main menu is displayed, as shown in Figure 3-3.

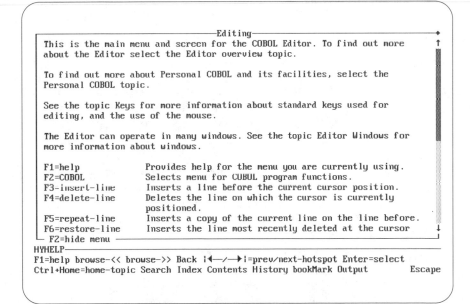

```
                              ─Editing─                                        ◆
  This is the main menu and screen for the COBOL Editor. To find out more     ↑
  about the Editor select the Editor overview topic.

  To find out more about Personal COBOL and its facilities, select the
  Personal COBOL topic.

  See the topic Keys for more information about standard keys used for
  editing, and the use of the mouse.

  The Editor can operate in many windows. See the topic Editor Windows for
  more information about windows.

  F1=help              Provides help for the menu you are currently using.
  F2=COBOL             Selects menu for COBOL program functions.
  F3-insert-line       Inserts a line before the current cursor position.
  F4=delete-line       Deletes the line on which the cursor is currently
                       positioned.
  F5=repeat-line       Inserts a copy of the current line on the line before.
  F6=restore-line      Inserts the line most recently deleted at the cursor   ↓
   ─ F2=hide menu ─
  HYHELP─
  F1=help browse-<< browse->> Back |◀─╱─▶|=prev/next-hotspot Enter=select
  Ctrl+Home=home-topic Search Index Contents History bookMark Output      Escape
```

Figure 3-3: Help Topic

The topic is displayed in a window. As in this case, a topic may contain more information than can be seen in the window at one time. If it does, the right hand border of the window contains a scroll bar with up and down arrows at each end and a slider.

The size of the slider indicates the size of the window relative to the size of the topic.

To see the extra information you scroll (move up or down one line at a time) or page (move up or down by the height of the window) the topic text. Try this now. (If your screen is set up to display more than 25 lines, there may be room to display the whole topic. In this case no scroll bar is displayed, and you will not be able to try the following actions.)

2. To scroll the text, press the **up/down cursor** keys or, if you have a mouse, place the mouse cursor on the up or down arrow in the scroll-bar and click.

3. To page the text use the **PgUp** and **PgDn** keys, or click in the dark background of the scroll bar. Click below the slider to page down and above the slider to page up.

Whether scrolling or paging, the slider moves to indicate the position of the text in the window relative to the rest of the topic.

4. Press the **Home** key to take you back to the start of the topic, and the **End** key to take you to the end of the topic.

Many topics contain "hotspots" which contain hypertext links to other topics. Hotspots are usually colored in a particular way, so you can see where they are. They are also highlighted in turn when you press the **Tab** or **Backtab** keys.

5. To see the hotspots in this topic press the **Tab** key and watch the highlighting cycle from one hotspot to the next. Press **Backtab** to cycle through the hotspots backwards.

Notice that the topic automatically scrolls or pages to ensure that the hotspot to be highlighted appears in the window.

To jump to the topic linked to the hotspot, you either select it using the **Tab/Backtab** keys, and press **Enter**, or place the mouse-cursor on the hotspot and double-click the left mouse-button.

6. Press **Tab** until the hotspot "Personal COBOL" is highlighted. Press **Enter.** (If you have a mouse, scroll the topic until the hotspot become visible, place the mouse cursor on it and double-click the left mouse-button.)

The selected topic appears.

7.   To return to the previously displayed topic, press **B** for **B**ack.

The previous topic appears. You can use the back function at any time to return to the previously displayed topic.

The Personal COBOL topic selected above gives you access to information about each of the components of Personal COBOL, as well as a number of additional topics about using Personal COBOL. To learn a bit more about Personal COBOL you should make time to go back to this topic and browse the information available.

Every file contains a contents list and an index.

8.   To view the contents press **C** for **C**ontents.

A listbox is displayed containing a list of the topics in the file. When there are more entries than the listbox can show, the right-hand border of the listbox contains a scroll-bar, just as for the window. To see more entries, scroll or page the information in the same way as you scroll and page the information in a window, only use the scroll-bar in the listbox border rather than the one in the window border

You select a topic by moving the scroll bar to the name of the topic using the **cursor-up/down** keys or the mouse and then pressing **Enter.** Alternatively, use the mouse and double-click on the required name.

9.   To view the index, press **Escape** to leave the contents listbox if necessary, and press **I** for **I**ndex.

A listbox is displayed containing a list of index entries for the file. You move around the list using the scroll-bar or cursor keys as described above. With the index, you can also position at the start of any letter by pressing the required letter key.

10.   Press **M.**

The index is positioned so that the first entry starting with the letter M is at the top of the listbox as shown in Figure 3-4.

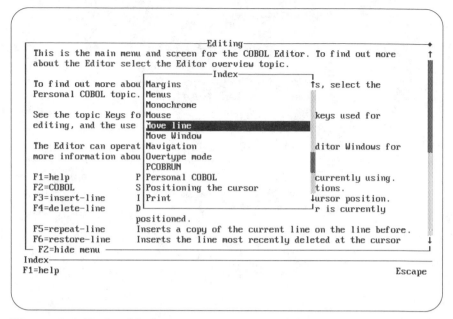

Figure 3-4: Index Listbox

11.   Use the **cursor-down** key to move the selection-bar to the
      index entry "Move line" and then press **Enter**. Alternatively,
      move the mouse cursor to the entry "Move line" and
      double-click the left mouse-button.

The topic associated with the index entry is displayed.

You can create your own index of topics using the Bookmark
facility.

12.   To add the currently displayed topic to your bookmarks,
      press **M** for book**M**ark then press **A** for **A**dd.

You are given the option to enter a new name for the bookmark,
or to use the name of the topic. We will enter a new name.

13.   Press the **Del** key repeatedly to clear the name from the
      entry-field. Type in the name **"Handling lines"** and press
      Enter.

The bookmark listbox disappears, but the name has been entered
in it.

14.   Press **Ctrl+Home** to get to the home topic for this file. Press

M for book**M**ark again.

The bookmark listbox is redisplayed, and it now contains your entry. As you add names they are placed in the list in alphabetical order. You can display the topic associated with a name by selecting it in the usual way. From this menu, you can also rename or delete any entry. The bookmarks list is permanent, and all entries are available to you in future Personal COBOL sessions.

15.   Select the entry "Handling lines" and press **Enter.**

The topic you associated with this name is now displayed.

Each time you view a topic its name is placed at the top of the History list. The History list is a chain of the topics you have viewed, held in reverse order to the order you viewed them. Pressing the **Back** key at any time takes you back to the previously displayed topic. Successive presses takes you back through the topics in the History list.

Finally, if you get lost, press **Ctrl+Home** to take you to the home topic of the current file.

16.   Press **H** for **H**istory to display the History list.

The History list is displayed in a listbox, and you can select any topic in the usual way.

17.   From the History listbox, press **Escape** twice to leave the On-line Help System and return to the Editor main menu.

Editing TICTAC

To create your own applications you first need to create your COBOL source code. Use the COBOL Editor for this purpose. For this example, we will process the source of a sample program.

When invoked, Personal COBOL brings up the Editor main menu and an editing window, as shown in Figure 3-5.

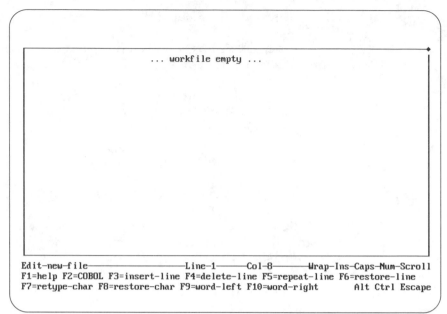

```
                         ... workfile empty ...



















Edit-new-file─────────────────Line-1─────Col-8────────Wrap-Ins-Caps-Num-Scroll
F1=help F2=COBOL F3=insert-line F4=delete-line F5=repeat-line F6=restore-line
F7=retype-char F8=restore-char F9=word-left F10=word-right         Alt Ctrl Escape
```

Figure 3-5: COBOL Editor Main Menu and Editing Window

The Edit main menu appears at the bottom of the screen. It displays an information line containing the file-name (at present "new file") and Line, Column, Wrap, Ins, Caps, Num and Scroll indicators. The next two lines contain the function key options you use to edit the file.

If you were creating a new program you would type it now. However, the source of TICTAC is supplied on disk for you. You simply need to load it into the COBOL Editor. *Accessible from the main menu are two more menus - the Control (Ctrl) menu and the Alternate (Alt) menu - which you get to by holding down the **Ctrl** and **Alt** keys respectively.*

1.   Hold down the **Alt** key now. The Alternate menu appears as shown in Figure 3-6. Press **F3=load file.** You can then let go of the **Alt** key.

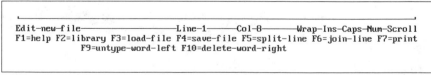

```
Edit-new-file─────────────────Line-1─────Col-8────────Wrap-Ins-Caps-Num-Scroll
F1=help F2=library F3=load-file F4=save-file F5=split-line F6=join-line F7=print
            F9=untype-word-left F10=delete-word-right
```

Figure 3-6: The Editor Alt Menu

The Load File menu appears. It includes a line on which to type the name of the file to load. The path (drive and directory) you are in is already displayed on this line.

2. If you are not in the directory where TICTAC is installed, you must replace the path shown with the path which contains TICTAC.CBL.

    If you installed the Sample and Tutorial programs during Setup then TICTAC is in the sample and tutorial directory, which defaults to C:\MFCOBOL\SAMPLES. If you did not install the Sample and Tutorials then TICTAC will be in the Personal COBOL system directory, which defaults to C:\MFCOBOL.

    Press **Home** and the **Space-Bar** until the name of the path is cleared. Now type the path and name of TICTAC, for example `c:\mfcobol\samples\tictac` and press **Enter.**

The source code is displayed with the cursor positioned under the first statement on line 1. The main menu returns.

Since TICTAC is a complete working program, there is no need to edit it. However, you can look at the program using the cursor keys and the **PgUp/PgDn** keys to scroll and page through it.

To find out more about getting started with the Editor:

3. press **Fl=Help** from the main menu.

This will place you in the On-line Help for the Editor.

4. Press **I** to bring up the index, then **G** to position on the first entry starting with "G", and select "Getting Started". (Refer to *On-line Help System* earlier in this chapter to learn how to access the help topics.)

The On-line Help contains information about how to use the Editor. Browse through this at your leisure.

5. Press **Escape** to return to the Editor.

On-line Reference

The On-line Reference contains information about the COBOL language and the Personal COBOL system. You enter the On-line Reference from the Editor.

1.　Return to the Editor main menu. Follow the instructions in the section *Editing TICTAC* to load TICTAC.CBL.

You can enter the On-line Reference at the main contents, or go straight to the information you require. For example, entering the On-line Reference using the name of any COBOL verb shows the syntax of that verb. Entering using the name "CBL " shows a full list of the COBOL System Library Routines available.

2.　Press **Ctrl+Home** to move to the start of TICTAC. Place the cursor on the first line of asterisks and press **Alt+l**.

The table of contents for the On-line Reference is displayed.

3.　Spend some time investigating the contents of the On-line Reference by using the hotspots. You can return to the main contents topic at any time by selecting the Contents hotspot at the top of every topic.

4.　Press **Escape** to return to the Editor.

 If you place the cursor on a word and enter the On-line Reference, the On-line Help System looks for a topic matching the name and, if found, displays it. If it cannot find a topic it displays the main contents.

5.　Type **CBL_OR** (delimited by spaces), position cursor under **CBL_OR,** and press **Alt+l**.

The topic for the CBL_OR routine is displayed. It is often useful to take the information from the On-line Reference and paste it into your program.

6.　Press **Output**.

The Output menu appears and a cursor is placed on the first line. You position the cursor on the first line of the area you wish to paste using the **cursor up/down** keys or the **PgUp** and **PgDn** keys.

7.   Press the **cursor-down** key to move the cursor to the line headed "Syntax".

8.   Press **M** for **Mark-on** key to switch marking on, and press the **cursor-down** key twice to mark the lines to paste.

9.   Press **C** for **Copy-to-file** key to copy these lines to the paste file.

10. Press **Escape** twice to return to the Editor, and press **F2=COBOL, F3=cmd-file** and **F2=insert-paste-text**.

The selected lines are inserted preceding the current line. They can now be edited as required.

Checking TICTAC

You check the sample program by invoking the Checker from the COBOL Editor's menus.

Ensure you are in the COBOL Editor at the main menu.

1.   If you have a copy of TICTAC loaded, to ensure that you are using an unchanged version, press **Ctrl+F4=clear**, and answer **Y** if you are asked if you are sure.

2.   Load TICTAC by pressing **Alt+F3=load**, ensuring TICTAC is entered as the filename and pressing **Enter**.

3.   Press **F2=COBOL**.

The COBOL menu appears.

4.   Press **F2=check/animate**.

The Checker menu appears.

5.   Press **F2=check/anim** until the word "Check" appears on the information line.

With this key you select whether you will check or animate your program. A word on the information line changes each time you press **F2.**

6.   Press **Enter.**

The COBOL Editor screen disappears and you see the source listing scrolling rapidly up the screen. The Checker is checking the program for syntax errors and producing intermediate code. It outputs this code in a file with extension .INT. When the check has finished you are returned to the Editor main menu.

Animating TICTAC

Now use Animator to watch the source code executing.

Ensure you are in the COBOL Editor at the main menu, with TICTAC loaded, as described in the section *Editing TICTAC* earlier in this chapter.

1.   Press **F2=COBOL.**

The COBOL menu appears.

2.   Press **F2=check/animate.**

The Checker menu appears.

3.   Press **F2=check/anim** until the word "Animate" appears on the information line.

With this key you select whether you will check or animate your program. A word on the information line changes each time you press **F2.**

4.   Press **Enter.**

The Animator starts and displays the screen shown in Figure 3-7.

```
89 play-game section.
90 play-1.
91     perform with test after
92         until char not = "Y" and char not = "y"
93         display spaces upon crt
94         display
95             "To select a square type a number between 1 and 9"
96             upon crt
97         perform init
98         move "Shall I start ? " to question
99         perform get-reply
100        if char = "Y" or char = "y"
101            move 10 to check(5)
102            perform put-move
103        end-if
104        perform new-move until game not = spaces
105        move "Play again ?     " to question
106        perform get-reply
107    end-perform.
108
109 play-stop.
Animate-TICTAC————————————————Level=01-Speed=5-Ins-Caps-Num-Scroll
F1=help F2=view F3=align F4=exchange F5=where F6=look-up  F9/F10=word-</> Escape
Step Go Zoom next-If Perform Reset Break Env Query Find Locate Text Do 0-9=speed
```

Figure 3-7: The Animate Main Menu

The source code is displayed with the cursor positioned under the first executable statement on line 91:

```
perform with test after
```

The Animate main menu appears at the bottom of the screen. It displays an information line containing the program name TICTAC and level, speed, Ins, Caps, Num and Scroll indicators. The next two lines contain the function and letter key options you use to control the way the program is animated.

To find out more about getting started with Animator:

5.   Press **Fl=Help** from the main menu.

This will place you in the on-line help for the Animator.

6.   Press **I** to bring up the index, then **G** to position on the first entry starting with "G", and select "Getting Started". (Refer to *On-line Information System* earlier in this chapter to learn how to access the help topics.)

The on-line help contains information about how to use the Animator. Browse through this at your leisure.

7.   Press **Escape** to return to Animator.

Controlling the Speed

You can execute your program in one of three modes: Step, Go and Zoom. When you execute your program in Step mode, you manually control the execution of each statement. In Go mode, you initially set the speed of execution, then watch as each statement is automatically executed. Zoom mode executes the entire program without displaying the source code until it reaches the end of the program (you can interrupt it, or set a breakpoint where it will stop). These modes of execution are described in the following sections.

Stepping Through the Program

1.   The first letter command on the Animate menu is Step. Press **S** to begin stepping through your program.

The cursor is now positioned under the next executable statement:

```
display spaces upon crt
```

2.   Press **Step** again twice.

This positions the cursor on the DISPLAY statement and then executes the statement, causing a brief display of the user screen in its current state. (The user screen briefly appears each time you execute a DISPLAY statement.) The cursor then moves to the beginning of the statement:

```
perform init
```

on line 97.

3.   Now press **F2=view**.

The user screen appears with the display of the executed DISPLAY statement:

To select a square type a number between 1 and 9

You use the view facility to view the user screen at any time during animation.

4.   Press any key to return to the Animator screen.

5.   Now execute the next three statements in the program by pressing **Step** three times. Each time you press **Step** another statement is executed, and you can see what is actually happening in the program.

Executing in Go Mode

In Go mode, your program is automatically executed at the speed you select, and you can watch exactly what is happening in the program.

6.   To start Go mode, press **G.**

The Go menu as shown in Figure 3-8 appears at the bottom of the screen as execution begins.

```
Go-TICTAC─────────────────────────────Level=01-Speed=0-Ins-Caps-Num-Scroll
F1=help F2=view F3=align F4=exchange                                 Escape
0-9=speed Zoom
```

Figure 3-8: The Go Menu

The program is currently executing at a speed of 5, the default setting.

7.   Press **7** to increase the speed.

This change in speed is displayed on the information line.

You can set execution speed from either the Animate main menu or the Go menu. The range of speeds is from 0 to 9, with 0 the slowest speed. You can change this speed at any time during execution by pressing a key between 0 and 9.

Program execution halts when an ACCEPT statement is encountered. The system now pauses on the user screen after executing the ACCEPT statement on line 114 anticipating data entry.

8.   Respond by typing **N** (indicating that you will be the first to start the game).

The system continues animation in Go mode at a speed of 7 and pauses after the next ACCEPT, displaying the user screen and prompting again for data entry.

9.   Select square 9 by pressing **9** on your keyboard.

This places an X in square 9 and resumes program execution in Go mode.

Remember, you can press **F2=view** at any time to see the user program's screen.

Execution stops again when you are prompted to select another square. Notice that the system has placed a 0 in square 5.

10.   Press **8** to select the square and to resume execution.

11.   Now temporarily halt execution to change to Zoom mode. Press **Escape** while the source code is visible.

The message:

```
Keyboard interrupt
```

appears at the bottom of the screen. The cursor is positioned on the next executable statement.

Executing in Zoom Mode

12.   Now press **Z** to begin execution in Zoom mode.
The program resumes execution at full speed and displays only the user screen. Continue playing until the game is complete.

13.   When the message:

```
Play again?
```

appears, respond by typing **N** (**No**).

The source code returns to the screen with the cursor positioned under STOP RUN, indicating that the program has completed execution. The message:

```
STOP RUN encountered with RETURN-CODE- =  +00000: use
Escape to terminate
```

appears at the bottom of the screen.

Exiting Animator

14.   Press **Escape** to terminate your Animator session.

The message:

```
Exit from animator? Y/N
```

appears at the bottom of the screen. Press **Y** (**Yes**) to return to the Editor. The Editor screen with the source and the main menu are displayed.

Examining Data Items Using Animator

In the Animator you can monitor and change the contents of data items. You can view the contents in hexadecimal or ASCII, as well as create lists of data values for future use.

You will now see how to monitor and change the contents of a data item in TICTAC.

1.   First, invoke Animator again by pressing **F2** twice to get to the Checker menu, pressing **F2** again several times until the word on the information line becomes "Animate", and then pressing **Enter.**

2.   After the Animator screen appears, press **S** to step through

the program until you reach line 97:

```
perform init
```

3.   Use the **cursor-left, cursor-right** and **cursor-up** keys to
     position the cursor anywhere under the data-name CHAR
     on line 92.

4.   Press **Q** (Query) on the Animate menu. The Query menu
     appears, as shown in Figure 3-9.

```
Query-data────────────────────────────Level=01-Speed=5-Ins-Caps-Num-Scroll
F1=help F2=view F3=align F4=exchange F5=where F6=look-up  F9/F10=word-</> Escape
Cursor-name Enter-name Repeat Monitor-off Dump list
```

Figure 3-9: The Query Menu

5.   Now press **C** (Cursor-name). The submenu shown in
     Figure 3-10 appears.

```
Query:    CHAR────────────────────────Level=01-Speed=5-Ins-Caps-Num-Scroll
F1=help F2=clear F3=hex  F4=monitor                       ↑ ↓ =up/down data
F7=containing F8=contained F9=same level                  ↵    Alt  Ctrl  Escape
  ]
```

Figure 3-10: The Query Cursor-name Menu

The data-name CHAR appears on the information line; the current
value of CHAR appears at the bottom of the screen. At the mo-
ment CHAR contains spaces.

6.   Press **F4** (Monitor) on this menu to cause the value of CHAR
     to be displayed constantly in this field during execution. The
     Animate menu returns to the screen.

7.   Press **Step** to step to the next executable statement. The
     cursor is now positioned on line 120:

```
move 'y' to char.
```

8.   Press **Step** again.

Notice that the current value field at the bottom of the screen now displays "y". The value of CHAR has been changed by the execution of the previous statement.

Notice that the word Monitor appears in place of Animate on the menu. This tells you that the data item CHAR is being monitored throughout the execution of the program.

9.   Now press **Step** until the user screen is displayed, prompting you to respond to "Shall I start?"

10.   Type **N** (**N**o).

When the Animator screen returns, notice that the previous value "y" of the current field has been replaced by "n". Once again, the value of CHAR has changed.

11.   To turn monitoring off, press **Query** from the Animate menu to invoke the Query menu and press **M** (**M**onitor-off).

The data field at the bottom of the screen disappears.

Running TICTAC

Having created your application, and debugged it using Animator, you subsequently run it from the operating system command line using PCOBRUN.

1.   Leave Personal COBOL by pressing **Escape** and answering any "are you sure" prompts with **Y**.

2.   Type at the command line:

```
pcobrun c:\mfcobol\samples\tictac
```

and press **Enter**. If TICTAC is installed in a directory other than c:\mfcobol\samples, type the name of that directory in the above instead of c:\mfcobol\samples. If you are in the same directory as TICTAC you can omit the path.

The system runs the program, which starts off by displaying the first message of the game on your screen. Have fun playing it; it can be beaten!

Using Screens

If you wish to display forms from your program in which you can present information or input information, then use Screens. Screens enables you to design forms easily and quickly, and then automatically generates COBOL source code to use in your program.

From the Editor main menu, if you have a program loaded remove it using **Ctrl+F4=clear**. Otherwise the program generated by Screens will be added to it rather than replacing it.

1. Press **Ctrl+F6=draw/scrns,** then press **F7=screens** to start Screens.

This brings up a blank work area and the Screens main menu as shown in Figure 3-11:

```
New form——————Attribute——————————————Row:01-Col:01-Ins-Caps-Num-Scroll
F1=help F2=mark/unmark F3=field F4=group F5=paint-attribute F6=attribute-roll
F7=cut-to-block F8=copy-to-block F9=restore-block F10=field-order Alt Ctl Escape
```

Figure 3-11: Screens Main Menu

The Screens sample session is a step-by-step guide to some of the features of the Screens facility. It will show you how to:

- design the sample form
- alter attributes
- define fields
- define groups
- define and manipulate a block of text
- define an input field acceptance order
- generate COBOL for the sample form

Designing the Sample Form

Having invoked Screens, use text characters and the cursor movement keys to create on your screen a form similar to that shown in Figure 3-12.

```
name:                              tel:
address:




                    WARNING
                    MESSAGE




————————————Attribute————————————Row:01-Col:01-Ins-Caps-Num-Scroll
F1=help F2=mark/unmark F3=field F4=group F5=paint-attribute F6=attribute-roll
F7=cut-to-block F8=copy-to-block F9=restore-block F10=field-order Alt Ctl Escape
```

Figure 3 -12: Sample Form

Altering the Current Attribute

We will now change the attribute of the message.

1.   Position the cursor under the W in WARNING MESSAGE.

2.   Press **F6=attribute-roll** repeatedly to roll through the available attributes. Notice how the word "Attribute" changes on the information line.

3.   Select the desired attribute and press **F5=paint-attribute.** This assigns the desired attribute to the character at the cursor position and moves the cursor one character to the right.

4.   Continue to press **F5** until WARNING is displayed with the new attribute setting. Move the cursor to the M of MESSAGE and press **F5** until this is displayed with the new attribute setting.

You can set the attributes for "Name:", "Tel No:", "Address:" and any other part of the screen by following the steps outlined above.

Defining Fields

1.   Position the cursor at the first character position after "Name:".

2.   Enter carets (^) to begin defining the Name field. Notice that the carets (^) that you are entering are displayed in the current attribute setting. This screen now appears as shown in Figure 3-13.

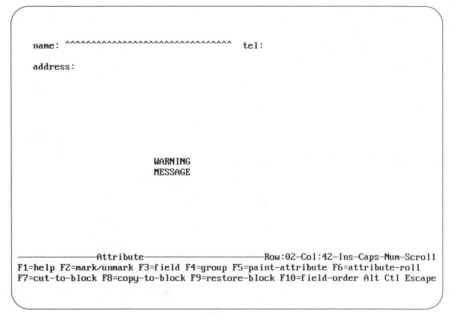

```
    name:  ^^^^^^^^^^^^^^^^^^^^^^^^^^^^^^^^^^   tel:

    address:




                          WARNING
                          MESSAGE




 ────────────Attribute────────────────Row:02-Col:42-Ins-Caps-Num-Scroll
 F1=help F2=mark/unmark F3=field F4=group F5=paint-attribute F6=attribute-roll
 F7=cut-to-block F8=copy-to-block F9=restore-block F10=field-order Alt Ctl Escape
```

Figure 3-13: Defining a Field

3.   Position the cursor in the carets.

4.   Press **F3=field** to define the carets as a field.

The carets are replaced by a COBOL picture string (X's), and a pop-up menu of Screen Section clauses appears. The word "Field" appears on the information line, as shown in Figure 3-14.

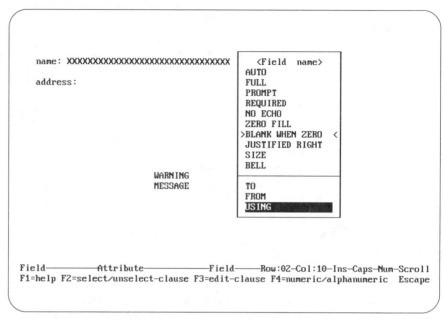

Figure 3-14: Form with Screen Section Clauses

We will use the AUTO clause as an example of how to select Screen Section clauses to be included in your program. The AUTO clause automatically terminates an ACCEPT when the last character position is filled, with no explicit terminator key being required. Screen section clauses are documented in the *Screen Section Reference* chapter.

Note: You can select more than one Screen Section clause to be included in your program. Some require additional input (for example, a COBOL identifier for the TO clause). You can also assign a Screen Section name to the current field by selecting <fieldname> in the pop-up.

5. Use the ↑ key to move the pointer (">" and "<") to the AUTO clause in the pop-up menu.

6. Select the AUTO clause by pressing **F2**.

7. Use the ↓ key to move the pointer to the USING clause.

8.   Press **F3=edit-clause** to edit the USING clause.

9.   Enter **ORD-NAME** as the name of this field and press **Enter.** *This name is used as a data-name in your COBOL program, so it must not be a COBOL reserved word.*

10.   Now press **Escape** to return to the main menu. The selection of the AUTO clause is saved. The COBOL picture string is replaced by carets.

11.   Now define the "Tel No:" field following the steps outlined above. Give it the name **TEL-NO**. Note that you might want to define it with numeric characters. This option **(F4=numeric/alphanumeric)** is available on the Field menu. You can also define any legal COBOL picture string.

Defining Groups

We will now define the "Address:" field as a group. Note that before you can define groups, you must define all fields that are to be repeated; there must be at least one.

1.   Define the Address field immediately after "Address:" by following the steps outlined in section *Defining Fields* above. Give it the name **ORD-ADDRESS.**

2.   Now position the cursor at the first caret in the "Address" field.

3.   Press **F2=mark/unmark** to activate the mark option. A reverse video attribute is painted over the character at the cursor position.

4.   Use the $\longrightarrow$ key to move the cursor to the right so that it expands the marked area to cover the entire "Address:" field.

5.   Press **F4=group** to define the marked area as a group and invoke the Group menu, as shown in Figure 3-15.

```
┌─────────────────────────────────────────────────────────────────┐
│                                                                   │
│   name: ^^^^^^^^^^^^^^^^^^^^^^^^^^^^^^^^^^^   tel: ^^^^^^^^^^^^     │
│                                                                   │
│   address: ^^^^^^^^^^^^^^^^^^^^^^^^^^^^^^^^^^^^^^^^^^^^^^^^^^^^     │
│                                                                   │
│                                                                   │
│                                                                   │
│                           WARNING                                 │
│                           MESSAGE                                 │
│                                                                   │
│                                                                   │
│                                                                   │
│                                                                   │
│   Group──────────Attribute-ORD-ADDRES  Group──────Row:04-Col:60-Ins-Caps-Num-Scroll │
│   F1=help F2=assign-properties F3=repeat-horizontally F4=repeat-vertically │
│   F5=delete-horizontally F6=delete-vertically                Escape │
│                                                                   │
└─────────────────────────────────────────────────────────────────┘
```

Figure 3-15: Form with the Group Menu

6. Press **F4=repeat-vertically** four times to vertically repeat the defined area to a total of five lines.

7. Press **Escape** to fix the group definition and return to the main menu. This removes the highlighting and restores the field to its original attribute setting.

Defining and Manipulating Blocks of Text and Data

We will now move the highlighted WARNING MESSAGE to a new position.

1. Position the cursor on the W in WARNING MESSAGE.

2. Press **F2=mark/unmark** to set the mark option. A reversed video attribute is painted over the character under the cursor.

3. Use the ⟶ and ↓ keys to expand the marked area to cover all of the characters.

4. Press **F7=cut-to-block**.

The marked area is now separated from the rest of the form although its appearance does not change. The Block menu appears on the screen, as shown in Figure 3-16.

```
name:  ^^^^^^^^^^^^^^^^^^^^^^^^^^^^^^^^^^   tel:  ^^^^^^^^^^^^
address:  ^^^^^^^^^^^^^^^^^^^^^^^^^^^^^^^^^^^^^^^^^^^^^^^^^^^^^^
          ^^^^^^^^^^^^^^^^^^^^^^^^^^^^^^^^^^^^^^^^^^^^^^^^^^^^^^
          ^^^^^^^^^^^^^^^^^^^^^^^^^^^^^^^^^^^^^^^^^^^^^^^^^^^^^^
          ^^^^^^^^^^^^^^^^^^^^^^^^^^^^^^^^^^^^^^^^^^^^^^^^^^^^^^
          ^^^^^^^^^^^^^^^^^^^^^^^^^^^^^^^^^^^^^^^^^^^^^^^^^^^^^^



                        WARNING
                        MESSAGE






Block————————Attribute———————————————Row:13-Col:27-Ins-Caps-Num-Scroll
F1=help F2=paste-block F3=copy-from-block F4=store-block
cursor-keys=move-block                                        Escape
```

Figure 3-16: Form with the Block Menu

5. Use the cursor keys to move the block to a new position.

6. When you are satisfied, press **F2=paste-block** to paste the block to its current position. The highlighting disappears and you are returned to the main menu.

Altering the Input Field Acceptance Order

If more than one input field exists on a form, you can define the order of field input when the form is ACCEPTed. To demonstrate this, we will enter the fields in the following order: Name, Address, Tel No.

1. Press **F10=field-order** to set the field input order. The three defined fields display 5's by default.

2. Position the cursor on one of the 5's following the word "Name".

3. Press **4**. This field now displays 4's and will be accepted before the other two fields at run time.

4. Now position the cursor on one of the 5's following the word "Tel No".

5. Press **6**. The "Tel No:" field displays 6's and will be the last field accepted at run time.

6. Now press **F10** again to turn off the field-order option. The order is saved.

Saving the Form

You must now save your form so you can use it again.

1. Press **Alt+F4=save** from the main menu.

The file-name prompt appears.

2. Type the file-name **MYFORM**.

The file will be saved as MYFORM.SRN. The extension .SRN is assigned by the system as the default file extension for a form created with the Screens facility.

3. Press **Enter** to save the form. The system once again returns you to the main menu.

4. When you use Screens at a later stage you can reload this form using **Alt+F3=load**.

Generating COBOL

You can now generate COBOL code for the form you have just created. (Ensure that you have saved the form before proceeding.)

1.   Hold down the **Alt** key while you press
     F5=generate-COBOL.

If you receive the message:

```
Generate without saving? Y/N
```

answer **N** and save the form as described in the above section
Saving the Form. Then repeat Step 1.

The file-name prompt appears at which you enter the name of the
COBOL file you wish to generate. The name MYFORM.SS will
already be shown. (If it is not you should press **Escape** and follow
the instructions in the above section *Saving the Form.*)

2.   Press **Enter**. The Generate COBOL menu appears.

3.   Press **F3=skeleton-program** from this menu. This generates
     the COBOL code to display and accept the screen form you
     have just created.

The code is generated as a skeleton program, that is, as only the
screen section code plus the COBOL statements essential to be
able to compile the program. The screen section code is generated
as a separate "COPY" file, and is included in the program by the
COPY statement.

After the program is generated, you are returned to the Editor
main menu with the skeleton program loaded.

4.   Save the skeleton program by using **Alt+F4=save** before
     continuing. Use the default name supplied MYFORM.CBL.

The skeleton program code in MYFORM.CBL reads as follows
(the directory name may differ if you were in a different
directory):

```
IDENTIFICATION DIVISION.
DATA DIVISION.
WORKING-STORAGE SECTION.
COPY "C:\MFCOBOL\SAMPLES\MYFORM.wks".
SCREEN SECTION.
COPY "C:\MFCOBOL\SAMPLES\MYFORM.ss".
```

```
PROCEDURE DIVISION.
    DISPLAY G-MYFORM.
    ACCEPT G-MYFORM.
    STOP RUN.
```

As you see, Screens has generated a skeleton program with very little code. The program contains a DISPLAY statement and an ACCEPT statement, and two COPY statements. The COPY statements include into the program two other files which Screens generated: a file for the working-storage called MYFORM.WKS, and a file for the screen section called MYFORM.SS.

You can edit either of the copy files by putting the cursor on the line containing the COPY statement and pressing **Alt+F2=library**. If you do so, you can return to editing the main program by pressing **Escape.**

You can now compile and animate your program, in the same way as explained in the sections *Checking Tictac* and *Animating Tictac* earlier in this chapter.

Creating an Index Program

The Screens facility also lets you generate an entire COBOL program based on a form that you design. The program generated enables you to create, display, change and delete records in an indexed sequential file. Each record contains all the details defined on the form. Thus, you can create and maintain "databases" of information.

An indexed sequential file is a data file for which an alphabetic index is automatically maintained. The index is based on a prime key (and optionally three alternate keys) that you specify on your screen form.

In addition to storing data, the index program lets you recall any record from disk, change or delete records, and conduct an alphabetic search through the file regardless of the order in which records were entered.

1.   From the Editor main menu, clear any program loaded into the Editor using **Ctrl+F4=clear.**

2. Re-enter Screens - press **Ctrl+F6** then **F7.**

3. Load the form you created earlier by pressing **Alt+F3=load**, typing the name **MYFORM** and pressing **Enter.**

4. Return to the Generate COBOL menu by pressing **Alt+F5**, and then **Enter** to accept the name of the screen you are using. If you get the message:

   ```
   File already exists. Overwrite? Y/N
   ```

   answer **Y**.

Before creating an index program you need to indicate which fields are to be used as keys into the file.

5. Press **F7=mark-fields** in the generate-COBOL menu. This will take you into the mark-fields sub menu.

6. Using the cursor keys move the cursor onto the NAME field. Press **F2=mark-prime-key**.

You will notice that the field has been marked with "P"s to indicate that it is the prime key field. Now, when the index program is generated it will store the records in NAME order.

7. Using the cursor keys move the cursor onto the TEL NO. field. Press **F3=mark-alternative-key-1.**

You will notice that the field has been marked with "1"s to indicate that it is the first alternate key field. Now, when the index program is generated it will still store the records in NAME order but you will have the option of retrieving them in TEL NO. order.

If you had more fields on your screen you could mark one or two more alternate key fields. If you mark a key field incorrectly you can remove the mark using the **F6=unmark-key-field** option.

8. Press **Escape** to return to the generate-COBOL menu.

9. Press **F5=index-program** to generate the index program.

When the program has been generated, you are returned to the Editor main menu with the index program loaded. You should save it using **Alt+F4=save** before continuing.

This chapter completes the *Getting Started* part of this book, and does not cover the more advanced topic of using the index program you have just generated, but we suggest you use the program in your exploration of Personal COBOL. The index program is a useful tool either to create and maintain a "card-index" file, or as a learning aid for indexed (ISAM) files. Compile and animate the index program, as described in the sections *Checking Tictac* and *Animating Tictac* earlier in this chapter.

You will see from the index program source code how it uses an ISAM file based on the interface you designed with Screens. When you start the index program (by zooming in Animator for instance), it runs in automatic mode, reading and writing records to the ISAM file. If you switch the program to manual mode by pressing **F10** on its menu, then it enables you to experiment with the various COBOL verbs which manage indexed files, such as START, WRITE, READ and DELETE.

Sample Session

PART II

TOOLS

Chapter 4

Editor

The Personal COBOL Editor is a very powerful, yet easy-to-use, utility for developing and editing COBOL source code programs under the DOS operating system. It is designed with the COBOL programmer in mind, but it can also be used to create and edit other types of files.

Overview

The Personal COBOL Editor has a hierarchical menu system that lets you easily access each function with a simple keystroke. From within the Editor you can access the On-line Reference directly, enabling you to obtain information about syntax or library routines at the very point you need to know about the information - when you are writing your program. When you use the COBOL Editor, you can syntax-check and/or animate your program from within the Editor by simple keystrokes. After checking and/or animation, the system returns you to the Editor so that you can immediately resume work on your program.

The COBOL Editor includes general text editing features as well as features specific to COBOL program development.

General Editing Features

■ Simple insertion, deletion and restoration of characters, words, entire lines and blocks of text.

■ Find and Replace operations, including global replacement.

- A directory facility which allows you to load files from the current directory or from another one defined by entering the full path name.

- Easy movement through your file using special keyboard keys and function keys defined on the menus.

- A line drawing facility to draw diagrams or enclose text in a box anywhere in your file.

- The ability to edit multiple files and have multiple views on files simultaneously.

- Wide records, up to 132 characters.

- Large files, up to 999,999 records.

- Visible file tags.

- File and window navigation listboxes.

- Mouse support for selecting, resizing and moving windows.

- Configurable margins and file search extensions.

COBOL Program Editing Features

- A margin default setting specifically for COBOL programs which is easily adjustable.

- COPY-library support which allows you quick access to parts of program source code held in separate files.

- Screens, a screen painter with which you design a screen and then generate COBOL code to display the screen and accept user input.

- An index program, generated by Screens, to create and maintain data files.

- Checker/Animator support which allows you to check and/or animate your program from the editor.

■   Multiple error handling of checked programs.

Operation

Invoking the COBOL Editor

The COBOL Editor is automatically invoked upon entry to Personal COBOL. As the Editor is loaded, copyright and other information is displayed on the screen. After pressing any key, the initial screen of the Editor appears.

The Editor Screen

The screen that appears when you first invoke the COBOL Editor displays a work area in which you can create a new file (or edit an old one), and three lines of text at the bottom of the screen: an Information Line and two lines displaying the options on the current menu. A fourth line is reserved for displaying messages such as reminders or errors; this is the message line and is initially blank. Each of these parts of the screen is described below.

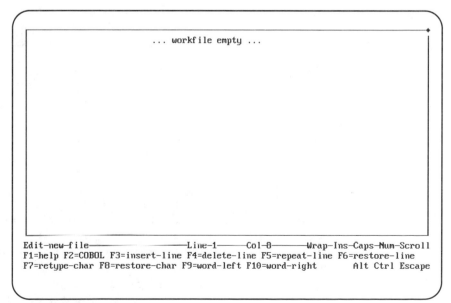

Figure 4-1: Editor Screen

The Work Area

The work area initially contains a single window within which all editing operations are performed.

If you invoke the Editor to create a new file, the message:

```
...workfile empty...
```

appears at the top of the window. If you are working with an old file, the line:

```
...top of text...
```

marks the beginning of the text file and

```
...end of text...
```

marks the end of all text entered in the file.

Since the Editor is designed for the development of COBOL programs, the work area by default is initially divided into three sections that conform to COBOL programming standards, although this is configurable. Using this default setting, each time you invoke the Editor the cursor is positioned in column 8, the first column in which you can enter COBOL code. You can enter text and other characters from column 8 through column 72 inclusive. Columns 8 through 72 correspond to Areas A and B in a COBOL program.

You can enter text such as sequence numbers or indicators in columns 1 through 7. (Note, however, that these numbers are not mandatory and will only be checked if the SEQCHK checker directive is used.) You can also use columns 73 onwards for comments you wish to include in your program. Since the default margin settings are 7 and 73, you use the cursor movement keys or **Home** and **End** keys to move into these two areas. You can change these default settings of the right and left margins so that you can use the Editor to create and view other types of files; this is described in the section *Entering Text*. Text lines of up to 132 characters can be created and viewed within an edit window.

The Information Line

The Information Line is the first line displayed by the Editor at the bottom section of the screen. Although the contents of this line vary, it appears on every screen invoked by the Editor.

The Information Line displays:

- the current function being performed, often referred to as the name of the current menu (for example, Edit).

- the name of the file being edited (for example, new-file).

- the line number within the file of the current cursor position (for example, Line-1). Maximum file size 999,999 line sequential records.

- the column number within the file of the current cursor position (for example, Col-8). Maximum record size 132 characters.

- the current status of the word-wrap option (Wrap) which is highlighted when "on" (active) - its default setting.

- indication of whether exclusive access (lock or "Lck") has been obtained on the current file being edited (for environments that support file locking).

- the Ins, Caps, Num and Scroll indicators which are also highlighted when active; their associated toggle keys are described later in this chapter.

- the number of lines in the file (if at least 1) displayed between the file-name and the line number indicator.

The Menu

The menu always appears below the Information Line. It displays the options, defined by keyboard keys and function keys, that you can access from the current menu. The number of options displayed varies according to the menu. When you first invoke the COBOL Editor, the screen displays the main menu. You access two other menus - the Alternate menu and the Control menu - by pressing and holding down the **Ctrl** and **Alt** keyboard keys, respectively. The Alternate and Control menus display further options available in the Editor.

```
Edit-new-file──────────Line-1────Col-8────────Wrap-Ins-Caps-Num-Scroll
F1=help F2=COBOL F3=insert-line F4=delete-line F5=repeat-line F6=restore-line
F7=retype-char F8=restore-char F9=word-left F10=word-right       Alt Ctrl Escape
```

Figure 4-2 : Main Menu

When you access options from the Alternate or Control menus, you continue to press the **Alt** or **Ctrl** key while you press the desired function key. This instruction is documented as **Alt+Fn** or **Ctrl+Fn**, where **n** is the function key number.

```
Edit-new-file──────────Line-1────Col-8────────Wrap-Ins-Caps-Num-Scroll
F1=help F2=library F3=load-file F4=save-file F5=split-line F6=join-line F7=print
             F9=untype-word-left F10=delete-word-right
```

Figure 4-3 : Alternate Menu

```
Edit-new-file──────────Line-1────Col-8────────Wrap-Ins-Caps-Num-Scroll
F1=help F2=find F3=block F4=clear F5=margins F6=draw/scrns F7=tags F8=word-wrap
F9=window         ←/→ (move in window) Home/End (of text) PgUp/PgDn
```

Figure 4-4 : Control Menu

You can also set the Alternate and Control menus to remain visible on the screen by pressing **Shift+F1** and **Shift+F2**, respectively. Press the appropriate key combination again (or **Escape**) to toggle back to the main menu.

Help

The definition of function keys may vary according to the particular menu displayed. However, one function key carries the same definition throughout the COBOL Editor system. This is the **F1=help** option. When you press **F1** from any menu, you access an on-line help system which displays information about the current function as well as defining the options available from within that function. If there is more than one screen of help text, pressing **F1** again will display the next screen. To return to the current function from the help screen, simply press **F1** (from the last screen) or the **Space** bar.

Escape

The **Escape** option, though not shown on every Editor menu or submenu, is consistent in its use where available: when you press the **Escape** key, you return to the previously displayed screen or function. Pressing **Escape** from within certain menus causes a reminder to appear on the message line (the last line on the screen). For example, if you press **Escape** from the main menu without saving your file, the Editor prompts you to make sure you want to do this. When you are editing a single file and you press **Escape** at the main menu, you exit from the Editor. If you have loaded more than one file for editing, you are presented with the next file to edit.

The Message Line

The message line is the bottom line of the screen. This line is reserved for system messages such as error messages and reminders.

Multiple Files and Views

It is possible to edit more than one file at a time, or to open windows on different parts of the same file, as detailed below. The procedures for doing these things are explained in the section *Using Windows*.

You can load a program and its COPY member files into one window, and bring any one of them to the front to view and edit. The others are temporarily hidden.

You can also open more than one window, and load one or more files into each of them. This allows you to see several files at once if you wish. As with a single window, you can bring any file you want to the front of a window. There is still only one menu, since

Editor

you can only edit one thing at a time: it applies to the window which you have selected.

If you load the same file into two or more windows, then you can see two or more views of the file at once. It's important to note that this doesn't create multiple copies of the file. Changes made in one window will be present in another window as soon as you select it.

Exiting from the COBOL Editor

There arc two ways in which you can exit from the COBOL Editor. These are described below:

■ By closing your last open file - pressing **Escape** when only a single file is open will cause you to exit from the Editor.

■ By closing your last open window - the **F10=close-window** function on the Window Control menu will automatically cause you to exit from the Editor if you close the last open window.

In all cases, the Editor first checks to see if any files or blocks exist which have been modified but not saved. If this is so, the message:

```
unsaved files exist - exit without saving Y/N ?
```

is displayed. Where only a single file is loaded, the message is shortened to:

```
exit without saving Y/N ?
```

Pressing **Y** (**Y**es) tells the Editor to continue to exit and discard any unsaved modifications. Pressing **N** (**N**o) abandons the exit, allowing you to save your changes. If you have many files open, you might find the facilities offered by the save file listboxes helpful in saving a number of modified files in one go - see the section *The Save File Listboxes* for further details.

Functions

This section explains how to perform editing procedures. The section *Using Windows* explains how you can edit more than one file at a time.

Loading a File

If you are creating a file or files from scratch, you will not need to load anything: you can just start typing in the window which is present when the Editor starts up. See the next section for details of the functions available for entering new text.

The COBOL Editor offers two ways in which to load files for editing. You can either specify a file-name at a file prompt or you can select the file-name from the Directory facility. This next section briefly describes loading files by specifying the file-name or by selection via the Directory facility. For details on how to access files which have already been loaded into the Editor, see the section *Accessing Files in a Window* in the section *Using Windows*.

You access the Load-file menu by pressing **Alt+F3** from the Editor main menu. The load-file function inserts the specified file at the current cursor location. This makes it easy to build a program from individual pieces of code stored as separate files. For each segment, just move the cursor to the insertion point and use **Alt+F3**.

Using the File Prompt

The file prompt appears below the Load-file menu. It displays the current path by default. You can change to another drive and directory by typing over the current one. You can use the **Backspace** key to delete the characters at the file prompt.

You enter the name of the file you wish to edit at the cursor position. If you do not specify a file-name extension then by default the system searches for that file-name with an extension of either .CBL, .CPY or spaces, in that order. If no file exists with the specified file-name and one of the search extensions, the system displays the following message:

```
file not found with defined extension
```

After you enter the file-name, press **Enter** . The system loads the file for editing. The Editor main menu then appears with the file displayed in the work area of the screen.

Using the Directory Facility

You use the Directory facility to display the names of all files available for editing. You select the file-name of the file you wish to edit from this listing.

To access the default Directory, press **F2=directory** on the Load-file menu. The default directory displays those file-names with the same extension as shown at the bottom of the screen. If you want to load a file-name with another file extension, type the extension at the file prompt. Then when you press **F2=directory,** the listing of all files with that extension appear on the screen.

To select a file-name from the directory listing, use the **up/down** keys to place the cursor on the desired file-name. Then press **Enter**. The selected file-name now appears at the file prompt on the Load-file menu. Press **Enter** again to load the file into the COBOL Editor.

File Access Considerations

When a file is specified for loading, either at the File prompt on the Load-file menu or on the command line when the Editor is started, the following search method is employed to locate the file:

1.   The file requested is compared with all files currently loaded within the Editor - if a match is found, the Editor presents the already loaded file for editing. The Editor matches files requested or already loaded without a path description to those specified with a path description. It will not match file-names specified with different paths. For example,

C:\PROGRAMS\MYAPP.CBL matches MYAPP.CBL;
C:\PROGRAMS\NEWAPP.CBL does not match
C:\DEMO\NEWAPP.CBL.

2.   If no match is found among files already loaded, the Editor
      searches for the file on disk. If a path is specified then the
      Editor looks only in the specified path. If no path is specified
      the Editor looks only in the current directory. If the file-name
      was specified without an extension, the Editor by default
      looks for files with one of the extensions CBL, CPY or spaces.
      If the file is not found either with a specific name or using
      the search extensions then the message:

      `file not found with defined extension`

      is displayed.

Entering Text

This section describes the keyboard keys used to enter text within
a window. It will also show you how to change margin settings
and turn on and off the word-wrap feature of the COBOL Editor.

As you enter text, the Editor beeps at you when the cursor ap-
proaches the right hand margin. This is a reminder that you are
nearing the end of the line.

Note also that the current line (the one on which the cursor is
positioned) is always highlighted.

Caps Lock

The Editor accepts text entry in either upper or lowercase alphabetic characters. To set text entry to uppercase characters, you
press the **Caps Lock** key. This is a toggle which you press to turn
the key on and off. The status of the **Caps Lock** key is displayed
by the change in appearance of the Caps indicator on the Information Line. To set entry to lowercase characters, simply press the
Caps Lock key again.

Num Lock

The **Num Lock** key is a toggle key similar to the **Caps Lock** key. You press the **Num Lock** key to lock the numeric keyboard so that it produces numbers rather than cursor movement key functions. The status of the **Num Lock** key also appears on the Information Line; the indicator is highlighted when **Num Lock** is on.

Word-wrap

When you reach the end of the line, the word-wrap feature (on by default) moves the last word to the next line if the number of characters in the word exceeds the available character positions on the current line. If word-wrap is off, the word splits over the two lines. When word-wrap is on, the indicator Wrap is displayed on the Information Line.

The word-wrap option is located on the Control menu. You first press the **Ctrl** key to access the Control menu, then, while holding down the **Ctrl** key, you press **F8** which toggles between word-wrap on and off.

The Enter Key

The **Enter** key has three functions within the COBOL Editor:

■ When you are editing a file, pressing the **Enter** key places the cursor on the next line (carriage return). If insert is on, this inserts a new line.

■ When you are specifying a file-name from the file prompt, accessing a file from the Directory or selecting an item from a listbox, this key enters the desired action into the system.

■ When you are in the Checker menu, pressing the **Enter** key starts the check and/or animate functions.

This section discusses the key in its role as the **Carriage Return** key.

When you are entering text and have not reached the end of the current line, you use the **Enter** key to position the cursor on the next line. The first time you press **Enter**, the cursor returns to the same column in which the previous line began.

For example, the current line is indented 4 spaces from the left margin and begins in column 12. When you press **Enter** once, the cursor moves to column 12 on the next line. If you press **Enter** again, the cursor returns to the beginning of the next line (column 8).

When you are working with a file you have already created, pressing **Enter** from any character position on the current line places the cursor at the first character entered on the next line. However, if Insert mode is "on"(set by the **Ins** key), pressing **Enter** inserts a new line below the current line and moves all characters to the right (including the character at the current cursor position) to this new line.

Margins

The default margin settings for standard COBOL files (.CBL, .COB, .CPY, .BAK or spaces) conform to COBOL program development standards. The left margin is set at column 7, the right margin at 73, allowing you to enter your source code between those columns. You can use the remaining columns (1-7 and 73-132) for sequence numbers and comments.

If the file loaded into the Editor does not have one of the standard COBOL extensions, the margins by default will be set to 0 and 81.

If margins other than the COBOL margins are selected, then tabbing will include tabs every 4 columns at columns 4, 76, 80 and every 4 columns up to column 132 (with COBOL margins, the tab keys skip these positions).

You can change the margins to settings between columns 1 and 132, as well as take advantage of the full window, by using the margins option on the Control menu. This option consists of a Margins menu which displays various ways to change margin settings.

Editor

From the Editor main menu, press and hold down **Ctrl** to access the Control menu. Continue to press the **Ctrl** key as you press **F5=margins**, then release both keys. The Margins menu appears on the screen. Two vertical bars may also appear within the window, displaying the boundaries of the current margin settings if they are within the region of text enclosed by the window.

There are various ways to change the margin settings depending on the results desired. These are listed below:

■ To set margins wider or narrower than the current settings, you can use either of two sets of function key combinations:

   a. **F3=left-margin-to-cursor** and **F4=right-margin-to-cursor:**

   Move the cursor to the column in which you want to begin entering text. Then press **F3=left-margin-to-cursor** to position the left vertical bar at the new left margin setting.

   Move the cursor to the last column in which you want to enter a character. Then press **F4=right-margin-to-cursor** to position the right vertical bar at the new right margin setting.

   b. **F5/F6=left-out/in** and **F7/F8=right-in/out:**

   Press **F5=left-in** to move the left vertical bar to the left (out) one position and **F6** to move it to the right (in) one position.

   Press **F7** to move the right vertical bar to the left (in) one position and **F8** to move it to the right (out) one position.

■ You can access the maximum record length (132 columns) for text entry by using either of the methods described above. However, a faster way to do this is to use **F9=fullpage-left** and **F10=fullpage-right.**

   Press **F9=fullpage-left**. The left vertical bar disappears from the window verifying that you can begin entering text in column 1. The left margin position is set to column 0.

Press **F10=fullpage-right** to extend text entry through column 132. The right vertical bar also disappears from the window, and the right margin position is set to column 133.

The vertical bars reappear when you reset the margins to another location, within the window. The margin settings are also displayed in the message area below the Margins menu.

Of course you can use **F9=fullpage-left** and **F10=fullpage-right** individually to quickly set the left margin at column 0 and the right margin at column 133.

■ To return the margins to the COBOL default settings, press **F2=Cobol-margins**. The vertical bars automatically move to columns 7 and 73, allowing text entry between columns 8 and 72.

Note: You can enter text outside of the margin boundaries by using the **cursor up/down** keys or **Home** and **End** keys to position the cursor in these areas. Note, however, that when you press **Enter,** the cursor remains in the current area. You must use the cursor movement keys to reposition the cursor inside the margins.

If you change the margin settings within a window, they remain set until you exit from and close the window. A new window has its margins set to those initially defined for the Personal COBOL system.

Press **Escape** to continue editing with the currently set margins.

Inserting, Deleting and Restoring Text

This section describes the keyboard keys and function key options that you use to insert and delete text. You will also learn how to restore text that you have deleted within the same editing session. This section is divided into three subsections:

■ Characters

■ Words

■   Lines

Some of the function and keyboard keys you use to insert and
delete characters can also be used to insert and delete words.
Those procedures you use to insert and delete words, in turn, can
be applied to inserting and deleting lines of text. However, each of
the above categories also has its own specific function key to
provide the fastest and easiest way of executing the procedure.

Characters

This section describes how to insert and delete individual characters from your text. You can restore in sequence up to 132 characters deleted at a time during the current editing session.

Inserting Characters

You can insert text between characters, words and lines by turning on Insert mode. The **Ins** key is a toggle key that turns this
mode on and off. When Insert mode is on, the Ins indicator on the
Information Line appears highlighted. The shape of the cursor
also changes.

To insert a character(s) on a line, move the cursor to the character
position before which you want to insert text. (This is because
insertion is always made at the cursor position with the current
text moved one character position to the right.) Then type the
character(s).

Remember that when you press **Enter** while Insert mode is on, all
the characters to the right and including the current cursor position move to the next line within the window.

Deleting and Restoring Characters

You can use three different keyboard keys to delete characters
from the screen. These are the **Space** bar (with Insert mode off),
the **Del** (delete) key and the **Backspace** key.

Pressing the **Space** bar, with Insert mode off, overtypes the character at the current cursor position with a space.

The function of the **Del** key erases the character at the current cursor position and causes the text following the deleted character to move one character space to the left.

The **Backspace** key functions differently according to the setting of Insert mode. When Insert mode is on, the **Backspace** key behaves similarly to the **Del** key: it deletes the character to the left of the cursor position and causes all text to the right to move one character position to the left.

When Insert mode is off, pressing the **Backspace** key deletes the character to the left of the cursor position and restores any characters that were previously overtyped.

The Editor remembers up to a maximum of one line of characters deleted during an editing session. It places them in a buffer, allowing you to recover them by using **F7=retype-char** or **F8=restore-char** on the main menu. The buffer is used by all windows enabling deleted characters to be restored in any window. The use of these keys is slightly different.

You use the **F7=retype-char** option to recover the character last deleted with the **Backspace** key. Its behavior depends on the status of Insert mode. If Insert mode is on, the recovered character is inserted at the current cursor position. If Insert mode is off, pressing **F7=retype-char** types the recovered character over the character at the cursor position. You can change the case of the recovered character by pressing the **CapsLock** key before you press **F7=retype-char.**

The **F8=restore-char** option lets you insert the character last overtyped or deleted with the **Del** key at the current cursor position, inserting it into the line regardless of insert mode.

If you change a word by typing over it, you can use the **Backspace** key to replace the original word. You simply press the **Backspace** key to restore the most recently replaced characters.

Words

This next section describes how to insert and delete entire words from your file. You recover deleted words using the same method to recover deleted characters.

Inserting Words

Inserting entire words into your text is the same as inserting characters. You place the cursor at the position at which you want to insert text. Then, with Insert mode on, you begin typing the inserted material as the characters to the right and including the cursor position move further to the right.

Deleting and Restoring Words

The Editor lets you delete entire words with one keystroke. The options to do this are located on the Alternate menu and are defined by **F9=untype-word-left** and **F10=delete-word-right.**

Note: The COBOL Editor defines a word as a string of characters preceded and followed by a space, as well as two or more contiguous spaces.

If the cursor is positioned on a non-space character, deleting a word left/right means deleting all characters left or right until a space is encountered.

If the cursor is positioned on a space character and the adjacent character(s) left or right are spaces, deleting a word means deleting all spaces left or right until a non-space character is encountered.

The behavior of the **F9=untype-word-left** option depends on the setting of Insert mode. If Insert mode is off, the word disappears, and the most recently overtyped characters appear in its place. If Insert mode is on, the word to the left and the character positions it occupied are deleted, bringing the text at the right to the current cursor position. You can recover the deleted word by pressing **F7=retype-char** on the main menu.

Press **Alt+F10=delete-word-right** to delete the word to the right of the cursor position. You can recover the deleted word by pressing **F8=restore-char** on the main menu.

Lines

The Editor offers various ways to insert and delete entire lines of text. All of the menu options for these functions are located on the main menu.

Inserting Lines

You can insert entire lines of text in your file using either Insert mode or the **F3=insert-line** option on the main menu. Using Insert mode (by pressing the **Ins** key), you insert a blank line below the current line by positioning the cursor at the end of the current line and pressing **Enter.** The cursor moves to the beginning of the blank line.

To insert a blank line above the current line in Insert mode, place the cursor in the first column of the current line and press **Enter.** The blank line is inserted, but this time the cursor remains with the current line.

A faster way to insert lines is to use the **F3=insert-line** option. This inserts a line above the current line. Position the cursor anywhere on the current line and press **F3=insert-line**. The existing text moves down one line while the cursor remains in place.

Deleting and Restoring Lines

You can delete an entire line of text using one keystroke. Place the cursor on the line you want to delete and press **F4=delete-line**. The line is deleted and the text below moves up one line.

Any lines that you delete within an editing session remain in a buffer so that you can restore them to the file. The system restores the most recently deleted line first. The buffer is used by all windows enabling deleted lines to be restored in any window.

Restored lines are inserted on the line above the cursor. To restore the deleted lines, place the cursor on the line below the one where you want the insertion. Then press **F6=restore-line**. You can press **F6=restore-line** again to insert the next line or move the cursor to another location to restore the next line in the buffer. You can use the combination of the **F4=delete-line** and **F6=restore-line** function keys to move lines of text from one location in your file to another. When all of the deleted lines held in the buffer have been restored, the Editor beeps at further attempts to restore. The action of restoring a line removes that line from the buffer.

Repeating Lines

The Editor also lets you repeat the current line. It inserts this line above the current one. You do this by using the **F5=repeat-line** option.

Note: You can copy multiple consecutive lines to another location in your file. To first store them in the buffer, alternately press **F5=repeat-line** and **F4=delete-line** for each consecutive line you want to copy. Then move the cursor to the desired location and repeatedly press **F6=restore-line** until all the lines have been copied to the new location.

Splitting and Joining Lines

Other features of the COBOL Editor allow you to split a line of text and, optionally, join it back together. You can then insert text at a specific character position or eliminate unnecessary gaps in your file. The **Alt+F5=split-line** and **Alt+F6=join-line** options are located on the Alternate menu.

Pressing **Alt+F5=split-line** splits a line at the current cursor position. All text from the cursor to the end of the line moves to the next line, causing the following lines of text to move down one line. The columns occupied by the text remain the same.

Pressing **Alt+F6=join-line** joins lines at the current cursor position. To join lines, place the cursor on the first of the split lines. Press **Alt+F6=join-line**. The text on the line below appears to the right of the word on the line containing the cursor. If the number of characters on the second line exceeds the available space on the line above, the **Alt+F6=join-line** feature moves as many whole words as possible and then places the cursor on the second line with the remaining text. The join-line option is particularly useful for formatting paragraphs. To do this, position the cursor on the first character of a paragraph and press **Alt+F6=join-line** until the paragraph is formatted.

Moving Through a File

You can move the cursor to any location in your file by using special keyboard keys, key combinations, and function keys defined on the Main and Control Menus. This section lists the different ways you can move through a file and describes the use of the keys associated with the particular operation.

You use the cursor movement keys to place the cursor anywhere within the file. However, there are quicker ways to position it at specific locations.

Moving Across a Line

You move the cursor back and forth across a line using the **Home**, **End** and **Tab** keyboard keys, and the **F9=word-left** and **F10=word-right** function keys defined on the main menu.

Home and End Keys

The effect of using the **Home** and **End** keys depends on the current cursor position and whether text exists within each region of the line. The following sequence for the **Home** and **End** keys assumes that the current cursor position is within the margin settings and not at the beginning of the line and text only exists within the text area between the margin settings.

Pressing the **Home** key once places the cursor at the left margin on the current line. Pressing **Home** again then places the cursor in column 1 of your window, regardless of the margin setting. If you press **Home** a third time, the cursor then moves to column 1 of the first line within the window.

The function of the **End** key is opposite to that of the **Home** key. You press **End** to position the cursor after the last character on the line. Pressing **End** a second time moves the cursor just outside the right margin. Pressing **End** again moves the cursor to column 132. If you press **End** one more time, the cursor moves to the column 132 of the last line within the window.

If text exists in the left or right margin areas, the **End** key first positions the cursor after the last character within the region, pressing **End** again moves the cursor just outside the region.

If you were editing a non-COBOL file, you would probably not press these keys more than twice in succession. However, for COBOL program development, you might use these keys to position the cursor inside columns 1-7 and 73 onwards for entering comments.

Tab Keys

You can use the **Backtab** and **Tab** keys to move the cursor 4 positions to the left or right. To indent an existing line of text, place the cursor at the beginning of the first word on the line. Then press **Ins** to turn on Insert mode, and press **Tab**. The entire line moves 4 character positions to the right.

Moving to the Next or Previous Word

The Editor also lets you move word by word through the screen using the **F9=word-left** and **F10=word-right** options on the main menu. Remember that the COBOL Editor defines as a word a string of characters preceded and followed by a space, as well as two or more contiguous spaces.

Press **F9=word-left** to move the cursor to the first character of the word to the left of the current cursor position. If the cursor encounters two or more spaces, it moves to the first of these spaces. Using the **F10=word-right** option moves the cursor to the beginning of the next word to the right. Again, if it encounters two or more spaces, it stops on the first of these spaces.

Moving to the Next/Previous Line

As you reach the end of a line, pressing the **Tab** or **F10=word-right** keys (described above) places the cursor on the first tab position or word on the next line. Pressing **F9=word-left** eventually moves the cursor to the first word encountered on the previous line. However, a more expedient way to move the cursor to the next line is to use the down key or **Enter** (with Insert mode off). Simply use the up key to position the cursor on the previous line.

When you are entering text, you press the **Enter** key to position the cursor at the first character position on the next line. However, if wrap is on, when you reach the end of the line, the text you are typing automatically wraps to the following line. If you are working with a previously created file, pressing the **Enter** key places the cursor on first character of the following line.

Moving to the Beginning/End of a File

When used with the **Ctrl** key, the **Home** and **End** keys place the cursor at the beginning and end of a file. These two functions are defined on the Control menu.

Press and hold down **Ctrl** to display the Control menu. The Home/End (of text) option is displayed on the second line. Continue to hold down the **Ctrl** key and press **Home** to position the cursor at the top of the file, the cursor moving to the first column to the right of the left margin. Pressing **Ctrl+End** places the cursor at the end of the file (on the "end of text" indicator) the cursor retaining the same column position from which it moved.

Moving Up/Down Through a File

You use specific keyboard keys or combinations of keys to view parts of your file not visible within the window.

Page-up and Page-down Keys

The **Page-up** and **Page-down** keyboard keys display the previous or following page of text not currently visible on the screen. You simply press **Page-up** to view the previous page, and **Page-down** to display the following page.

The height of the window determines the size in lines of a page. The page height is the number of text lines available within a window minus 1. For example if a window is 19 lines high, excluding the border, then the page height is 18 lines.

The **Page-up** and **Page-down** keys behave differently when used with the **Ctrl** key. These two keys are defined on the Control menu. Press **Ctrl** for the **Page-up/Page-down** option.

Press **Ctrl+Page-up** to move the cursor up 200 lines of text. Press **Ctrl+Page-down** to move the cursor down the same number of lines.

Scrolling

There are three different ways to scroll through a file. These are described below.

- Scrolling line by line. This allows you to scroll through the entire file, displaying a new line of text at the top or bottom of the window as needed.

- You can also use the up and down keys with the **Scroll Lock** key set to scroll text up and down, line by line, as the cursor remains in place.

- Press the **Scroll Lock** key to turn on the scroll function. Then press up to move the text up and down to move the text down.

See information on the **Page-up, Page-down, Home** and **End** keys for other ways to move through a file.

Tagging Text Lines

You can use the tag facility of the Editor to tag a text line so that it can be selected by other keystrokes while editing the file. Any number of text lines can be tagged while editing the file.

To access the tag facility, press and hold down **Ctrl** from the Editor main menu to display the Control menu. Continue to press on the **Ctrl** key as you press **F7=tags**, then release both keys. The Tags menu appears.

Setting a Tag

A tag is set by pressing **F2=set-file-tag**. The tag is set on the current text line. The tagged line is displayed using an alternative screen attribute making the tagged lines visible within the displayed file. Any text line within a file or block may be tagged.

Clearing a Tag

A tag is cleared from the current text line by pressing **F3=clear-tag**. All the tags are cleared from a file or block if **F4=clear-all-tags** is pressed. Tags are only maintained while the file is being edited. If a file is saved and escaped from then the file tags are lost. Deleting a tagged text line also clears the tag. Creating, inserting or restoring blocks does not include tags on any text line.

Locating a Tag

A tag can be located by pressing **F7=previous-tag** or **F8=next-tag**. The search is made from the current text line. If when searching the start or end of the file is reached then searching wraps to the end or start of the file, depending upon the search direction. When a tag is located the Editor is positioned to the text line. The column number is unchanged.

Finding and Replacing Text

You can use the Find facility of the COBOL Editor to locate a string of text within a file and optionally replace it with another string. You can either replace individual occurrences of a string of text or globally replace all of them. As you use this facility, you can edit the file but you cannot use those editing functions that require the use of function keys. This section describes all of the features of the Find facility.

The Find facility of the Editor is region-orientated with the search area being defined by the cursor position in relation to the current margins when the search is begun. Depending on the particular margins you are using, a line can consist of up to three different regions - the columns margins and the columns beyond the right margin. Taking COBOL margins as an example, if the cursor is in column 5 when the search is started then only columns 1 through 7 of each line are searched. Similarly, if the cursor lay in column 25 then the search region is columns 8 through 72. In practice this means that if a word you are searching for overlaps a margin column then the Find facility will not recognize the word, since it is not wholly within the search region. To find the word you must adjust the margin settings so that the word does not cross a margin column.

To access the Find facility, press and hold down **Ctrl** from the Editor main menu to display the Control menu. Continue to press on the **Ctrl** key as you press **F2=find**, then release both keys. The Find menu (including the Information Line) appears.

```
Find─────────stp-239-lines───Line-1─────Col-8─────────Wrap-Ins-Caps-Num-Scroll
F1=help F2=set F3=line F7/F8=REPLACE-back/fwd F9/F10=FIND-back/fwd       Ctrl Esc
Find                                        Replace
```

Figure 4-5 : FIND Menu

The variety of functions within the Find facility require more than one menu to display all of its options. Therefore, further options are displayed on the Find Control menu. Press and continue to hold down the **Ctrl** key to display the Find Control menu.

```
Find————————stp-239-lines————Line-1————Col-8————————Wrap-Ins-Caps-Num-Scroll
F1=help F3=cursor→Find F4=clear F5=punc F6=case F9=repl-mode(step,all)
Find                                        Replace
```

Figure 4-6 : FIND Control Menu

Refer to these two menus as you read through this next section.

Entering the Text String

You use the Find and Replace buffers below the Find menu to enter the string of text you want to locate and optionally replace in your file. When you first select the Find option, the cursor appears in the Find buffer.

There are a number of ways in which you can enter the text string to be found and, optionally replaced, in the Find facility. You can simply enter the text string at the cursor position in the Find or Replace buffer; each buffer accepts a maximum of 32 characters .

Another way is to position the cursor on an occurrence of the character string you wish to locate in your file. Then press **Ctrl+F3=cursor-Find** to place the text string in the Find buffer.

You can also use this method to enter text in the Replace buffer. Press **F2=set** twice and position the cursor on the replacement string in the file. Now press **Ctrl+F3=Cursor-Repl** to place this character string in the Replace buffer.

Moving Through the Find and Replace Buffers

Pressing **F2=set** cycles you through the Find and Replace buffers and then back to the window. You can use the **Tab** and **Backtab** keys to move back and forth between the two buffers.

Clearing the Find and Replace Buffers

The **Ctrl+F4=clear** key combination lets you clear the Find and Replace buffers so that you can enter another text string. All characters from the cursor position to the right are deleted.

You can use the **Space bar, Backspace** or **Del** key to erase characters from the Find and Replace buffers. However, you should be careful using the space bar in replace buffers - you may add unexpected trailing spaces.

Locating the Text String

Once you have entered the text string in the Find buffer, you can search back and forth through the file to find each occurrence of the string. To search forward through the file, you press **F10=FIND-fwd**.

Each time the cursor locates the text string, the following message appears at the bottom of your screen:

```
"F8=forward" to replace, "F10=forward" to find next
```

You have the option of either continuing with the search or replacing the text string at this time (see the section *Replacing the Text String* below). If you use **F8** and there is nothing in the Replace buffer, the find text string is deleted.

You can move backward through the file to locate the previous occurrence of the text string by pressing **F9=FIND-back**. Each time the cursor finds an occurrence of the text string, the message:

```
"F7=back" to replace, "F9=back" to find previous
```

appears at the bottom of the screen. You can continue to locate each previous occurrence, or you can choose to replace the text string with the text string in the Replace buffer (see below)

Note: If you press **Enter** when the cursor is in the Find or Replace buffer, you will find only the first occurrence of the string.

There are two other options which you can specify to further define the text you want to locate. By default, the cursor searches for a text string without attention to alphabetic case. You can specify a search with alphabetic case by pressing **Ctrl+F6=case**. This causes the Editor to find only those occurrences that match the alphabetic case specified in the Find buffer. When you specify case, the word "case" appears on the Information Line. For example, if case is turned off and you specify "Abc" as the find string, the Editor finds both "abc" and "ABC", If case is turned on it will find only "Abc". To turn off case sensitivity, press **Ctrl+F6=case** again.

The three punctuation characters comma (,), period (.) and semicolon (;), are, by default, treated as spaces during a search. However, you can include these characters in the search by pressing **Ctrl+F5=punc**. The abbreviation "punc" appears on the Information line. Pressing **Ctrl+F5=punc** a second time turns "punc" off.

Moving to a Specific Line

You can also move to a particular line of text by specifying the line number. You do this by pressing **F3** (line). The word "Line" replaces the word "Find" in the Find buffer. A message appears at the bottom of the screen prompting you to enter the line number at the cursor position. Then press **Enter**. The specified line becomes the current line on the screen.

Replacing the Text String

You can change each occurrence of a text string either individually or by global replacement.

Individual or "Step" Replacement

When you first access the Find menu, the Information Line displays the indicator "stp" (for "Step"). This means that the replacement mode is set to step to each occurrence of the text string specified in the Find buffer. The first time you press **F8=REPLACE-fwd** to locate the next text string, the cursor moves to that text string. The same message that appears when you use press **F10=FIND-fwd** also appears when you press **F8=REPLACE-fwd**:

```
"F8=forward" to replace, "F10=forward" to find next
```

If the cursor is not currently on an occurrence of the text string, it moves to the next occurrence the first time you press **F8**. Pressing

Editor

F8 a second time confirms that you do indeed want to change the text string and makes the replacement. You use **F7=REPLACE-back** to replace the previous text string in the file. If the cursor is not currently on an occurrence of the text string, it moves back to the previous occurrence the first time you press **F7**. Pressing **F7** a second time confirms that you do indeed want to change the text string and makes the replacement.

The difference between the **F7/F8=REPLACE-back/fwd** function and the **F9/10=FIND-back/fwd** function is that the former replaces the text string while the latter simply finds the next or previous occurrence. You can use them interchangeably depending on the desired results.

Global Replacement

You can choose to replace all occurrences of a text string with another using global replacement. The cursor moves either forward or backward from the current cursor position through the file making all changes. To change to global replacement mode, you press **Ctrl+F9=repl-mode** (step, all). The indicator "all" replaces "stp" on the Information Line.

To go forward through the file, press **F8=REPLACE-fwd**. The following message appears:

```
WARNING: next "F8=forward" will replace ALL remaining
occurrences
```

This warning message reminds you that global replacement mode is active.

When you press **F8=REPLACE-fwd** a second time, the cursor begins its movement through the file, changing each occurrence of the text string on its way. The cursor stops to the right of the last change made. The number of occurrences replaced appears on the Message Line at the bottom of the screen. You use the same procedure to go backward through the file in global replacement mode. However, you use the **F7=REPLACE-back** option instead. The following message appears the first time you press **F7=REPLACE-back** to locate the text string:

```
WARNING: next "F7=back" will replace ALL remaining oc-
currences
```

Pressing **F7=REPLACE-back** again will replace all occurrences of the text string with the string specified in the Replacement buffer. The cursor stops on the last change made. The number of occurrences replaced appears on the Message Line at the bottom of the screen.

Note: You can interrupt the search or replace process at any time by pressing **Ctrl+Break**.

Moving and Copying Text

You can move or copy text from one part of a file to another using the Block function within the COBOL Editor. You first copy or move the block of text to a temporary buffer in which you can edit it. You then insert it anywhere in your current file or into any other file loaded into an Editor window. You can define and use multiple blocks within the same Block session. Even entire files can be loaded as a block into the current file.

These features are displayed on the Block menu, available from the Control menu. This section describes all of the functions available to move or copy blocks of text.

To access the Block function, press **Ctrl+F3=block**. The word "Block" appears on the Information Line above the menu.

Defining Blocks of Text

You must first define the block of text you want to copy or move to another location in the file. Press **F4=define-block** to begin this process. The submenu appears displaying further options.

An instruction also appears on the Message Line at the bottom of the screen. This tells you to use the cursor movement keys to mark the block of text. As you press the down key, the marked text appears highlighted. You press the up key to unmark the text. You can also use the **Page-up, Page-down, Home** and **End** keys to mark a larger block of text.

Editor

You can use the **F2=find** option on this menu to locate the string of text you wish to include in the block. This lets you access the Find facility of the Editor (described above). When you press **F9=FIND-back** or **F10=FIND-fwd**, all text from the current cursor position to the first occurrence of the text string specified in the Find buffer becomes part of the block. When you exit the Find facility, you return to the Block menu shown above.

You can define multiple blocks of text for insertion elsewhere in your file. To do this, you simply define one block of text at a time, which is then placed in a buffer.

Moving/Copying Blocks of Text

You now have the option of copying the marked text or removing it entirely from its current location. If you wish to simply copy it to another location in your file, press **F3=copy-to-block**. If you want to move it to another location, press **F4=remove-to-block**. You can also exit from this Block submenu without defining a block by pressing **Escape**.

When you press **F3=copy-to-block** or **F4=remove-to-block**, the initial Block menu reappears. You can now move to any location to insert the defined block of text.

Place the cursor on the line before which you want to insert the block of text. Press **F3=insert-block** to place the entire block of text in this location. You can continue to insert a copy of this block of text anywhere in your file.

If you defined multiple blocks of text, you can use **F6=restore-block** to restore the blocks in the reverse order in which you defined them. First, place the cursor on the line above which you want the last-defined block to appear. Then press **F6=restore-block**. Then move the cursor to the location where you want the next block in the buffer to appear and press **F6=restore-block** again.

Note: When you move or copy a block of text, the Editor places the block in a stack. When you define multiple blocks to be moved or copied, they are located in the stack in the reverse order in which you selected them. For example, the second block selected sits on top of the first selected block.

When you press **F3=insert-block**, a copy of the first block on the stack is inserted at the desired location. You can then insert this same block at other locations in your file.

Pressing **F6=restore-block** removes the top block from the stack and inserts it at the desired location.

Editing Blocks of Text

If you want to edit a block of text before you insert it in a file, press **F2=edit-block** on the initial Block menu. The block appears alone in the work area of a screen below which is the Editor main menu. The cursor is positioned at the left margin if this is the first time the block has been edited or at the previous cursor position if the block has been edited before. This cursor positioning can be useful if a particular string is to be edited before each insertion (when the block is to be inserted in many places). Notice that the file-name on the Information Line is "Block". All of the COBOL Editor functions are available from this menu.

Once you have finished editing the block of text, you press **Escape** to return to the current file. Then, to return to the Block menu, press **Ctrl+F3=block**. Move the cursor to where you want to insert the block. Then press **F3=insert-block** or **F6=restore-block**. As part of the function of block editing, you can load an entire file into a block (see the section Loading a File below). The file is opened and the records copied into the block. The file is then closed. You can also save the block as you would save any other file (see the section *Saving a File* below).

Each save operation is performed as if a new file is being created. If a file had been loaded into a block which was now being saved to the same file-name, the Editor will warn you that this file already exists on starting the save operation.

Note: If you exit the COBOL Editor while there are still modi-fied blocks of text in the buffer, the following warning message is displayed on the Message Line below the

Editor

Editor main menu:

```
unsaved blocks outstanding in Editor -
exit without saving? Y/N
```

Saving the file does not automatically save blocks of text. If you want to save the blocks of text remaining in the buffer, press **N** (**No**) in response to this message. Then press **Ctrl+F3=block to return** to the Block menu.

Now press **F2=edit-block** to display the last block you defined. (To save all blocks, you must combine them into one block - see below.) The Editor main menu appears at the bottom of the screen. You can now save this block by pressing **Alt+F4=save-file**. During your next editing session, you can load this file into any location in your current working file.

Combining Blocks of Text

If you have multiple blocks in the stack, you can combine these blocks into one block and then save this block as one file or insert it in your current file.

To do this, press **F2=edit** from the Block menu (**Ctrl+F3=block**). The first block on the stack appears on the screen. The Editor main menu is also displayed.

Now press **Ctrl+F3=block** to invoke the Block menu again. Then press **F6** (restore-block). The second block appears on the screen on the current line. You can now either save the combined block as you would save any other file or insert it into your current file. To insert this block into your current file, press **Escape** twice. Your main file appears on the screen. Once again, press **Ctrl+F3=block**. Then from the Block menu, press either **F6=restore-block** or **F3=insert-block**. The combined block now appears on the current line.

Saving a File

The procedure for saving a file is similar to that for loading a file. You invoke the Save-file option by pressing **Alt+F4=save-file** from the Editor main menu.

The Information Line is the same as that for the Load-file option except for the name of the function. The Save-file menu displays the same options **F1=help**, **F2=directory** as the Load-file menu. Two listbox functions are also accessible from this menu. These listboxes give you the ability to save one or more files at a time and are described in the section The Save-file Listboxes

The **F3=backup-file** option allows you to have a backup file automatically created when you save a file. Pressing **F3=backup-file** will alternately select and de-select the option. When selected, the word Backup appears on the status line. The backup-file option renames the original file with a file extension of .BAK and gives the edited file the original file-name and extension.

Additional information is displayed at the file prompt the first time you are saving a file. The system supplies the extension .CBL as the default file-name extension for the new file. You enter the name you want the file to have. If you want to change the default file-name extension to any other extension, just enter the file-name followed by . and the new extension.

If you are saving a file that already has a name, its file-name appears by default at the file prompt. You can retain this or enter another one. Once the desired file-name is shown at the file prompt, you press **Enter** to save the file. To save multiple files with their current names, see the section *The Save-file Listboxes*.

The Save-file Listboxes

The Save-file listboxes are used to specify one or more files that you wish to save in one operation. They contain the names and details of files you are editing. You will bring up one of the lists, mark those files you want saved, and then give the go-ahead to save them.

F7=files-in-window brings up a list of all the files which can currently be viewed in the selected window, for instance a program and its COPY members.

F8=list-all brings up a list of all the files which have been loaded into the Editor, irrespective of which window they can be seen in.

The steps are as follows:

Ensure that the window you want to work in is selected. From the main menu, select the Save-file menu (press **Alt+F4=save-file**) and press **F7=files-in-window** or **F8=list-all** as appropriate.

The appropriate listbox will be displayed.

For each file, the length in lines is shown, together with an M indicator in the "mod" column if the file has been modified. A third indicator shows whether the file is marked for saving, and if so, whether a backup is to be kept.

To mark a file which you want to be saved, first of all move the highlight over its entry using the **cursor up/down** keys. (If there are too many entries in the list to be shown in the box, they will scroll when the highlight comes to the top or bottom of the box. If the entry is too wide to fit in the box, use the **cursor left/right** keys to scroll it.)

Pressing the **F2=toggle-save** key will rotate between selections in the Save column. If the column entry is blank the file will not be saved. Save means the file will be saved. Bak+Save means the existing file on disk will be renamed with a .BAK extension and the file saved. Note that the setting of the "Backup" toggle on the Load and Save-file menus is not connected with the Bak+Save setting of this toggle. Use the cursor keys and **F2=toggle-save** key until you are happy with your selections, then press **Enter** to perform the save. Only those files marked Save or Bak+Save will be included.

In some circumstances the Editor may not be able to save a file you have marked. In this case, it pauses and tells you so, and invites you to press the space bar to continue. One likely cause is that the file has not been saved before, and so has no name. In this case, the message:

```
no name active on file, save from menu - press space bar to go
to next file
```

is displayed. In this case you must save the file manually using the
File prompt on the Save-file menu. Once the file has a name and
exists on disk you will be able to subsequently save it using the
listboxes.

When the save operation is complete, the listbox will be removed
leaving the workspace as it was. You can also use a mouse to
operate the listbox. See the section *Using the Mouse* for further
details. If you want to escape from the list and return to the Save-
file menu without performing a save, press **Escape** rather than
Enter.

COBOL Support Functions

The Editor's COBOL menu, reached by pressing **F2=COBOL** at
the main menu, provides access to the Checker (syntax-checker
and compiler) and Animator debugger, and associated functions.

Functions supplied on the COBOL menu are:

■ Checking and Animating

■ Checker error handling

■ Command file processing

These functions are described below.

The COBOL Editor uses the first file loaded into a window as the
main COBOL program root file for that window when accessing
any of these functions. It is possible to have more than one program loaded in the Editor provided that each main program file is
loaded in a different window and is the first file loaded for each of
those windows. Any files loaded after the initial file in a window
by using the library facility (**Alt+F2=library** from the Editor
Alternate menu) are assumed to be components of the main
program file. Blocks are assumed to contain only temporary
information related to editing any of these files.

When accessing any of the COBOL support functions, the particular function uses the program file associated with the current window. If you are editing more than one program in different windows then you need to make the window containing the main file for that required program active (that is, highlighted) before you access the function - the main program file does not necessarily have to be the file.currently being viewed in that window however. It is sufficient to simply select the window. For details on how to select windows see the sections *Using Windows* and *Using the Mouse*.

Note: If your program has been changed since you loaded it, you must save it (**Alt=F4** from the main menu) before you can check and animate it. If you don't save, the message:

```
exit without saving?   Y/N
```

reminds you to do this.

Checking and Animating

The COBOL compiler in Personal COBOL is called the Checker, because as it compiles your program's COBOL source code it performs a syntax check. If it finds an error it interrupts the compilation process and displays an error message. It then gives you the option of returning to the Editor to correct the error immediately or continuing the compilation. If you choose to continue compilation after an error, you can use the Checker error handling function on the COBOL menu later to move to each error in the source code in turn.

Once checking is completed with no errors, program animation can begin. Program animation, under the control of the Animator, lets you control and view the execution of your source code. Animator enables you to find bugs in programs very easily and quickly. When you exit Animator, you are returned to the Editor and you can correct any logic errors in your program.

For details on Checking and Animating, see the chapters *Checker* and *Animator* which follow.

Checker Error Handling

During the checking phase any errors encountered are displayed on the screen and written to an error file. The error file produced by the checker is used by the Editor to position at the identified errors. The file is created with the root name of the program being checked and is given a file extension of MSG.

If errors are encountered during the check phase then on return to the Editor the error file and program main file are loaded. The Editor reads the first error file record and positions to the identified error line. The error message associated with the error line is displayed on the message line.

If the error is in a copy file, the Editor first loads the main program file and then loads the copy file containing the error and positions to the required line. The copy file load action is similar to the library function (**Alt+F2=library**), that is the current edit view (onto the main program file that has just been loaded) is stacked and the COPY-file is loaded.

To position the Editor on the next program error, press **F8=locate-next** from the COBOL menu. To position on the previous program error, press **F7=locate-previous**. The current error position can be relocated by pressing **F9=locate-current**.

If it is not convenient to process the errors immediately after checking the program then the error message file can be closed and processed at some later time. The error message file can be opened and closed explicitly from the Command File menu. See the section *Command File Processing* below.

Command File Processing

The command files created during checking and animation of a COBOL program together with pasted text copied from the on-line documentation system can be loaded at any time into the COBOL Editor. The functions to load these files are provided, through the COBOL menu (**F3=cmd-file**), by the Command File menu.

Text copied from the on-line documentation system can be inserted at the current point in your file by pressing **F2**. The Editor will look for a file called PASTE.TXT in the current directory. If the file is found the Editor loads the entire contents of the file and inserts the text immediately before the current line. The same text can be inserted as many times as you require, either at the same place or at different locations within your files.

The error message file created by the Checker can be loaded by pressing **F3=load-error-file**. The Editor will search for a file with the same name as the main program file associated with the current window but with a file extension of MSG. If the file is found, the Editor positions to the first error defined in the error message file and returns to the COBOL menu with the error message displayed on the message line.

The Editor can be positioned to other error locations using **F7=locate-previous**, **F8=locate-next** and **F9=locate-current** from the COBOL menu.

On next entry to the Command File menu, the Information Line contains "Error-File-Active". The currently active file can be closed by pressing **F5=close file**.

Using Edit Windows

This section describes the creation and use of edit windows Initially the Editor has one window which is used to contain a textual view of the line sequential file being created or updated. The line sequential file can contain up to 999,999 records and each record can contain up to 132 characters. Navigation of the file is presented through the window, the window appearing to scroll vertically or horizontally over the underlying file contents.

Creating a New Window

The initial window created when the Editor is started fills the available work area and includes a border. The border can be turned off if the full work area is required for Editor operation.

Each new window is created half the size of the work area including a border, the border providing a visual indication of the extent of the window. Once the window has been created you can either load an existing file into it or you can create a new file.

When a file is specified for loading into a window, the Editor checks to see if the file has already been loaded, either in the current window (for example, as a COPY member) or in a different window. If the file is already loaded in the current window, the Editor represents that view in the window. If the specified file is already loaded in another window, the Editor opens another view onto the file, in the current window. The file can then be edited in any of the windows which have a view onto it, although changes are displayed only in the current window. Any changes made are reflected in the other windows as and when they are selected.

The active window has a highlighted border and contains the cursor. When a new window is created it becomes the active window.

The window functions are available in a menu entered from the Editor main menu. Press and hold down the **Ctrl** key to access the Control menu. Continue to press the **Ctrl** key as you press **F9=window**, then release both keys. The Window Control menu appears.

A new window may be created using the open window function **F5=open-window**. Windows may also be created using the window listbox - see the section *The Window Navigation Listbox* for more details.

The border of the window can be removed or added using the border on/off function (**F2=border-on/off**).

Selecting a Window

When a new window is created it overlays previously created windows and becomes the active window.

Previously created windows can be selected as the active window using the **F7=previous window** and **F8=next window** functions.

The previous window function allows you to select windows created prior to the current active window. When the current window is the first window created, this function wraps and selects the last window that was created. Similarly the next window function selects windows created after the current one. If the most recent window to be created is current when the next window function is used, then the command wraps and selects the first window to be created.

In addition to being able to cycle between windows in terms of creation time, it is also possible to select windows you wish to work with directly using either a mouse or the window listbox. See the sections Using the Mouse and *The Window Navigation Listbox* for more details.

Sizing a Window

When using multiple windows you may wish to vary the size of the windows and position them to enable a number of windows to be viewed simultaneously. You can re-size and move the windows to provide non-overlaid windows.

To size a window using the keyboard press **F3=size** on the Window Control menu. The Window Control menu is updated to provide re-sizing using the cursor control keys.

The sizing of a window is controlled by first selecting a border and then moving the selected border. The first cursor control key pressed selects the border of the window corresponding to the cursor control key, cursor left selects the left border, cursor up selects the top border, cursor down selects the bottom border and cursor right selects the right border.

When a border is selected the screen attribute of the border line is changed to indicate that it is selected. If the top or bottom border is selected then the **cursor up/down** keys move the selected border up/down. If the left or right border is selected then the **cursor left/right** keys move the selected border left/right.

When using the keyboard to size a window, two borders can be selected at any time, but only one each of the top and bottom, or left and right borders can be selected. If the border is at the edge of the work area further attempts to move in this direction cause the Editor to beep. The minimum window size is four characters high by four characters wide. To deselect the active borders and to re-enable the Window Control menu functions press the **Escape** key. Alternative borders can then be selected by pressing **F3=size** to re-enable the sizing functions.

As the window sizing operates on the border of the window it is advisable to have the border switched on. The keyboard sizing functions operate in the same way with the border switched off but it will not be apparent from the window display which borders are selected. When using a mouse to size a window, the borders must be turned on.

A window can be re-sized to the complete work area by a single keystroke, press **F9=max/restore-window** to maximize the window. Other windows are then hidden as the active window overlays the complete work area. As other windows are selected, they will each in turn become the active window overlaying the inactive windows. To restore the window to its pre-maximized size, press **F9=max/restore-window** again. This key toggles a window between its maximized and "current" size.

Moving a Window

A window can be moved anywhere within the work area. To move a window using the keyboard press **F4=move** on the Window Control menu. The Window Control menu is updated to provide window movement using the cursor control keys.

The cursor movement keys now move the window within the work area. The cursor up and cursor down keys move the window up and down respectively within the work area, and the cursor left and cursor right keys move the window left and right respectively within the work area. If the window is at the edge of the work area, further attempts to move in this direction cause the Editor to beep.

A window can also be moved using a mouse. This is described in the section *Using the Mouse*. As with sizing a window, the keyboard controls for moving a window operate regardless of

Editor

whether the window's border is on or off. When using a mouse to move a window, the border must be on. To re-enable the Window Control menu functions press the **Escape** key.

Closing a Window

A window remains open until you explicitly close it using the close window function (**F10**) or you exit from the last file contained within the window which automatically closes the window.

When you close a window using either method, the Editor checks to see if any of the files loaded into the window have been modified and are not loaded in any other window. If such files exist you are informed and asked if you wish to "exit without saving?". Replying no cancels the close function. If you reply yes, then the modifications are discarded and the window closed. The first available window is then selected as the active window. If no open windows remain, you exit from the Editor.

If a modified file is being viewed from more than one window then the "exit without saving?" message is displayed only on exit from the last window with access to the file.

The Window Navigation Listbox

The Window Navigation listbox ("window listbox") is a facility to enable you to open new windows and select existing windows for editing. It is useful for quickly accessing a window that is completely hidden behind others. The listbox is accessed using the show windows function (**F6**). It can also be accessed easily using a mouse. This method is described in the section *Using the Mouse*.

When accessed the window listbox displays a list of all open windows detailing the file currently being viewed in each, together with the file's size (in lines) and an indicator showing whether the file has been modified but the changes not saved. The first entry in the list is always "— Open New Window —" - selecting this item opens a new window, the same as if you had used the open window function (**F5**) on the window control menu. The current selection in the list is shown in highlighted text.

A window is selected or created by moving the highlight to the appropriate entry and pressing the **Enter** key. The highlight is moved using the cursor keys. The **up/down** keys move the highlight up and down the list while the **left/right** keys scroll the text of the entries right and left respectively. If the listbox contains more entries than can be displayed, a vertical scroll bar is displayed on the extreme right of the listbox. As the highlight reaches the top and bottom extents of the displayed items then the listbox contents scroll revealing further entries, one at a time. If you attempt to move beyond the first or last item in the list, the Editor will sound the bell. If you select an existing window, then that window is made active with the cursor placed at the same position it was at when the window was last accessed. In addition if any modifications have been made to the file in another window then the display is updated to show these changes.

If you select the "Open New Window" entry then a new window is created and the cursor placed at the left margin column in the window.

You can exit from the listbox without changing the current active window by pressing the **Escape** key. This removes the listbox and places the cursor back in the current window. On making a selection the listbox is automatically removed.

Accessing Files in a Window

From the Load-files menu (**Alt+F3=load-files** from the main menu), you can access files which are already loaded, but are either hidden behind others in the same window, or were originally loaded into another window.

F7=files-in-window brings up a list of all the files which can currently be viewed in the selected window. Selecting one brings it to the front, with the cursor where it was last time you edited it. The previous view is hidden behind it.

This facility is useful for switching between a program (previously loaded using **Alt+F3=load-file**), and its COPY members (previously loaded using **Alt+F2=library**).

F8=list-all brings up a list of all the files which have been loaded into the Editor, irrespective of which window they can be seen in. Selecting one adds it to the files which you can view in the selected window, and brings it to the front.

This is useful if you want to see two or more parts of one file at the same time.

The steps are as follows: Ensure that the window you want to work in is selected. From the main menu, select the Load-files menu (press **Alt+F3=load-file**) and press **F7=files-in-window** or **F8=list-all** as appropriate.

The appropriate listbox will be displayed; they are very similar, and each contain a list of files. For each file, the length in lines is shown, together with an M indicator in the "mod" column if the file has been modified.

To select a file to view, move the highlight over its entry and press **Enter.** The **up/down** keys move the highlight up and down the list while the **left/right** keys scroll the text of the entries right and left respectively. If the listbox contains more entries than can be displayed, a vertical scroll bar is displayed on the extreme right of the listbox. As the highlight reaches the top and bottom extents of the displayed items then the listbox contents scroll revealing further entries, one at a time. If you attempt to move beyond the first or last item in the list, the Editor will sound the bell. When an entry has been selected, the listbox will be removed leaving the selected file being viewed in the window. The previous view (if any) is stacked ready for possible re-use later by the same method.

You can also use a mouse to operate the listbox. See the section *Using the Mouse* for further details.

If you want to exit from the listbox and return to the Load-files menu without selecting a file to view, press **Escape** rather than **Enter**.

Clearing a File

After you save a file, it remains within the window until you either clear it, close the window, or exit from the Editor.

To clear a file and present an empty workfile for editing or loading another file, ensure that the required window is the currently active window and press **Ctrl+F4=clear** from the Editor main menu. If you have loaded more than the current file into the window none of those files will be affected by the clear operation - it applies only to the current file being edited and/or viewed.

If you are in danger of losing modifications to a file, you are warned and given the chance to cancel the clear operation. A message such as:

```
clear without saving? Y/N
```

appears on the Message Line. Respond by pressing **Y** (**Yes**) to clear the current file and discard any unsaved changes or **N** (**No**) to cancel the operation.

You can also use the clear option when you want to clear an edited block of text. When you are editing a block of text, all of the Editor editing features are available for use. If you press **Ctrl+F4=clear** without first saving the block, it cannot be recovered. If you save the block of text (**Alt+F4=save-file**), you can then use **Ctrl+F4=clear** to clear the block (and still be able to recover it later from the file).

Using the Mouse

If you have a mouse attached to your workstation and you have included the necessary commands in your operating system configuration files then you may use the mouse within the CO-BOL Editor to perform such operations as moving, sizing and selecting windows and moving the cursor. This section describes how to perform each operation. Each operation uses the following terminology to describe actions with the mouse:

Editor

click	press and then release the left mouse button once;
double-click	press and release the left mouse button twice in rapid succession;
drag	press and hold down the left mouse button then move the mouse in a particular direction. The dragging ends when you release the left mouse button, regardless of whether the mouse is moving or not.

Moving the Cursor Within a Window

To move the cursor to a particular row and column within the displayed extent of your text in a window, move the mouse pointer to the desired location and click the left-hand mouse button. The cursor will then move to that position and the line will be highlighted to mark it as the current line.

If you click the left button while the mouse pointer is beyond either the "top of text" or "end of text" markers then the bell will sound and the cursor will not be moved from its present location. This facility is also available when using the Draw function to position the cursor for draw or erase operations directly.

Selecting a Window For Editing

If you have more than one window open you can select a particular window to become current by positioning the mouse pointer on any visible part of the required window and clicking the left mouse button once. The border (if on) of the particular window will then change color to indicate that the window has become current and will be the one used when further commands or text are entered. The border (if on) of the window that was previously active will also change color, to indicate that that window is no longer current.

When the window has been selected, the cursor is positioned at the same position as it was when the window was last active. If you "double click" the left mouse button when selecting a window, then in addition to selecting the window the cursor is also moved to the text position lying beneath the mouse pointer, if that is a valid location as described above in the section Moving the Cursor Within a Window.

Note: It is not possible to select and therefore switch between windows while a file is loading or printing in the current window. If you attempt to do so, the bell will sound and a message will be displayed indicating the function is disabled. Pressing the **Space** bar clears the message and allows the file loading or printing to continue.

Moving a Window

You move a window using the mouse by positioning the mouse pointer on the top border of the window, pressing and holding the left mouse button and dragging the window to the desired position on the screen. It is not possible to move a window with the mouse if the window does not have its border turned on. As you click on the border, the text within the window is temporarily removed from the display and the entire window border changes color to indicate that you are moving the window. When you release the left mouse button, the text is restored to the display and the border resumes its normal "current" color.

It is not possible to move a window over the menu area or off any edge of the screen - any attempt to do this results in the bell sounding, the window remaining in its previous position.

Sizing a Window

You can size a window by moving either its left, right or bottom border in the desired direction to shrink or enlarge the window's extent (the top border is used to move a window with the mouse and therefore cannot be used to size a window). It is not possible to size a window with the mouse if the window's border is turned off. The procedure is the same as moving a window - you click on the border you wish to shrink or enlarge and drag the border to achieve the desired effect. As you click on the particular border, it changes color to indicate it is currently active for resizing. When you release the left mouse button the border resumes its previous color.

Unlike moving a window with the mouse, when you size a window the text displayed within the window is not temporarily removed - this is so you can see the effect on the visible text as the window's size changes. The Editor always keeps the current cursor position within the text visible, regardless of the size of the window.

Note: It is not possible to size a window to the effect that a particular border lies beyond the edge of the screen or over the menu area - any attempt to move a border beyond these limits causes the bell to sound, the border remaining in its previous position.

Maximizing and Restoring a Window's Size

The COBOL Editor provides an easy method for instantly sizing a window to occupy all of the work area and to restore it to its pre-maximized size. An indicator on the upper right corner of the window's border displays which of these two states the window is currently in. If the indicator is an upward pointing triangle, then the window can be maximized. If the indicator is a diamond, the window is already maximized and can be restored to its pre-maximized state. If you size a window by dragging one or more of its borders then the indicator is changed depending upon the size of the window when you release the left mouse button and end the dragging of the particular border.

If the indicator is showing that the window can be maximized, clicking on the indicator maximizes the window. Conversely, clicking on the indicator when the window is already at its maximum size restores the window to its previous size.

It is not possible to access this function with the mouse if the border of the window is turned off.

Note: When the Editor is started, the initial window by default is maximized, the indicator showing this. Clicking on the indicator will cause the window to shrink to half its maximized height automatically. Until you explicitly size the window using some other method (either mouse or keyboard), this is the default pre-maximized size.

Accessing the Window Navigation Listbox

The Window Navigation listbox ("window listbox") lists and gives access to all windows currently open within the Editor. In addition to allowing you to select windows for editing, it allows you to create new windows easily. The window listbox facilities are described in more detail in the section The Window Navigation Listbox. To access this listbox using the mouse instead of the **F6=show-windows** function on the Window Control menu, click the left mouse button while the mouse pointer is over any unused portion of the Editor work area or the menu area. Provided the listbox is not already active, it will then be displayed.

The use of the mouse to select listbox items or cancel a particular listbox is described below. The window listbox is the only listbox that can be accessed using the mouse - to access the other listboxes, you need to use the actual key functions on the Load and Save-file menus.

Note: You cannot access the window listbox while a file is loading or printing or you are marking a block. If you attempt to do so, the bell will sound and a message of the form:

```
Function disabled while file loading
```

will be displayed. Pressing the **Space** bar will remove the message. If you were marking a block, you can then continue to define the block, while if you were printing or loading a file, the print or load operation continues as before.

Using the Mouse with Listboxes

The mouse can be used in conjunction with all of the file and window listboxes provided by the Editor. However, the window listbox is the only listbox where access is provided by clicking the left mouse button on any unused portion of the Editor work-area or menu.

Once a listbox has been displayed, the mouse can be used to select items, scroll the list of items displayed (where applicable) and cancel the listbox. To move the selection highlight to a list entry, position the mouse pointer over the entry and click the left mouse button. The current entry will then lose the selection highlight and it will be supplied to the entry clicked on. To select a particular entry and thus remove the listbox, double-click on the particular entry. For example, in the window listbox, to open a new window double-click on the "Open New Window" entry - the listbox will then be removed and the new window created. If the list contains more entries than can be displayed at any one time, a vertical scroll-bar is displayed on the extreme right of the listbox. The dark shaded slider represents the portion of the list currently being displayed. Clicking above this slider causes the list to page up. Similarly, clicking below the slider causes a page down. Clicking on the slider itself has no effect.

To cancel a listbox without making a selection simply click on either the window that was active before the listbox was accessed or another window that you want to edit. The listbox will then be removed and the window that you clicked on made current. Note that cancelling a listbox in this way is slightly different from just pressing the **Escape** key - if you press the **Escape** key you are placed back into the menu from which you accessed the particular listbox. Using the mouse bypasses this menu and returns straight to the main menu.

Printing a File

You can send a file to the printer using the print option on the Editor's Alternate menu. You press **Alt+F7=print** to access the print submenu from which you can define how the file is printed.

You can set the system to pause at each page by selecting the **F3=pause-at-new-page** option. Printing stops each time a "/" (page-break character) is encountered in the column where the left hand margin is set. For example, if you are using the default COBOL margins, you would enter page break characters at column 7. You restart printing by pressing the **Space** bar.

You can also print the entire file without pausing by pressing **F4=no-pause**. However, a new page is still begun each time the page-break character is encountered. Pressing

F3=pause-at-new-page or **F4=no-pause** initiates the printing process.

If you wish to cancel printing at any time, simply press **F2=cancel-print**. You return to the Editor main menu as printing is aborted.

You exit from the print menu without printing anything by pressing **Escape**.

See section *Printer Control Codes* for more information.

Drawing Lines

The COBOL Editor draw feature lets you be creative in the display of your text on the screen. You can draw diagrams and charts as well as enclose text in boxes.

The draw feature has its own menu which is accessed by pressing **Ctrl+F6=draw/scrns** from the Editor main menu, and **F2=draw** from the Editor draw/scrns menu.

```
Drawing────Join────239-lines────Line-1────Col-8────────Wrap-Ins-Caps-Num-Scroll
F1=help F2=draw/erase/move F3=│/‖ F4=join/over/under
                                  ↓←↑→=draw                                Escape
```

Figure 4-7: Draw Menu

When you invoke the Draw feature, the cursor changes shape, appearing similar to the cursor when Insert mode is on. As soon as you press one of the cursor movement keys the beginning of a single line appears on the screen. You can switch back and forth between drawing single lines and double lines by pressing **F3** (a toggle). When you press **F3** to draw double lines, the appearance of the Information Line changes to display a double line.

You change the mode indicator by pressing **F2=draw/erase/move**. This key toggles from one function to the next and changes the effect of cursor movement; its current function is displayed both on the Information Line and next to the movement keys on the Draw menu. The default behavior of the cursor is draw (which is displayed when you first invoke this menu). When you set the cursor to erase by pressing **F2=draw/erase/move**, you use the cursor movement keys to go back over those lines, deleting them. When you set this toggle to move, the cursor changes shape, and you can then move through the screen without drawing any lines.

Lines can be made to join, cross over or cross under when they meet by using the "Join" toggle. Pressing **F4=join/over/under** toggles between the settings "Join", "Over" and "Under". The default setting is "Join". When the toggle shows "Join", lines will be merged when they cross. "Over" causes the current line to appear to "pass over" the existing line while "Under" causes the current line to appear to pass below the existing line.

When drawing lines, the full record width (132 characters) of the Editor is available for use. The window contents will scroll in the same manner as that used when entering text if you attempt to move the cursor beyond the borders of the current window. In addition you have unlimited movement downwards - the Editor extends the number of lines in the file each time you attempt to move below the end of text marker. If you attempt to move above the top of text marker, to the left of column 1 or to the right of column 132 then the Editor will sound the bell. When drawing left and right, the current margin settings are ignored although the line highlighting will indicate the region on each line enclosed by the margins.

The text editing options are not available when you are in draw mode. You press **Escape** to return to the Editor main menu to continue editing your file. The lines you have drawn remain visible on the screen.

Editing Files Identified in Your COBOL Program

You use the library facility to edit a file identified in your COBOL program by one of the following statements:

CALL file-name
COPY file-name
INCLUDE file-name

You can then edit this file, save it and return to your main program file. You access this function of the COBOL Editor from the library option on the Alternate menu. When you press **Alt+F2=library**, the COBOL Editor scans the current line for a CALL, COPY, INCLUDE statement. If it locates one of these statements, the word following the statement is assumed to be a file-name and the system will attempt to locate a file with that name. If no extension is provided, then by default the Editor will look for a file with a .CBL, .CPY or spaces extension. If the file is located, the current file being viewed is "stacked" and the window displays the contents of the new file, with the name of the file being displayed on the Information Line. If the file is not found then the view onto the current file is stacked and a blank workfile is presented within the window.

If the Editor does not locate one of these statements, then the word at or to the right of the current cursor position becomes the file-name.

If multiple COPY, CALL, INCLUDE statements are located on the same line of text, the Editor selects only the first occurrence. The file-name must follow the statement identifier and be completed on the same text line; if the statement is continued onto a second text line then the required file will not be found.

The COBOL Editor searches for the named file as follows:

1. The list of files already loaded for editing is searched to see if a matching file root name exists. If a match is found the Editor represents the existing view for editing. If no match is found the Editor looks for the file on disk as detailed below.

2. If the file-name contains a path name, the Editor searches for the file in that path only.

3. If there is no path specification on the COPY statement, then it looks for the file-name in the current directory.

4. If not found, a new file is opened in the current directory. You can easily switch between files loaded using the library function by using the "Files-in-window" listbox, available from the Load-files menu. For further details, see *Accessing Files in a Window*.

The Directory Facility

The Directory Facility is available to find the disk file you want whenever you need to provide the Editor with a file-name. You enter the Directory Facility by pressing **F2-directory** while in a load-file or save-file menu (reached by **Alt+F3** and **Alt+F4** respectively).

The Directory Facility includes functions for listing, browsing, renaming and deleting files (you must not delete or rename a file that is currently loaded in the Editor), and for changing the current directory or drive. The default directory displays those file-names with the same extension as shown at the bottom of the screen, but you can use the file prompt in the load-file menu to pass a file specification to the Directory Facility, such as "*.TXT".

Printer Codes

This section describes how you can make the most of the features of your personal computer. It includes information on how to control the printer.

The COBOL Editor supports several facilities for printing text files. The print option (**Alt+F7=print**) prints the current file. As it is being printed, you can continue editing beyond the page being printed. The COBOL Editor lets you send form-feed characters to the printer to throw new pages. You key a "/" (slash) in column 7 (under the left margin). The "/" is not printed but causes a new page to be thrown.

Note that if you print the file under DOS, the "/" is treated as a text character and appears on the print-out. It does not throw a new page.

The documentation accompanying an IBM printer (designed to be inserted in the *IBM Guide to Operations*), includes a list of control codes that you use to control the printer. However, since it addresses programming in BASIC, this next section explains how to use these printed codes from the COBOL Editor.

Controlling the Printer

You can include printer control codes in text files created and edited in the COBOL Editor. You will notice from your *IBM Guide to Operations* that most control codes must be preceded by an ESC character. However, in the COBOL Editor, the **Escape** key exits the current function; it is not treated as a text character.

To produce an ESC character, hold down the **Alt** key and key 2, then 7 on the numeric keypad of your keyboard (an **Alt-27** is the alternate code for the escape character). Then release the **Alt** key. An arrow appears at the cursor position. This arrow is the text representation of the ESC character. You then key after the ESC character whatever control codes you want to send to the printer. These neither print nor take space on the line on which they appear; that is, they occupy a space on the screen but not on a printed line.

Example

The following example shows how to underline text on the IBM graphics printer. "I will try to arrange a meeting for May or June"

To underline the word "or":

1.   Position the cursor on the letter "o".

2.   Set insert mode by pressing the **Ins** key.

3.   Press **Alt+2**, then **7** on the numeric keypad.

4.   Release the **Alt** key.

5.   Key **-1** to begin underlining. The text now appears as shown below:

   "I will try to arrange a meeting for May ⟵ 1or June"

6.   Move the cursor to the character position following the "r"

7.   While still in insert mode, press **Alt+2**, then **7** once again.

8.   Key **-0** to end underlining. The text now appears as follows:

```
"I will try to arrange a meeting for May ←— lor
←— 0June"
```

and prints as:

```
"I will try to arrange a meeting for May or June"
```

Other printer control codes can be keyed in the same way using the **Alt** key and entering **2** and **7** from the numeric keypad. The control codes that you include in this way remain in the file when it is written to disk and are understood and acted on if you send your file to an appropriate printer under DOS.

There are a few control codes which are not preceded by an ESC character. To include these you use the same technique with the **Alt** key and the numeric keypad. For example, to set compressed characters, press **Alt+15**. To unset them, press **Alt+18**. For further information about printer control codes, see the section about printers in your *IBM Guide to Operations*.

These control codes are specific for the IBM Graphic Printer. Codes to control printing vary widely among different printers. Refer to your printer manual for details of these codes.

Chapter 5

Checker (Compiling)

The Checker compiles the program source code into intermediate code which can then be tested or run. Syntax-checking is synonymous with the phrase compiling in this system.

Invoking the Checker

The Checker is accessed through the Editor's main menu **F2=COBOL** option. Press **F2** from the COBOL menu to enter the Checker menu. From the Checker menu, the **F2** key toggles between Check and Animate. The selected option is displayed on the information line.

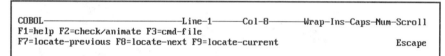

```
COBOL────────────────────Line-1────Col-8────Wrap-Ins-Caps-Num-Scroll
F1=help F2=check/animate F3=cmd-file
F7=locate-previous F8=locate-next F9=locate-current              Escape
```

Figure 5-1: Checker Menu

Using the Checker

When you press **Enter** the program to be checked is determined by the name of the file loaded in the editor. The root name and path of this program file is shown on the bottom line of the Checker menu. If the name shown is not that of the program required then you must first edit the correct program before pressing **Enter**. See *COBOL Support Functions* in the chapter *Editor*.

Checker

When you press **Enter** to initiate checking, the screen is initially blank except for the information displayed at the bottom of the screen. This line shows the name of the file being checked. It also tells you that you can terminate the checking process by pressing **Ctrl+Break**.

The first line that appears in the working area of the screen lists the options (Checker directives) that are pre-set by the system. It then displays the source code of your program.

Each time the checker detects a syntax error, it stops and displays the following message:

```
CONTINUE CHECKING PROGRAM ? Yes/No/Zoom
```

If you respond by pressing **N** (**No**), you are returned to the COBOL Editor screen on the first line that caused an error so that you can correct the error. To recheck the program, first save your changes, then press **F2=COBOL** to enter the COBOL menu followed by **F2=check/anim,** if required to access the Checker menu. Finally press **Enter** to restart the checking process.

If you press **Y** (**Yes**) in response to the "Continue checking..." message, the system continues to check the program, informing you about any further errors it detects.

If you press **Z** the compiler will check the whole program without pausing at errors.

The compilation process ends by displaying the number of errors found in your code. It also displays the size of the generated data area, the size of the generated code, and the size of the internal dictionary. On completion of the compilation phase the system returns you to the Editor. If the checking process detected errors the Editor positions you at the first line that caused an error.

Syntax errors are documented in the On-line Reference. To reach the On-line Reference information for a syntax error:

- in the Editor press **Alt-1** to enter the On-line Reference.
- press **C** to view the Table of Contents.
- select the Syntax Errors button (either double click with the mouse or use the **Tab** and **Enter** keys).
- select the error number for which you need information.

The compiler ends by showing the number of syntax errors found and the size of the data, code and internal dictionary produced. The system then returns you to the Editor. If errors were found, the Editor positions you at the first line that caused a syntax error.

Specifying Checking Options

You may wish to check a program with options other than the default. These options may be entered from the Checker menu.

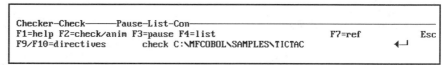

Figure 5-2: Checker Options

Pause (*F3*)

This key is a toggle that switches "Pause" on and off. The Information Line indicates when pause is on. The default setting is On.

When pause is on, the checker pauses if an error is found during syntax checking and the checker is suspended.

The Checker screen can then be viewed to establish the nature of the error. You can return to the Editor at the indicated error line by selecting 'N' to stop checking the program.

When pause is off, the Checker errors are stacked on the Checker screen in the normal way but no indication is given apart from the Checker sounding the bell.

List (*F4*)

The **F4=list** option allows you to specify either no listing ("Nolist") which speeds up the checking process, list to file ("List-File"), print ("Print") or list to console ("List-Con"). Pressing **F4=list** cycles through these settings with the status line being updated to show the current setting.

Ref (*F7*)

Allows you to specify the "REF", "XREF" (or both) directives. The default setting for this toggle is both options off.

The REF directive makes the compiler include in the source listing the intermediate code address of each data item or Procedure Division statement. The address is four digits long and appears on the right hand side, needing a line width of at least 90. Thus the REF output cannot be seen in a screen listing, but only when the list output is directed to file or printer.

The XREF directive makes the compiler produce a cross reference listing. Extra information is added to the end of the .LST file produced:

- the name of each data item and procedure

- the type of each data item and procedure

- the line number where each was defined (n#)

- the line numbers where each data item was updated (n*)

- the line numbers where each data item was tested (n?)

- the line numbers where each procedure was used (n)

- the number of times each appeared in the listing (X n)

Directives (*F9/F10*)

To enter additional directives, press **F10=directives** to access the Checker Directives menu. Type in the directives you require and press **Enter** to return to the Checker menu. Pressing **F9=directives** on the Checker menu toggles the "opt-on" indicator on the Information Line. When "opt-on" is displayed, the directives entered on the Checker Directives menu will be passed to the checker. When "opt-on" is not shown, they are ignored. Checker directives are listed in the chapter *Compiler Directives*.

Chapter 6

Animator

The Animator is a powerful menu-driven tool for debugging your COBOL programs. It displays your source code on the screen, highlighting each line of the source as your program is executed. This process is referred to as animating.

This chapter describes the complete set of functions in the Animator.

Overview

Animator displays information about your program during execution, along with the corresponding part of your source code. Animator provides functions to enable you to control the pace at which your program runs, interrupt execution to examine and change data items, alter the sequence of execution or enter COBOL statements for immediate execution before your program continues. These facilities allow you to debug your programs quickly and easily.

Executing the Program

Animator can be used after you have checked your program with no errors. From the Editor, press **F2** to enter the COBOL menu, and **F2** again to enter the Checker menu. At the Checker menu, press **F2** until the Animator is selected and "Animate" is shown on the information line. At this point, pressing **Enter** will load the program into Animator and testing can begin.

Animator

A flexible set of execution functions enables you to execute the code at the speed to suit the problem you are examining. You can Zoom (execute at maximum speed) through code you do not wish to see execute, manually Step through each statement or set a convenient automatic execution speed in a problem area.

Breakpoints can be set throughout the source code by marking each statement where you want a break to occur or by defining a condition that should give rise to a break. This lets you define exactly when to get manual control of your program when it is executing automatically.

A backtracking facility can show you the path that has been taken through your code to arrive at a specific point.

Monitoring and Changing Data Items

Debugging a program often involves monitoring various data value in order to detect unexpected results.

Data queries allow you to see the before and after states of data values as each statement is executed. You can simply overtype the monitored data items if you want to manually set a new value in order to change the logic flow of your program.

Logic Testing

"Do" functions allow you to execute additional code without having to interrupt your testing session. These COBOL statements may be executed when you enter them.

"Reset" functions allow you to bypass code that you do not want to be executed.

Data items may be viewed and modified in either text or hex format.

Operation

Once you have compiled a program for animation, you can invoke Animator. This section explains:

- how to invoke Animator

- how the Animator screens are organized

- how you operate the display and access the Animator functions

Invoking Animator

Animator is selected via the Editor **F2=COBOL** function. A program that has been previously checked (and not subsequently changed) can access Animator directly by toggling the **F2=check/anim** switch. When "Animator" is highlighted on the information line pressing **Enter** loads the Animator.

A program that has not been has been previously checked (or checked but subsequently changed) can access the Animator only after checking with no errors has occurred.

Screen Description and Operation

The Animator screen appears after Animator has been invoked. The source code of your program appears on this screen. The cursor is positioned under the first executable statement in the Procedure Division, and this statement is highlighted. The bottom of the screen displays the Information Line and the Animator Main menu.

The Animator Main menu contains functions that you select to control the way your program is executed. A full description of these functions is presented later in this chapter.

Animator

When you use an option that causes statements to be executed, the cursor and highlighting follow the execution path, so they are always on the statement to be executed next. At other times, the highlighting remains on the statement that is to be executed next, but you can move the cursor around the screen to access different places in the source. The statement to be executed next, or currently being executed, is always highlighted, and is known as the current statement.

```
    89 play-game section.
    90 play-1.
    91    perform with test after
    92        until char not = "Y" and char not = "y"
    93        call clear-screen
    94        display
    95            "To select a square type a number between 1 and 9"
    96            upon crt
    97        perform init
    98        move "Shall I start ? " to question
    99        perform get-reply
   100        if char = "Y" or char = "y"
   101            move 10 to check(5)
   102            perform put-move
   103        end-if
   104        perform new-move until game not = spaces
   105        move "Play again ?     " to question
   106        perform get-reply
   107    end-perform.
   108
   109 play-stop.
Animate-TICTAC────────────────────────────Level=01-Speed=5-Ins-Caps-Num-Scroll
F1=help F2=view F3=align F4=exchange F5=where F6=look-up  F9/F10=word-</> Escape
Step Go Zoom next-If Perform Reset Break Env Query Find Locate Text Do 0-9=speed
```

Figure 6-1: Animator Screen

The Information Line

The Information Line displays the name of your program. It also shows the nested level performed of subroutines within the current program (Level=01) and the speed you have selected at which to animate your program. The **Ins**, **Caps**, **Num** and **Scroll** indicators, which appear on the right side of the information line, are highlighted when **Ins**, **Caps Lock**, **Num Lock**, or **Scroll Lock** respectively are active.

Moving the Cursor and Text During Animation

There are several keys that you can use to move the cursor through the displayed code. You can also change the portion of text displayed on the screen. These keys are listed below. Some of these keys are symbolic key names which may not be present on your keyboard. For IBM keyboards, the appropriate key combinations are shown in parentheses at the end of the symbolic key description.

You can also use a mouse to move the cursor position. Simply move the mouse pointer to the required position and click the left mouse button.

Key	Function
left-arrow	moves the cursor left one character position
right-arrow	moves the cursor right one character position
cursor-up	moves the cursor up one line; with **Scroll Lock** on, moves the text down one line
cursor-down	moves the cursor down one line; with **Scroll Lock** on moves the text up one line
Tab	moves the cursor to the next tab position to the right; tabs are set every four positions in columns 8 through 72
Backtab	moves the cursor to the next tab position to the left
Enter	moves the cursor to column 8 on the next line; with **Scroll Lock** on, moves the text up one line
Home	moves the cursor to column 1 of the current line; pressing **Home** a second time moves the cursor to column 1 of the top line; pressing **Home** a third time moves the cursor to the beginning of the file

Animator

End	moves the cursor to the end of the current line; pressing **End** a second time moves the cursor to the bottom of the screen; pressing **End** a third time moves the cursor to the end of the file
PgUp	displays the screen of program text preceding this screen
PgDn	displays the screen of program text following this screen
Top-of-text (**Ctrl+Home**)	moves immediately to the top of the program
Bottom-of-text (**Ctrl+End**)	moves immediately to the end of the program
Up-ten-screens (**Ctrl+PgUp**)	moves (10 x source screen size) lines up the program
Down-ten-screens (**Ctrl+PgDn**)	moves (10 x source screen size) lines down the program

Entering Text on Menus

Several of the Animator menus require you to enter text. In all cases, on entry to the menu, the previous contents of the field will be present. This can be cleared using **F2**. The **F2=clear** key acts as a delete-to-end-field, deleting all characters from the current cursor position to the end of the field. When entering or editing text, the cursor keys, **Home**, **End** and **Backspace** all operate as normal. Insert or overtype mode can also be selected using the **Ins** key.

Once you have completed a field, pressing the **Enter** key will confirm your update. If you wish to cancel the update, press the **Escape** key. Both keys will cause exit to a higher level menu if appropriate.

Where a selection of fields is presented, the cursor keys may be used to move up and down the list, and the **Enter** key will select the item you want and place it in the input field if appropriate.

Viewing Data

You can view a maximum of 80 characters in COBOL format. You can scroll through the contents of this data to view other parts of the data item. You also have the option of displaying a maximum of 16 bytes of the monitored item in hexadecimal format.

Note: Numeric values are viewed as equivalent edited PICTURE strings.

Keyboard keys and special keystrokes allow efficient editing of the item's contents. See the section *Key Functions for Updating Queried Data Items* below.

Key Functions for Updating Queried Data Items

The following keys and key combinations have special effects when updating the contents of data items.

Key	Function
Home	moves cursor to beginning of data item
End	moves cursor to end of data item
cursor-left	moves cursor left one character position
cursor-right	moves cursor right one character position
F2	clears contents of data item
Ins	toggles between insert and replace modes; in insert mode, **Ins** is highlighted on the information line; cursor changes shape
Del	deletes character at current cursor position and causes all other characters to right of cursor to shift left one position
Backspace	deletes character before cursor position; if insert mode is on, causes all characters to right of cursor to shift left one position

Menus

The Animator menus are organized to provide rapid access to the most commonly used functions.

Help menus can be accessed from any Animator menu by pressing **F1=help**. This calls the help screen for the option from which it is called.

The menus described in this section appear in alphabetical order according to their menu name, which is displayed on the left-hand side of the information line.

Animator Main Menu

The Animator Main menu is displayed when Animator is started. The Main menu provides access both to direct functions and to submenus. The direct functions allow you, with a single keystroke, to execute the program and to reposition the program text on your screen.

To select a submenu or a function, use the appropriate function key or letter. To select the Alternate menu or the Control menu available in Animator, press the **Alt** or **Ctrl** keys respectively.

Breakpoints Menu

This menu is accessed by pressing **B** on the Animator Main menu.

You can set breakpoints in your program to halt execution when you are using Go or Zoom mode. They are useful for debugging programs quickly when you have some idea of where a problem lies.

This menu displays options that allow you to:

- set a breakpoint at the statement at the current cursor location.

- cancel either a single breakpoint at the current cursor location or all breakpoints throughout the program.

■   set a conditional breakpoint.

■   examine the set breakpoints.

■   automatically execute a specified COBOL statement at
     a breakpoint.

■   set the frequency with which a breakpoint is activated.

Re-checking a program causes breakpoints to be lost. If you leave
Animator without unsetting a breakpoint, the breakpoint will be
set next time you Animate the program, unless you have re-
checked it. You can set up to 100 breakpoints in each program.

When a breakpoint is reached, you will see the message:

```
Breakpoint encountered
```

at the bottom of your screen.

Environment Menu

The Environment menu is accessed by pressing **E** on the Animator
Main menu.

The Environment function allows you to set parameters to control
some general execution aspects of the program you are executing.
These include:

■   specify the name of a program at which to interrupt
     execution.

■   set a level below which PERFORMs and CALLs are
     executed as single steps (Threshold).

■   set a conditional program break which causes execution in
     Go or Zoom mode to halt when the condition is
     encountered (Until).

Animator

Go Menu

The Go menu is accessed by pressing **G** on the Animator Main menu.

The Go function automatically executes each statement in the program one by one, displaying the source code on the screen as it is executed. Go mode is an automatic Step mode; you do not have to press a key to execute each statement as you do in Step mode.

You can set the Go execution speed by pressing a key from **0** to **9**, where 0 is the slowest. You can also set the speed of execution from the Animator Main menu by pressing a number from **0** to **9** before selecting the Go function. The current speed is shown on the Information Line. The default speed is **5**.

Locate-declaration Menu

The Locate-declaration menu is accessed by pressing **L** on the Animator Main menu.

The Locate-declaration function finds the location in the source code where a data item, file-name, or procedure is declared.

From the Locate-declaration menu you can locate an item either by using the cursor as a pointer or keying in the name of the item you wish to locate. The cursor control keys can be used to position the cursor in the program text. Data items and file names may be located from their name in the text. Procedure names may be located from their names within the program text.

Perform-level Menu

The Peform-level menu is accessed by pressing **P** on the Animator Main menu.

The Perform-level function lets you zoom through performed paragraphs, in-line PERFORM statements and called subprograms. This is useful if you are looking for a bug and are sure it isn't in a particular PERFORM range or subprogram.

The perform functions allow you to Zoom through the code specified by a PERFORM or CALL statement, or the code that completes such a statement if you have already begun to execute it.

Query Menu

The Query menu is accessed by pressing **Q** on the Animator Main menu. The Query menu functions enable you to look at and change the contents of data items.

From this menu and its submenus, you can query data items, create a file containing a list of data values, and monitor data items.

Following a successful query, the Query Data-name submenu appears on the screen with the queried data name on the information line and the value of the data item at the bottom of the screen.

If you are using Animator, you should be aware that exiting Animator causes the monitor to be lost.

Query Data-name Menu

The Query Data-name menu appears after you have selected the item to be queried. The data name appears on the information line; the value of the data item appears at the bottom of the screen.

The Query Data-name menu is actually a set of two menus: an ASCII (text) menu and a Hex menu. You switch between them using a toggle key.

The ASCII menu is the menu which first appears after selecting the data item to be queried. Selecting the Hex function invokes the Hex menu. On this menu, the Hex function is replaced by a Text function which switches back to the Text menu.

On the Hex menu, the content of the queried data item appears on the bottom left of the screen in hexadecimal form. The corresponding ASCII representation appears on the bottom right.

Animator

Reset-execution Menu

The Reset-execution menu is accessed by pressing **R** on the Animator Main menu.

The Reset function allows you to alter the sequence of program execution by changing the current statement, which is the statement that will be executed next. You can simply skip one statement, reset to the current cursor position, reset at the next (higher) Perform level, or reset at the start of the program. Reset does not change the values of any data.

Text Menu

The Text menu is accessed by pressing **T** on the Animator Main menu. The Text function enables you to split, join, and redisplay the screen.

Functions

Animator functions are accessed from menus. The function names are sometimes abbreviated on the menus; however, this description uses the full names.

The following section contains a quick reference listing all of the functions available in Animator. This listing is followed by detailed descriptions of these functions.

Function Access

The following table lists the functions in alphabetical order and indicates the keys you must press to access them. Thus, to determine the path to access a given function, follow the sequence of keystrokes. For example, to reach the Set Breakpoints function from the Animator Main menu, you press the Breakpoints key (**B**) followed by the Set Breakpoints key (**S**).

For the purposes of this table, it is assumed that you are using the cursor to identify data-names rather than keying them in;

therefore, a C on the menu access path indicates the selection of a data name using the cursor. If, however, you are not using cursor, simply substitute **Enter** and the name of your data-item for the key C to identify fields.

Function	Menu Access Keys
0-9	**0-9**
Add List	**Q, C, Alt+F3**
Align	**F3**
Breakpoints	**B**
Cancel Breakpoints	**B, C**
Cancel Program Break	**E, P, C**
Clear	Several
Contained Data	**Q, C, F8**
Containing Data	**Q, C, F7**
Cursor-name Locate	**L, C**
Cursor-name Query	**Q, C** or Double mouse-click
Cursor-position Reset	**R, C**
Do	**D**
Do At Breakpoint	**B, D**
Delete List	**Q, C, Alt+F4**
Down List	**Q, C, Alt+F4**
Down-table	**Q, C, F6**
Dump List	**Q, D**
Enter	**Enter**

Function	Menu Access Keys
Enter-name Locate	L, E
Enter-name Query	Q, E
Environment	E
Escape	Esc
Examine Backtract	E, B, E
Examine Breakpoints	B, E
Examine Until Conditions	E, U
Exchange	F4
Exit Perform	P, E
Find String	F
Go	G
Hex	Q, C, F3
Hex/ASCII	Q, C, F10
If Breakpoint	B, I
Insert List Left	Q, C, Alt+F7
Insert List Right	Q, C, Alt+F8
Join Text	T, J
Locate-declaration	Q, C, Alt+F9
Look-up	F6
Monitor	Q, C, F4
Monitor+fixed	Q, C, Ctrl+F5

Function	Menu Access Keys
Monitor-off	Q, M
Next Reset	R, N
Next-if	I
On Count Breakpoint	B, O
Perform-level	P
Query	Q
Query data-name	Q, C
Query data-name Alt	Q, C, Alt
Quit-perform	R, Q
Refresh	T, R
Repeat Query	Q, R
Reset-execution	R
Same Level	Q, C, F9
Select Program Break	E, P, S
Set Backtrack	E, B, S
Set Breakpoint	B, S
Set Threshold Level	E, T, S
Set Until Condition	E, U
Split Text	T, S
Start	R, S
Step	S

Animator

Function	Menu Access Keys
Step Perform	**P, S**
Text	**T or Q, C, T**
This Program Break	**E, P, T**
Un-set Backtrack	**E, B, U**
Un-set Breakpoint	**B, U**
Un-set Threshold Level	**E, T, U**
Un-set Until Conditon	**E, U, U**
Up List	**Q, C, Alt+F5**
Up Table	**Q, C, F5**
Update List	**Q, C, Alt+F2**
Up-perform Level	**L, U**
View	**F2**
Where	**F5**
Word Left	**F9**
Word Right	**F10**
Zoom	**Z**

Function Descriptions

This section describes the functions available with Animator.

0-9

Enables you to vary the speed at which execution progresses in "Go" mode, where 0 is the slowest and 9 is the fastest.

Add List

Adds the value you have keyed in to the end of the list of values for the queried data item.

Align

Repositions the program text so that the line on which the cursor is currently positioned becomes the third line on the display screen.

Breakpoints

This function displays the Breakpoints menu which is described in the section Animator Menus. For a description of the functions on this menu, see Cancel all Breakpoints, Do at Breakpoint, Examine Breakpoints, If Breakpoint, On Count Breakpoint, Set Breakpoint, Un-set Breakpoint, Zoom Breakpoint.

Cancel All Breakpoints

Resets all active Breakpoints.

Cancel Program-Break

Cancels the currently set program break; that is, a breakpoint that is activated when execution reaches the specified program. See also Select Program Break.

Clear

Clear the current input field.

Contained Data

Displays the contents of the first sub-level of the item that is being queried. This query function is active when a group item is being queried.

Containing Data

Displays the contents of the data item in which the selected item occurs. This query function is active when a member of a group item is being queried.

Cursor-name Locate

Finds the location in the source code where a data item, filename or procedure is declared.

The cursor control keys or the mouse can be used to position the cursor in the program text. Data items and filenames may be located from their name in the text. Procedure names may be located from their names within the program text.

Cursor-name Query

Displays the contents of the data item at either the current cursor position or the position of the mouse pointer (use a double click to activate this function). It gives you access to other functions which allow you to modify and monitor the item. To alter the contents of the queried data simply type in a new value. The new value replaces the item's previous value. If the data item is a dynamic stream you can update it by using the Do function.

You can place the cursor or select with the mouse anywhere withing the data item. If you do not select the name of a data item, the message:

```
Not data item
```

appears at the bottom of the screen.

Following a successful query, the Query data-name submenu appears on the screen with the query data name on the information line and the value of the data item at the bottom of the screen.

Curson-position Reset

Enables you to alter the sequence of program execution. The statement at the cursor position becomes the current statement. Execution will continue from this statement. This function does not change the value of any data.

Delete List

Deletes the current value displayed from the list of values for the data item being queried.

Do

Enables you to enter a COBOL statement to be executed immediately. This command allows you to insert a statement in the sequence of execution but does not add it to your program code. To add it, you must key it in using a text editor, then recompile your source code file. Alternatively, you may enter it as a Do At Breakpoint, in which case it will be saved in a file.

The COBOL statement cannot exceed 71 characters.

Note: Although most COBOL statements are supported by the Do command, Animator cannot handle some complex statements. An appropriate error message will be issued in these cases.

Animator

Do at Breakpoint

Prompts you for a valid COBOL statement which will be executed along with the current line. Execution is not interrupted. The line containing the breakpoint is highlighted.

When Animator encounters a breakpoint set with the Do option, the COBOL statement is executed immediately before the statement containing the breakpoint. In Zoom or Go mode, execution continues without a break. In Step mode, the Do-statement is executed when the statement containing the breakpoint is stepped onto. A message indicating that the statement has been executed appears at the bottom of the screen. You can repeatedly execute the COBOL statement without retyping it.

Entering an invalid COBOL statement will give an error message.

On exit from Animator, all the COBOL statements that are currently set using this function are written to a file called progname.EDO, where progname is the name of your main program, in the same directory as the source of that program.

Note: Although most COBOL statements are supported by the Do command, Animator cannot handle some complex statements. An appropriate error message will be issued in these cases.

Down List

Displays the next item in the list of values for the data item being queried.

Down Perform Level

Cancels the result of Up Perform Level, which allows the current execution path to be examined at the PERFORM level.

Down Table

Displays the contents of the next table entry. The display of the variable used as the table subscript (shown with the data name) reflect the current value and is changed by this function. This query function is only active when a table data item is being queried.

Dump List

Saves test data that you have created using the Query List functions. The list is written to disk in the current directory using the program name plus an .ILS extension. If the specified filename already exists, the file is overwritten with the new values. This list will be loaded when you re-enter Animator and execute the program you have created the list for. The file must be in the current directory.

Enter

Confirms any selections you have made or data you have keyed in. It may return you to a higher level menu. Where both **Escape** and **Enter** options are available, **Escape** exits without making the update you have keyed in, whereas **Enter** makes the update and then exits.

Enter-name Locate

Displays a menu where you can type in the name of the item to be located in the source code.

Moves the cursor to one of the following locations:

- the line in which the data item is declared, or

- the first occurence of the filename in your program, or

- the paragraph or section name at the head of a procedure

depending upon what you enter at the prompt. If you are working with nested programs, you must be positioned in the program in which that data item is defined for this function to work success-fully.

Enter-name Query

Prompts you for a data item name, which can be entered in upper- or lower case. Following a successful query, the Query data-name submenu appears on the screen with the queried data name on the information line and the value of the data item at the bottom of the screen. To alter the contents of the queried data simply type in a new value and press **Enter**. The new value replaces the item's previous value.

If you are working with nested programs, you must be positioned in the program in which that data item is defined for this function to work successfully.

Environment

Displays the Environment menu which is described in the section Animator Menus. For a description of the functions on this menu see This Program Break, Select Program Break, Cancel Program Break, Set Threshold Level, Un-set Threshold Level, Set Until Condition, Un-set Until Condition, Set Backtrack, Un-set Back-track, Examine Backtrack.

Escape

Returns to the higher level menu or exits from Animator alto-gether if you are at the top menu. Where both **Escape** and **Enter** are available options, **Escape** exits without making the update you have keyed in, whereas **Enter** makes the update and then exits.

Examine Backtrack

Enables you to traverse the recorded execution path. The Set Backtrack function must have been used prior to the execution of at least one line of source code in order for this function to operate.

You use the **cursor-up/up arrow** key to backtrack through the execution path starting from the current statement. At any stage you can move forward through the execution path by using the **cursor-down/down arrow** key.

Note: Execution does not occur during backtracking; back-tracking is purely a viewing facility. During backtracking, statements are stepped in accordance with the current Threshold Level. See the Set Threshold Level function.

Examine Breakpoints

Enables you to review your breakpoints. Each time you execute this function, the cursor is placed on the next COBOL statement that has a breakpoint set on it. After displaying the last breakpoint in the program, the function displays the first breakpoint in the program.

In addition, if the Breakpoint menu is active, whenever the cursor is positioned on a statement containing a breakpoint, a message appears on the bottom line of the screen.

Exchange

Toggles to move the cursor, and therefore the display of execution, between screens in split-screen mode. You can split the screen in two using the Split Text function.

Exit Perform

Executes the remainder of outstanding code in the PERFORM range that the current statement is within. Execution stops on the statement following the end of the PERFORM range.

This function operates only if the current statement is within a PERFORM range. If you select this function when you are not in the range of a PERFORM (PERFORM LEVEL = 01) and you are currently in a subprogram, you are asked if you wish to leave the program. If you reply "Yes", the program execution will continue in Zoom mode until the calling program is reached. If you are not in a subprogram, you will be reminded that the PERFORM LEVEL = 1 by an error message.

Find String

Finds the next occurrence of a text string in the source program file. You can find a text string in both the main program and copy files or in just the main program. By default, the Find function searches all files in the program. Once the find is completed, the cursor is positioned at the beginning of the text string located.

The string can be up to 32 characters long and must be entered exactly as written in the source code, using upper- and lower-case letters as appropriate.

If you want to include spaces at the end of the string, enter the spaces and terminate them with a **#**. If you wish to find a string in the main program only, enter the string, terminated by a **#** and an **M**. The **M** tells Animator to search just the main file.

If you have previously used the Find function during the current session, the last specified string appears in the prompt field. You can use the clear function to clear the string or **Enter** to search for the same string again.

The Find function searches forward only from the current cursor position. You cannot find a string that you have already passed.

Go

Executes automatically each statement in the program one by one, displaying the source code on the screen as it is executed. Go mode is an automatic Step mode; you do not have to press a key to execute each statement as you do in Step mode.

You can set the Go execution speed by pressing a key from **0** to **9**, where **0** is the slowest. You can also set the speed of execution from the Animator Main menu by pressing a number from **0** to **9** without selecting the Go function. The current speed is shown on the Information Line. The default speed is **5**.

To stop execution in Go mode and return to the Animator Main menu, press **Escape**.

To change to Zoom mode from within Go mode, press **Z**. The program then executes at full speed without animation. You can break out of Zoom mode by pressing **Ctrl+Break**.

Hex

Toggles to change the display of a queried data item to hexiadecimal format and to change the menu displayed. You can type over the data using either text or hexadecimal code.

Hex/ASCII

Toggles to move the cursor between the hex and ASCII data representations. It is available when you are displaying a queried data item in hex format. You can type over the data using either text or hexadecimal code.

If Breakpoint

Enables you to set a conditional breakpoint. A conditional breakpoint is a breakpoint that takes effect only if the specified condition is true when the breakpoint is reached. The line containing the breakpoint is highlighted.

The submenu prompts you to enter a condition in COBOL format. Once you have entered a valid statement, pressing the **Enter** key sets a conditional breakpoint at the current cursor position. Execution stops at this breakpoint only when the condition is true.

If the condition you specify is false or does not become true, the Animator ignores the breakpoint and continues executing the program. You can enter any condition allowed by COBOL syntax, including combinations of conditions. You cannot set a conditional breakpoint on a statement that already has an ordinary breakpoint, and vice versa.

Animator

If you wish to set a conditional breakpoint that is not tied to a particular statement, you should use the Until function.

Insert List Left

Inserts a new data value entered into the input field into the list immediately before the currently displayed list value. This function is one of the Query Data list functions.

Insert List Right

Inserts a new data value entered into the input field into the list immediately after the currently displayed list value. This function is one of the Query Data list functions.

Join Text

Cancels the effect of the Split Text function and returns you to a single screen display of source code. You can use the Refresh Text function to repaint the screen after using the Join function.

Locate-declaration

Displays the Locate-declaration menu if accessed from the Animator Main menu. For a description of the functions on this menu see Cursor-name Locate, Enter-name Locate, Up-perform Level and Down Perform Level.

Alternatively, if accessed from the Query Alternate menu, the Locate-declaration function finds the location in the source code of the current query item.

Look-up

Repositions the program text so that the line number specified at the prompt becomes the third line on the screen. This provides a quick and easy means of locating a line in your code without having to scroll through it line by line.

Monitor

Enables you to display the content of a query data item as it changes during program execution.

Monitor-off

Switches off the monitor display of a queried data item. See also Hide Monitors.

Next Reset

Causes the next statement to become the current statement without executing any code. This function does not change the value of any data.

Next-if

Zooms through all statements until the next IF statement is encountered. Program execution then stops, and the source code is returned to the screen.

On Count Breakpoint

Enables you to set periodic breakpoints that halt execution when a statement has been executed a specified number of times. The frequency must be in the range 2 to 255 inclusive. Once the frequency has been entered, the normal Breakpoint menu appears, allowing you to set the breakpoint or to specify a breakpoint with the Do function. The number selected for the desired frequency appears on the information line.

Perform-level

Displays the Perform-level menu which is described in the section Animator Menus. For a description of the functions on this menu see Step Perform and Exit Perform.

Animator

Query

Displays the Query menu, which is described in the section Animator Menus. For a description of the functions on this menu, see Cursor-name Query, Enter-name Query, Repeat Query, Monitor-off, and Dump-list.

Query Data-name

Displays the Query Data-name menu, which is described in the section Animator Menus. For a description of the functions on this menu, see Contained Data, Containing Data, Down Table, Hex, Hex/ASCII, and Up-table.

Query Data-name Alternate

Displays the Query Data-name Alternate menu, which is described in the section Animator Menus. For a description of the functions on this menu, see Add List, Delete List, Down List, Insert List Left, Insert List Right, Locate-declaration, Up-list and Update List.

Query Data-name Control

Displays the Query Data-name Control menu, which is described in the section Animator Menus.

Quit-perform

Exits from the current PERFORM range without executing the remaining statements. The next executable statement after the PERFORM statement becomes the current statement. You can select this function only when inside the range of a PERFORM.

This function does not change the value of any data.

Refresh

Refreshes the display of all monitors and the source text.

Repeat Query

Displays the content of the item which was last queried and displays the Query data-name submenu.

Reset-execution

Displays the Reset-execution menu which is described in the section Animator Menus. For a description of the functions on this menu, see Start, Next Reset, Quit-perform and Cursor-position Reset.

Same Level

Displays the contents of the next data item that has the same level as the queried data item. The data name appears on the information line.

Select Program Break

Prompts you for the name of the program you wish execution to halt at, that is a program break. A Program break is a breakpoint that is activated when execution reaches the specified program.

Set Backtrack

Causes the execution path to be recorded from the set point onwards. See the Examine Backtrack function for details of how to view the recorded details.

Set Breakpoint

Enables you to set a breakpoint at the current cursor position. When Animator encounters the breakpoint, execution halts before executing the statement. The statement containing the breakpoint becomes the current statement. The line containing the breakpoint is highlighted.

Animator

Program breakpoints remain set , so if you leave animation without un-setting (canceling) a breakpoint, the breakpoint will be set the next time you animate the program. You can set up to 100 breakpoints in each program.

When a breakpoint is reached, you will see the message:

`Breakpoint encountered`

at the bottom of your screen.

Set Threshold Level

Enables you to specify a nesting level of subroutines and called subprograms below which PERFORMs and CALLs are executed in Zoom Mode rather than being animated.

The level will be set according to the level of the current line. The set level then appears on the Information Line and can be un-set by using the Un-set Threshold Level function.

The Threshold Level remains set until you explicitly change it.

Set Until Condition

Enables you to set a conditional program breakpoint that causes execution to halt when the condition becomes true. This function only operates if you are in Go or Zoom mode.

This function is similar to a conditional breakpoint except that it is not tied to a particular COBOL statement but to the entire program. With a conditional program breakpoint, the Animator tests the condition before executing each statement and halts if it is true.

The condition must conform to the syntax rules for COBOL conditions.

You can set only one Until breakpoint in a program.

Split Text

Enables you to split a screen horizontally in two at the current cursor position. You must have a minimum of four lines in a splitscreen.

When you have split the screen, you can execute in either half. The Exchange function moves the cursor between the halves.

Split-screen mode is particularly useful if you wish to query data declarations or a set of variables in one screen while executing in the other.

Start

Makes the first executable statement in the program the current statement. No code is executed.

This function does not change the value of any data, so if you use this function to test your program as though you had not executed any code, make sure you reinitialize all of your variables before continuing.

Step

Executes the current statement and places the cursor on the next executable statement, which it also highlights.

Step Perform

Causes execution of the entire PERFORM range or subprogram in zoom mode if the current statement is a PERFORM or CALL statement. Execution stops on the statement following the end of the PERFORM range or subprogram.

Text

Changes the display of a queried data item to text format and changes the menu displayed if accessed from the Query data-

name menu. You can type over the data using either text or
hexadecimal code.

Alternatively, if accessed from the Animator Main menu, this
function displays the Text menu which is described in the section
Animator Menus. For a description of the functions on this menu
see Split Text, Join Text and Refresh.

This Program Break

Sets a program break; that is, a breakpoint that occurs when the
selected program is re-entered. For example, if This Program
Break specifies a program break for the current program, a
breakpoint will occur when the program is re-entered after a
subprogram call.

You must set the program break before using the Zoom
command.

Un-set Backtrack

Stops the recording of the execution path.

Un-set Breakpoint

Cancels a breakpoint at the current cursor position.

Un-set Threshold Level

Cancels the current Threshold Level. See Set Threshold Level.

If no level is set, then the Information Line displays the message:

```
Threshold-level = un-set
```

Un-set Until Condition

Cancels the Until Condition if one is active. See the Set Until
Condition function.

Up-list

Displays the previous item in the list of values for the queried data item.

Up-perform Level

Enables the current execution path to be examined at the PERFORM level. This shows where execution will return to when the current PERFORM range is exited. The related function, Down Perform Level, cancels the result of Up-perform Level.

Up-table

Displays the contents of the previous table entry. The display of the variable used as the table subscript (shown with the data name) reflects the current value and is changed by this function. This query function is only active when a table data item is being queried.

If you select an entry that is before the first table entry, a warning message appears.

Update List

Changes the value of the displayed item in a list of Query data to a new value which you key in.

View

Enables you to view the user screen during animation. The screen changes whenever you execute a statement that echoes a character to the screen. Press any key to return to the source code.

Where

Moves the cursor to the start of the current statement, and repositions the program text so that the current statement becomes the third line on the screen.

Animator

Word <-

Moves the cursor to the previous word in the program text. If the cursor is positioned on the first word on a line, the function moves the cursor to the last word on the previous line and scrolls the text if necessary.

Word ->

Moves the cursor to the next word in the program text. If the cursor is positioned on the last word on a line, this function moves the cursor to the first word on the next line and scrolls the text if necessary.

Zoom

Executes the program at full speed, displaying the user screen rather than the Animator screen containing the source code. You can break out of Zoom mode by pressing **Ctrl+Break**. If you do not break out of Zoom mode, execution will continue until either a STOP RUN statement is encountered or a breakpoint is reached. At this point the Animator screen is restored and Step mode resumed.

Error Messages

A Run-time system error message is returned on a program that is syntactically correct but which encounters problems during the actual running of the intermediate code. You could receive such an error if you attempt to access a file in the wrong mode or if you use a corrupt file. Refer to the chapter *Run-Time System Error Messages* for complete descriptions of possible Run-Time errors.

When animating a program, run-time errors are displayed on the bottom line of the screen in the following format:

```
message-text        (error nnn)
```

where:

message-text   is the text associated with each error

nnn   is the error number

Chapter 7

Screens

Screens is a screen painter designed to enable you to rapidly specify screen layouts and generate COBOL code for screen handling. Powerful functionality is provided by Screens to support easy specification of screen layouts and their subsequent modification.

Overview

The Screens facility enables you to:

- Perform comprehensive block manipulation of text and/or data. You can cut, copy, store, restore, and move rectangular blocks of text and data.

- Group together associated fields and text, and repeat them horizontally or vertically, or both, thereby enabling the specification of tables.

- Define field specifications and maintenance. Fields can be defined and assigned names and Screen Section clauses (for example , NO ECHO, JUSTIFIED RIGHT, REQUIRED, etc.).

- Specify field acceptance order.

- Specify attributes (selection via a palette). You can fill an area with a particular attribute and specify a default screen attribute.

Screens

■ Generate a complete index program application (with alternate keys) using the Screen Section as the interface.

■ Transfer text to and from the Micro Focus COBOL Editor.

When using Screens, please note:

■ There is no checking of the name entry. You can enter data names, group names and screen names which can subsequently fail compilation. You should take care to enter names which comply with the normal COBOL data-naming conventions and also ensure that you do not enter duplicate names.

■ Screens performs only simple picture string validation. As a result, invalid picture strings can be generated which fail during compilation. Your picture string entries should comply with the COBOL picture string conventions. See the *Language Reference* chapter for further information.

Operation

This section describes how to invoke the Screens facility, the use of the cursor movement keys when designing screens and the menus and functions available in Screens.

Invoking Screens

To invoke Screens select **Ctrl+F6** from the Editor menu to enter the draw/scrns menu. Select **F7** to enter Screens or **F6** to enter Screens with the information on the current editor screen.

The initial screen that appears displays an information line and the main menu, which occupies two lines. The rest of the screen displays a stored screen form if filename is specified, otherwise it is blank. Other options are accessed from the **Alt** and **Ctrl** menus. Each menu and its options are described in later sections.

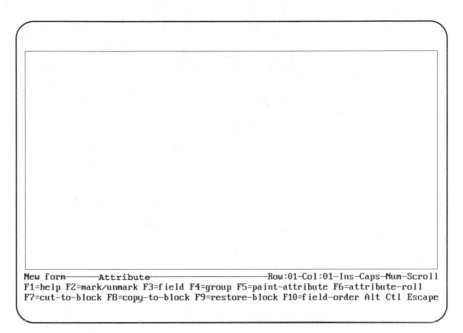

```
New form————Attribute——————————————————Row:01-Col:01-Ins-Caps-Num-Scroll
F1=help F2=mark/unmark F3=field F4=group F5=paint-attribute F6=attribute-roll
F7=cut-to-block F8=copy-to-block F9=restore-block F10=field-order Alt Ctl Escape
```

Figure 7-1: Screens Menu

The Information Line

The information line initially displays the name of the form, the word "Attribute", the present cursor position (row and column), and the state of the **Ins, Caps Lock, Num Lock** and **Scroll Lock** indicators. These four indicators are toggled by the appropriate keys to turn the respective function on and off. Upon entry into Screens, their status initially reflects their most recent setting. When toggled on, their color attribute changes (highlighted on a monochrome display). These indicators function as follows:

- The **Ins** key turns on insert mode. Notice the change in the shape of the cursor.

- The **Caps Lock** key locks the keyboard so that the alphabetic keys produce uppercase letters.

- The **Num Lock** key locks the numeric keys on the numeric key pad so that they produce numbers rather than the arrow key functions.

Screens

■ Moving the cursor up one line when **Scroll Lock** is on causes the text to move down one line. Alternatively, moving the cursor down one line when **Scroll Lock** is on moves the text up one line.

As you work with Screens, the information line is updated with the following information:

form name   The name given to the form when it was loaded or saved appears at the beginning of the information line. If the form is new, then "New form" is displayed.

attribute   The attribute currently associated with the next character to be typed is displayed as part of this word. If attributes are suppressed the word "Attribute" disappears.

field/group name   If the cursor is currently positioned on a field, then the word "field" appears on the information line. The name of the field is displayed if one has been given. If no name has been given, then the name in the USING, TO, or FROM clause is displayed. If the cursor is currently positioned inside a group, then the field display is replaced with the group display.

group order   This applies only to groups and displays H or V depending on whether the group is accepted first horizontally or vertically.

row and column   The position of the cursor is continually displayed.

The help function (**F1**) is available from each menu within the Screens facility. Press **F1** to display the help screen for additional information about the options available on the current menu.

Key Functions in Screens

In addition to the options available on each menu, the following keys have particular functions while you are using the Screens facility. Some of these keys behave differently when used with specific options within Screens. The table below shows the general use of these keys. Additional uses of these keys are described in the discussion of the specific option.

Some of them are notional key names which may not be present on your keyboard. For IBM keyboards, the appropriate key combinations are shown in parentheses at the end of the notional key description.

Key	Function
left-arrow	Moves the cursor left one character position.
right-arrow	Moves the cursor right one character position.
up-arrow	Moves the cursor up one line unless Scroll Lock is on, which instead causes the text to move down one line.
down-arrow	Moves the cursor down one line unless Scroll Lock is on, which instead causes the text to move up one line.
Tab	Moves the cursor to the next tab position to the right.
Backtab	Moves the cursor to the next tab position to the left.
Backspace	Deletes the character to the left of the cursor position, and moves the cursor left one character position.
Enter	Moves the cursor to the first character position on the next line.
Home	Moves the cursor to column one of the same line.

End	Moves the cursor to the position after the last character on the current line, or to column 80 if there are no characters after the current cursor position.
Del	Deletes the character at the cursor position.
Ctrl+End	Toggles menus on and off.

The Screens Menu System

You design your screens using the options available on three different menus. The Main Menu appears when you first invoke Screens. You access the **Alt** and **Ctrl** Menus using the **Alt** and **Ctrl** keyboard keys. These menus provide you with additional functionality.

The Main Menu

```
New form————Attribute————————————Row:01-Col:01-Ins-Caps-Num-Scroll
F1=help F2=mark/unmark F3=field F4=group F5=paint-attribute F6=attribute-roll
F7=cut-to-block F8=copy-to-block F9=restore-block F10=field-order Alt Ctl Escape
```

Figure 7-2: Main Menu

When you invoke the Screens facility, the main menu is displayed. You access the following options from this menu.

Mark/Unmark

The mark option (**F2**) causes a reverse video character to be placed at the cursor position. Moving the cursor using the cursor movement keys, **Tab, Backtab, Home** and **End** keys extends and contracts the marked area in a rectangular fashion from the original marked position. Following the use of the mark function with the cut-to-block (**F7**), copy-to-block (**F8**), paint-attribute (**F5**), field (**F3**) or group (**F4**) functions results in the application of those functions to the marked area. This function key is a toggle; selecting unmark cancels the mark option.

Field

Use the field option (**F3**) to define a field in either of two ways:

1. by placing the cursor on a set of caret characters and pressing **F3** , or

2. by marking an area and then pressing **F3**. This method inserts a set of carets over the marked area. Adjacent fields can be specified this way.

Once a field has been selected, the menu is also replaced by the Field menu. The caret characters are also replaced by a COBOL picture string. The picture string can be toggled between the numeric and alphanumeric characters using the numeric/alphanumeric (**F4**) function on the Field menu. The default character set is alphanumeric. Use the arrow keys to move along the picture string.

You can alter field sizes by positioning the cursor in the field and pressing the **Del** key (to reduce the size) or by turning on insert mode (**Ins**) and typing caret (^) characters (to increase the size).

Minimal validation is done on the field name, and only simple validation is performed on picture strings. The caret characters depict fields only when defined as fields; they can still be used as text characters.

When you exit from the field entry function, the field picture string is replaced with the carets. The picture string defaults to X's. These can be overtyped with the desired picture string characters.

A pop-up menu appears on the Field menu screen. This contains Screen Section clauses that you select by using the **up-arrow** and **down-arrow** keys to move the cursor through the list and then pressing the select-clause option (**F2**).

This pop-up menu also provides the option of assigning a Screen Section name to a field. If you select this option, a message appears prompting you for the name of the field. Enter the name, then press **Enter**. The field name then appears in the pop-up menu and on the information line. The field name applies to the name assigned to the screen item and is not a data item.

If you select a field name the field name prompt appears. This field name appears in the pop-up menu.

You use the **F2** toggle key to select and unselect the clauses. The current clause is identified by the "<" and ">" characters. Some of these clauses require additional text which you enter against the relevant clauses.

Previously selected items can be edited by selecting the Edit clause option (**F3**). Once you have selected an entry from the pop-up menu, the entry is highlighted and, in some cases, prompts you for further information.

If you select a clause that requires text entry but you do not enter text, this results in the generation of data identifiers, where necessary, for the missing entries at generation time. If literals are required for assignment, you must include them at the prompt. A brief description of the various Screen Section clauses is found in the section *Screen Section Clauses*.

Group

You assign fields to a group using the group option (**F4**) which displays the Group menu. The cursor must be positioned in a previously defined group, or an area must be marked. The marked area must contain at least one data field.

You can assign properties to the group by selecting the assign properties option (**F2**). Another menu appears offering options to select a clause (**F2**) and edit a clause (**F3**) from the pop-up menu on your screen. Selection of the clauses is the same as that for the Field menu. There are fewer clauses in this menu since some clauses are not applicable to groups. These entries are described in the *Language Reference* chapter.

If the group contains input fields, the direction of the initial repeat determines the way the group is accepted. Repeating horizontally (**F3**) first results in fields within the group being accepted row by row (from left to right). Repeating vertically (**F4**) first results in the acceptance of fields within the group being accepted column by column. To alter the acceptance manner for a group, delete occurrences and expand the group again. The information line displays "H" or "V" depending on the acceptance manner of the group.

A group can only be expanded in such a way so as not to overwrite any other data fields on the screen.

You can delete fields within a group both horizontally and vertically using **F5** and **F6**, respectively.

Paint-attribute

The paint-attribute option (**F5**) assigns the current attribute to the current cursor position. If the cursor is currently positioned on a field or group, then the entire field and its occurrences (if they are in group) are painted with the selected attribute. If the mark function (**F2**) is currently active, the entire marked area is painted.

Attribute-roll

The attribute-roll option (**F6**) rolls one by one through the five configured attributes, with the current attribute displayed on the information line. The five configured attributes can be changed using the attribute-palette (**F9**) function on the Alt menu.

Cut-to-block

The cut-to-block option (**F7**) places the marked block in a temporary buffer which remains visible on the screen in the position from which it has been cut. The menu then changes to the Block menu which offers further options.

When you paste a marked block (**F2**), the block is pasted onto the screen in its current position, and control is returned to the previous menu. You cannot paste a block in an area defined as a field or one having a group definition.

When you copy from a block (**F3**), the marked block is copied onto the screen in its current position. You remain in the Block menu.

Screens

You cannot copy a block over an area containing a field or group definition.

When you store a block (**F4**), the marked block is placed onto a "stack" on a last-in, first-out basis. The marked block is erased from the screen, and you are returned to the previous menu. This stored block can subsequently be restored if required.

You use the following keys to move the block around the screen leaving spaces in the block's original position.

- The cursor movement keys move the block in the desired direction.

- **Tab** moves the block to the next tab position.

- **Backtab** moves the block to the previous tab position.

- **Home** moves the block to column 1 of the same line.

- **End** moves the block to the right side of the screen.

Copy-to-block

The copy-to-block option (**F8**) places the marked block in a temporary buffer which remains visible on the screen in the position from which it has been copied. The menu then changes to the Block menu, from which you can select further options (see cut-to-block above). Subsequent cursor movements move the block around the screen leaving the original block unchanged.

Restore-block

The restore-block option (**F9**) enables you to retrieve the contents of a stored block from a stack of "stored" blocks. Blocks are stored within the Block menu as described under cut-to-block above. The restore-block option restores the last stored block and displays it in the temporary buffer which is visible on the screen.

Field-order

The field-order option (**F10**) enables data to be accepted in a sequence different from the standard order (that is, top-to-bottom, left-to-right). If the field order is not specified, the default specifies that the fields on the first line are accepted first in a left-to-right order, followed by the fields on the second line in a left-to-right order, etc. The significance of the numbering is that the field accept order is now all fields with field accept order number 0, followed by all fields with accept order 1, etc. Fields with equal acceptance order (that is, fields with the same order character) are accepted from top left to bottom right in a left-to-right manner. Valid order characters must be in the range 0-9, A-Z, and a-z; those fields with "0" order characters are accepted first while those with "z" are accepted last.

When the field order function is used, the fields on the screen are replaced with the number 5. If you now move the cursor to a field and enter another number, that field is replaced with the new number and the field acceptance order is changed. The numbers designate the order in which the fields are to be accepted.

When a group is displayed, only the original fields (containing the acceptance order numbers) of the group definition are displayed. When the code is generated for the new field orders, the group is accepted in its entirety. It is not possible to accept part of a group. If a group is two dimensional, then the horizontal or vertical order is determined by the order in which the group was first repeated.

The Alt Menu

Press the **Alt** key to display the Alt Menu from which you can select further options within Screens.

```
New form————Attribute————————————Row:01-Col:01-Ins-Caps-Num-Scroll
F1=help F2=attribute-on/off F3=load F4=save F5=generate-COBOL F6=clear
F7=delete-line F8=insert-line F9=attribute-palette F10=screen-name
```

Figure 2-3: Alt Menu

To select an option from this menu, press the appropriate function key while holding down the **Alt** key, then release both keys.

Screens

Attribute On/Off

The attribute option (**Alt+F2**) is a toggle key which turns the use of attributes on and off. If the toggle is on, the current attribute is painted as text is entered. The current attribute setting is displayed on the information line. If the toggle is off, the default attribute is the one that is painted and the word "Attribute" is not displayed on the information line.

Load

You use the load option (**Alt+F3**) to load previously saved screens. The Load menu prompts for the name of the form to be loaded. The default loads forms with the extension .SRN, the default extension for Screens. You can type in the name of the form at the prompt or access it from the Directory.

To access a file from the directory, press **F2.** A list of screen files appears on the screen. Use the cursor movement keys to position the cursor on the desired filename, then press **Enter**. The filename now appears at the prompt. Press **Enter** again to display the form on the screen.

Save

The save option (**Alt+F4**) saves the current screen. The default file extension is .SRN.

Generate-COBOL

The generate-COBOL option (**Alt+F5**) prompts you for the name of the output file. After you supply the filename and press **Enter**, the Generate-COBOL menu is displayed on the screen. The options on this menu are described below.

Screens generates standard COBOL COPY-files and source files which are written to your disk.

The **F2=data-descriptions** option generates a file with the extension .SS. This file contains the generated Screen Section code.

The **F3=skeleton-program** option generates a skeleton program with the extension .CBL. This program contains two COPY-libraries. The first COPY-library is the Screen Section file with the extension .SS. The other COPY-library is a file with the extension .WKS, which contains the Working-Storage entries necessary to handle the TO, FROM and USING entries, and any other phrase that requires data items. The complete program, which displays and accepts the screen, can now be checked and run.

The **F4=monochrome/color option** is a toggle which generates the COBOL necessary to run the painted form on a color or mono-chrome display.

The **F5=index-program** option generates an entire COBOL pro-gram based on the screen form that you designed. The generated COBOL enables you to key data into the screen form. The data is then stored as records in an indexed sequential file. It is important that you only use the top 21 lines of the screen for your screen form. The index program requires the last four screen lines for its menus. No warning is given if you break this rule.

The **F6=blank-screen** option is a toggle which generates the COBOL necessary to clear the screen before the painted screen is displayed.

Note: This toggle is ignored by both the skeleton-program and the index-program generation options.

The **F7=mark-fields** option enables you to select index key fields for use with the index program option. See the section *Mark Fields* below.

The **Escape** key returns you to the main menu.

Mark-Fields

When generating an index program it is imperative that you select the data fields that the generator can use as index keys. It is always necessary to have a prime key (**F2**) for the ISAM file but you can also select up to three alternate keys.

The fields that are flagged as index keys must have user-assigned data-names. Group items cannot be marked as index fields.

The **F2=mark-prime-key** option flags the cursor field as the prime key. The field is highlighted with the letter P.

The **F3=mark-alternative-key-1** option flags the cursor field as the first alternate key. The field is highlighted with the number 1.

The **F4=mark-alternative-key-2** option flags the cursor field as the second alternate key. The field is highlighted with the number 2.

The F5=mark-alternative-key-3 option flags the cursor field as the third alternate key. The field is highlighted with the number 3.

The **F6=unmark-key-field** option removes the index key mark from the cursor field. The field is lowlighted.

The **Escape** key checks the validity of the marked keys and returns you to the generation menu.

Index keys must be assigned in numerical order; for example, prime, alt1, alt2, alt3.

Clear

The **Alt+F6=clear option** clears the existing form from the screen.

Delete-line

The **Alt+F7=delete-line** option deletes the line on which the cursor is positioned and moves the lines below this line up by one. You cannot delete a line containing fields, nor can you delete a line in the middle of a group. To delete a line containing fields, you must first delete the fields using the **Ctrl+F9=delete-field-definition** option.

Insert-line

The **Alt+F8=insert-line** option inserts a line at the current cursor position. The lines below the cursor are moved down one line. If a line is inserted and the bottom line of the screen contains text, the bottom line is lost. (Forms can be no longer than 25 lines.) If the bottom line contains any fields, the line is not inserted; you must first delete the field definitions. You cannot insert a line in the middle of a group.

Attribute-palette

The attribute-palette option (**Alt+F9**) displays the attribute selection menu. From this menu you can select the five roll attributes from the set of attributes supported by your machine. These attributes are associated with five function keys (**F2, F3, F4, F5, and F6**).

You change the current default attribute of the characters associated with each function key to another attribute by moving the cursor to the desired character and then pressing one of the five function keys. This is useful for switching the whole screen to a particular attribute. You can change these attributes at any time while designing your form using the attribute-roll function (**F6**) on the main menu.

You can also select the default attribute by positioning the cursor over an attribute and pressing the default attribute option (**F7**). Setting the default attribute for a form alters all characters with the current default attribute to the new attribute. This is useful for setting the whole form to a particular attribute.

Pressing **Escape** returns you to the main menu.

Screen-name

The screen-name option (**Alt+F10**) prompts you to assign a name to your screen. If you do not specify a screen name, a name prefixed by "G-" is assigned by the system.

Screens

The Ctrl Menu

The **Ctrl** menu options are available when the **Ctrl** key is pressed. Continue to press the **Ctrl** key while accessing each of these options.

```
New form————Attribute——————————————Row:01-Col:01-Ins-Caps-Num-Scroll
F1=help F2=text→edit F3=char-left F4=char-right F5=select-char (!/033/21h)
F6=draw F7=read-char F8=read-attr F9=delete-field-defn F10=delete-group-defn
```

Figure 7-4: Ctrl Menu

Text Edit

The text edit option (**Ctrl+F2**) transfers an ASCII image of your form back into the COBOL Editor.

Character-left

The character-left option (**Ctrl+F3**) moves left along the set of special characters displayed at the bottom of the screen. Each time you press **Ctrl+F3**, the next character to the left is highlighted. At the same time the current character appears next to the select-character option (**Ctrl+F5**) with its corresponding hexadecimal and decimal values also displayed.

Character-right

The character-right option (**Ctrl+F4**) functions similarly to the character-left option described above. However, the character to the right is highlighted each time you press **Ctrl+F4**.

Select-character

The select-character option (**Ctrl+F5**) selects the currently highlighted character and displays it at the current cursor position.

Draw

The draw option (**Ctrl+F6**) option accesses the Draw menu. You use the **F2** toggle key to draw horizontal and vertical lines, as well as to move and erase them. The initial setting of the **F2** toggle switch is "Draw" as displayed on the information line.

You can erase lines by pressing **F2** to toggle to Erase mode. The word "Erase" appears on the information line. Then move the cursor over the lines you wish to erase. If you wish to move the cursor without drawing, press **F2** again. The word "Move" appears on the information line. You can now move the cursor anywhere on the screen without drawing a line.

You can select to draw either single lines or double lines by using the **F3** option. This key toggles between both types of lines.

The attribute-roll option (**F4**) enables you to change the background attribute at any time.

Read-character

The read-character option (**Ctrl+F7**) selects the character at the current cursor position as the current special character.

Read-attribute

The read-attribute option (**Ctrl+F8**) defines the attribute at the current cursor position as the current attribute.

Delete-field-definition

The delete-field-definition option (**Ctrl+F9**) removes all references to a field (containing the cursor) as a field.

Delete-group-definition

You use the delete-group-definition option (**Ctrl+F10**) to delete the group definition and to remove all group occurrences from the original marked item that was used to define that group. If the size of the fields inside a group requires editing, the group must first be deleted, then edited, and then redefined as a group.

Screen Section Clauses

This section lists the Screen Section entries found on the pop-up menus on both the Field and Group menu screens.

Auto

Selecting the AUTO option causes the AUTO clause to be included in the Screen Section of your program. This clause causes an ACCEPT operation on the screen item to be terminated automatically when a character is keyed at the last character position, if there are no further fields on the screen; otherwise it skips automatically to the next field.

Bell

The BELL option generates the BELL clause in the Screen Section. This causes the alarm to sound each time the field is displayed.

Blank When Zero

The BLANK WHEN ZERO option generates the BLANK WHEN ZERO clause in the Screen Section. A field is blanked out if the field contains only zeros.

From

The FROM option generates the FROM clause in the Screen Section. This results in the initial value of the field on the screen being taken from the identifier or literal specified with the FROM phrase.

Full

Select FULL to generate the FULL clause in the Screen Section of your program. This results in an ACCEPT of that field requiring the field to be full or empty.

Justified Right

The JUSTIFIED RIGHT option generates the JUSTIFIED RIGHT clause in the Screen Section. Data entry during an ACCEPT is right-justified in the field.

No Echo

Selecting the NO ECHO option generates the NO ECHO clause in the Screen Section of your program. This results in any ACCEPT of that field not displaying the entered characters. This is often used for password entry.

Prompt

Selecting PROMPT generates the PROMPT clause in the Screen Section which fills the field prior to an ACCEPT operation. When you select this option, you are prompted to enter a name. This name can either be a literal within quotes or a data name.

Required

Selecting this option generates the REQUIRED clause in the Screen Section which, in turn, results in an ACCEPT of this item requiring that the field not be empty.

Size

Selection of the SIZE option generates the SIZE clause in the Screen Section. This overrides the size specified by the number of carets in the field position. If the size is different from the number of carets in that field position, then when the COBOL code is generated, the smaller size is used for accepting that field. If an identifier is specified with the SIZE clause, the size of the field can be dynamically altered at run time by the COBOL program.

To

This option generates the TO clause in the Screen Section. This results in the accepted field being placed into the field defined after the TO entry.

Using

The field defined after the USING entry is used as both a sending and a receiving area. Note that USING and TO are mutually exclusive, as are using and from. However, to and from can be used together or independently.

Zero Fill

Selection of the ZERO FILL option generates the ZERO FILL clause in the Screen Section. This results in the replacement of trailing prompt characters by zeros instead of spaces. This clause is valid only with numeric fields.

Skeleton Program

The following skeleton program can be generated from the sample screen described in the Screens tutorial. This listing was generated from the Checker. Copy statements are expanded.

```
001   identification division.
002   data division.
003   working-storage section.
004*  copy "C:\MFCOBOL\MYFORM.WKS".
005   01 order-name pic x(12).
006   01 filler.
007   03 occurs 5
```

```
008   05 order-addr pic x(18).
009   01 order-tel-no pic x(7).
010   screen section.
011*  copy "C:\MFCOBOL\MYFORM.SS".
012   01 g-myform.
013   02 blank screen.
014   02 line 1 col 6 background-color 0 foreground-color 7
015   highlight pic x(12) using order-name  auto.
016   02 line 5 col 9.
017   02 g-001.
018   03 occurs 5.
019   04 pic x(18) using order-tel-no auto.
020   04 line + 1 col - 17.
021   02 line 1 col 51 pic x(7) using order-tel-no auto.
022   02 line 1 col 1 foreground color 1 highlight
023   value "Name:".
024   02 col 44 value "Tel No:".
025   02 line 5 col 1 value "ADDRESS:".
026   02 line 13 col 28 highlight value "WARNING".
027   02 line 14 col 28 highlight value "MESSAGE".
028   procedure division.
029   display g-myform.
030   accept g-myform.
031   stop run.
```

■ The "G-" before "MYFORM" in the DISPLAY and ACCEPT statements is the default screen name supplied by the system. See the preceding part of this chapter for information on assigning screen names.

■ Any variations in the code, in addition to the system drive and pathname, are due to the exact location of the fields on the screen and the attributes and sizes set for the fields.

The Screens Index Program

The index program created using Screens lets you key data into a form. This data is then stored as records in an indexed sequential file. You can change, delete and add records to this file.

The order in which records are positioned in the index depends on the collating sequence of this COBOL system. For most busi-

Screens

ness applications, the significant characters in the sequence are alphabetic characters. However, all 256 characters can be used in a file; this is why the collating sequence is important.

The design and implementation of the options available when running an Index program are patterned after the COBOL Indexed Sequential Access Method (ISAM). The options used to open files and the commands available for accessing records are those used in the COBOL language.

The section *Creating an Index Program,* describes how you create an index program. This section describes how you use it.

Preparing the Index Program

You can now compile and run the Index Progam, as described in this guide. When you run the Index Program, the form design is displayed on the screen.

You can continue to work with the file specified at the file prompt. Or you can access the Directory facility to work with a previously created data file. With the filename of the data file you wish to work with at the file prompt, press **Enter**.

The form you designed for data entry appears on the screen.

You can now begin entering data into the index program.

Using the Index Program

The index program operates in two modes: manual and automatic. The current mode is indicated on the right side of the Information Line. When the menu discussed above first appears, the setting is automatic which is the default setting. You press **F10** (manual) to toggle between the two settings.

When you are in Manual mode, the menu changes to display all of the options available in this mode. Most of these options are available when Automatic mode is set. See the section *Manual Mode* below to find out the options on the menu when Manual mode is set. The section later in this chapter, *Automatic Mode,* shows you how to use the **Enter** key to perform many of the same functions.

Moving Through the Form

You can use several keyboard keys to move through the form as you enter data.

Key	Function
left-arrow	Moves the cursor one character position to the left.
right-arrow	Moves the cursor one character position to the right
Home	Moves the cursor to the beginning of the first field on the screen.
Ctrl+Home	Clears the contents of all fields from the screen.
Tab	Moves the cursor to the beginning of the next field.
Backtab	Moves the cursor to the beginning of the current or previous field.

Manual Mode

Press **F10** (manual) to set the current mode to Manual.

Writing Records in Manual Mode

The current cursor position is the first character position in the first key field on the screen. To begin entering data into the fields, type the data into the first field on the screen. Use the tab or arrow keys to move from field to field. When you reach the end of one field, the cursor automatically moves to the beginning of the next field if there is one. When you reach the end of the last field on the screen, the system beeps.

Continue entering data until you have entered data in all of the desired fields on the screen. Then press **F7=write** to store the screen display as a record. The message at the bottom of the screen tells you whether the "write" was successful.

After you press **F7** to store the record, the cursor automatically moves back to the first field on the screen. You can then begin entry of another record.

Reading Records in Manual Mode

There are three ways in which you can establish starting points for reading the records you have entered into the index file. This depends on which record you wish to begin reading the file.

If a key field currently displays data on the screen, you press **F2** (**start=**) to position the current-record-pointer on the record indicated by this key. You then use the **F6=read-next** option to read the next record in the file.

You can use the **F3=start>=** to position the current-record-pointer either on the record indicated by the current record key, or on the next record in the index if the current one does not exist. Then press **F6=read-next** to continue reading the file.

To position the current-record-pointer on the record following that indicated by the displayed record key, press **F4=start>**. This also establishes a starting point for reading through the file. This option is also followed by the **F6=read-next** option.

Each time you press **F6=read-next** following either **F2, F3** or **F4**, you are displaying the next record on the screen and updating the current record pointer to point to this record. The current record pointer is displayed on the Information Line.

You can also locate an entire record by typing in the record key in one of the key fields on the screen. Enter the key in a key field, then press **F5=read-key**. The entire record associated with that key is displayed on the screen.

Rewriting Records

Another option on the menu in Manual mode is the **F8=rewrite** option. Press **F8=rewrite** to store the current displayed version of a record that already exists in the file. This is useful for changing existing data.

Deleting Records

You use the **F9=delete** option to delete the record key currently displayed on the screen from the file. When the function is complete, that option and the word "Successful" appears on the Message Line. If the operation is not successful, the appropriate message appears instead.

You press **Escape** to close the current file and return to the menu from which you opened the data file.

Using Alternate Keys

You use the **Shift-F10** option to select an alternative index key. If no alternative indexes were marked when the index program was generated, this option is not available.

The submenu displayed indicates the current index key. The function keys **F2, F3, F4,** and **F5** show the names of the fields that make up the alternative index keys. Pressing one of these alters the current index key to be that of the named field.

Automatic Mode

To use the index program in Automatic mode, you press **F10** (auto) to toggle to Automatic mode as seen by the word "Auto" on the Information Line. The options available in Automatic mode are limited to reading the next record, writing a new record, and finding an existing record. You cannot delete a record in Automatic mode.

Screens

Writing Records in Automatic Mode

If data has been keyed into the key and data fields, pressing **Enter** writes a new record for this data. This is equivalent to using the **F7=write** option in Manual mode.

Pressing **Enter** performs the following functions in Automatic mode. The current operation is displayed on the Message Line.

Reading Records in Automatic Mode

Pressing **Enter** reads the next record if no changes have been made to the key and data fields. This is equivalent to pressing **F4 (start>)** and **F6=read-next** in Manual mode.

You can also find an existing record by entering the key fields to be located and then pressing **Enter**. This is equivalent to using the **F5=read-key** option in Manual mode.

As in Manual mode, you press **Escape** in Automatic mode to close the file and return to the Index-name menu.

Error Messages

The following is an alphabetical list of error messages that you may encounter when using the Screens facility.

Block stack full

Block stack is full; you can only stack up to 16 blocks.

Clear without saving? Y/N

You are attempting to clear the screen without saving the current form.

Cut/Copy without paste? Y/N

The visible block has not been pasted/copied/stored. Exiting deletes the block.

Data on bottom line

You cannot insert a line because fields or groups exist on the 25th line of the screen.

Data on line

You cannot delete the line because it contains either fields or groups.

Error closing file

Could not close file - disk error.

Error creating file

Could not create file - possible disk full, or disk specified not found.

Error opening file

Specified file not found.

Error reading file

Possible disk error.

Error writing file

Disk error.

Exit SCREENS. Are you sure? Y/N

The system confirms that you want to exit from the Screens facility.

Exit without saving? Y/N

You have attempted to exit from the Screens facility without saving your form.

Field definition overlap

You cannot overlap fields.

Field not marked

You have tried to unmark a key field that had not been selected.

Field table full

The maximum number of screen fields has been reached.

File already exists. Overwrite? Y/N

You are attempting to work with a file that already exists.

File not found

The system cannot locate the specified file.

Generate without saving?

The form has not been saved. Do you want to generate COBOL without saving?

Group area

You cannot alter the size of a field in a group. You must first delete the group definition.

Group definition overlap

You cannot overlap groups.

Group nesting not allowed

The marked area already contains a group.

Illegal order character

Field order character is out of valid range.

Incorrect index sequence

The marked keys do not follow the order: prime, Alt1, Alt2, Alt3.

Index field not named

You have tried to generate an index program where a key field does not have a user-defined name.

Internal heap error

System error.

Invalid delete

You cannot delete a field if it is part of a group. You must first delete the group definition.

Invalid field definition

The cursor is not positioned on a caret character.

Invalid function

System error.

Invalid group definition

A marked area must be active and must not split any fields or include any existing group definitions. The area must contain at least one field.

Invalid insert

You cannot insert any more characters at the cursor position (field definition is blocking the way).

Invalid mark

The marked area is not valid for the selected function.

Load fail

> You were unable to load the file, possibly because of a disk read error.

Load without saving? Y/N

> The current form has been altered. The system prompts you to save the altered form.

Mark index fields first

> You have tried to generate an index program without marking any index fields.

No block defined

> The selected function requires a marked area.

No block to restore

> Block stack is empty.

No field definition

> You cannot delete a non-existent field.

No field in group definition

> The marked area does not contain at least one field.

No occurs

> You cannot contract the group.

Non-existent field

> The cursor is not on a field when attempting to enter a field order character.

Set lesser keys first

> You have tried to mark a key field out of numerical order.

Protected area - field

You cannot overwrite a field.

Save fail

You were unable to save the file, possibly because of a disk error.

Not a valid index key

The key you tried to mark is not an elementary item.

Screen limit reached

You have reached the last row or column on the screen.

Unknown file format

The specified file format is not recognized resulting in a load failure.

Unknown error code

System error.

Chapter 8

On-line Help and Reference (HYHELP)

The On-Line Help System displays information on the screen when you request it while using Personal COBOL.

Overview

The On-line Help System (HYHELP) allows you to view on-screen help information for the Personal COBOL tools, and to view reference information on COBOL syntax, library routines and other technical aspects of programming with Personal COBOL. The database containing the technical information is referred to as the On-line Reference. You use HYHELP to access this database and then display on screen, browse through, copy into text file or print any part of the selected reference information.

This chapter describes the functions of HYHELP, how to invoke it and how to use it for viewing the On-line Reference.

Operation

This section is split into two main subsections:

o   Invoking HYHELP

o   Using HYHELP

Invoking HYHELP

HYHELP is used in two different ways, to get help with the tool you are using, or to get technical information on some aspect of programming such as COBOL syntax or library routine parameters.

To display help for whichever tool you are using, press **F1**. This function is active at any of the Personal COBOL menus and can be used throughout the system. HYHELP will display the appropriate help topic for the tool being used.

From the Editor, the On-Line Reference technical information database is also available by pressing **Alt+1**. When you invoke HYHELP this way, the system will examine the word at the cursor. If the word is in the On-line Reference index then HYHELP will display the topic for that word, otherwise it will show a table of contents and display the topic you select. Thus if you need help on the syntax required by a COBOL word, just put the cursor under the word and press **Alt+1**. Similarly you can use HYHELP to show details of a library routine or compiler directive. The On-line Reference is only available from the Editor, not from other Personal COBOL tools.

Using HYHELP

Once you have invoked HYHELP, this section will help you to use it. It describes the user interface and various terms associated with this component.

When you have invoked HYHELP, it displays a bordered panel which contains the text for the selected topic. The title of the topic is displayed in the top border.

If the topic contains more lines than the panel the right side of the border contains a scroll bar. The scroll bar indicates what proportion of the text is visible, and the current position of the panel within the topic.

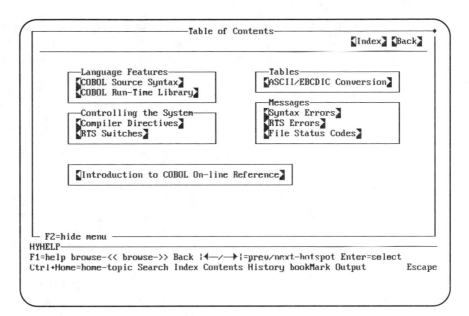

On-line Help

Figure 8-1: HYHELP Screen

You view the topic using the up and down cursor keys to move up or down one line at a time or the **Page-Up** and **Page-Down** keys to move up or down one panel at a time. If you have a mouse, click on the scroll bar to move up or down one panel of text or click on the up/down arrow icons to move up or down the topic by one line.

Some topics contain frozen lines. These lines always remain visible at the top of the screen while the rest of the text scrolls.

Below the text, a standard menu indicates the functions that can be performed by HYHELP. The menu can be made invisible and restored using the **F2** key. Any text that was on the screen prior to invoking HYHELP is revealed in the area previously occupied by the menu.

You can perform various operations in HYHELP using the keyboard or the mouse. All the functions indicated on the menu are activated by pressing the appropriate key. Several other functions can be performed using the various cursor-control keys or the mouse. These are described later.

In the following text, the terms clicking and double-clicking with the mouse refer to the operation of moving the mouse cursor to the relevant point and then clicking once or twice with the left mouse button. The mouse cursor is a solid block. It is visible only if you have a mouse. When you initially invoke HYHELP it is located at the bottom of the right hand side of the panel border.

Selecting and Activating

With HYHELP, a number of objects can be selected and/or activated. Selecting an object simply makes it the current object. Usually it becomes highlighted in some way. Subsequent keystrokes may take account of what object is selected.

Activating an object causes some process to take place related to the object.

For example, selecting a hot-spot (see later) simply causes it to be highlighted; activating it (by pressing **Enter** after selecting it) causes the topic that is cross-referenced by the hot-spot to be displayed.

Topics and Files

The information accessible to HYHELP is held in any number of On-line Help files. Topics from any of these files can be displayed using the facilities available.

In general, each file is self-contained and does not cross-reference to another file. However, in some instances (such as the On-line Reference), two or more files are used to contain a complete set of information. In this case you may switch from one file to another without knowing it. When a topic from a file is displayed, the file becomes the current file. Each file contains a set of topics. The topics are usually stored in the file in a logical sequence. Many files have a hierarchical structure. In general you should not need to understand the structure of a file to find the information you need. However, it can sometimes be helpful.

The first topic in a file is called the home topic. This topic provides a launch point to any of the information held in the file. In addition, most files also contain a contents list and an index of some form to help you.

Some files contain list topics. These topics contain a full width cursor bar. Each line in such a topic acts like a hot-spot, and as such is a cross-reference to another topic. You can select a line by moving the cursor bar to it using the cursor keys or by clicking on it. Press **Enter** to activate the selected list line. Double-clicking with the mouse on any line selects and activates that line.

Topic Names

To reference a topic from the command line or using the search function you need to know a topic name attached to the topic. A topic name is an ASCII string up to 30 characters in length. More than one topic name can point to a single topic.

The same topic name can exist in more than one file. When displaying information, the file containing the desired topic name can be prefixed to the topic name with an exclamation mark (!) as follows:

[file-name!][topic-name]

If file-name is supplied, then only that file is searched. Otherwise all files available are searched in the order shown in the file list (see the Files function). If topic-name is supplied, a topic with that name is searched for. Otherwise the first topic in the file specified - the home topic - is displayed.

The topic name is not the same as the topic title which appears at the top of the screen when a topic is displayed.

Hot-spots

A topic may contain areas which cross-reference other topics. These areas are called hot-spots. They are normally colored or enclosed in the horn characters (left and right arrow heads) to show their presence. Select a hot-spot by clicking on it or by using the **Tab** and **Backtab** keys. The hot-spot selected is highlighted.

If you double-click on a hot-spot, or press **Enter** when a hot-spot is selected, the system displays the topic cross-referenced by the hot-spot.

If you double-click on any other word in a topic, the system searches the On-line Help and help files for a topic with that name. The topic is displayed if found.

Functions Available in HYHELP

HYHELP provides functions to enable you to select menu functions and to navigate through displayed text.

List of Menu Functions

This section lists the functions available from the HYHELP main and output menus. See the section *Description of HYHELP Menu Functions* for details on individual functions.

Function	Description
Append-to-file	(output menu) append marked text to the end of a text file
Back	return to the previous topic displayed
bookMark	display a list of defined bookmarks and switch to the bookmark operations menu to go to, add, delete or rename bookmarks
browse->>	display the next topic in the browse chain
browse-<<	display the previous topic in the browse chain
Contents	display the contents for the current On-line Help file

On-line Help

Copy-to-file	(output menu) copy marked text to a text file
F1=help	display help information for the current menu from the HYHELP On-line Help file
History	display a list of the topics previously visited and switch to the history operations menu
Ctrl+Home=home-topic	display the home topic for the current On-line Help file
Index	display the index for the current On-line Help file
Mark	(output menu) mark a block of text for copying or printing
Print	(output menu) send all or part of a topic to a printer
Search	look for the specified topic in the available database

Keys and Mouse

This section lists the additional functions which can be activated using the keys and mouse operations described below.

Key	Function
Escape	exit from current menu
F1=help	display help for current menu
Enter	activate selected hot-spot or list item
Cursor-down	move topic text down one line in panel or move list topic cursor bar up one line

Cursor-up	move topic text up one line in panel or move list topic cursor bar up one line
Page-Up	move up topic by one panel height
Page-Down	move down topic by one panel height
Home	move to start of topic
End	move to end of topic
Tab	select next hot-spot (first if none are displayed)
Backtab	select previous hot-spot (last if none are displayed)
Ctrl+Home	display home topic of current file

The following mouse operations are available:

Action	Function
Click on vertical scroll bar above slider	move up topic by one panel height
Click on vertical scroll bar below slider	move down topic by one panel height
Click on up-arrow	move topic text down one line
Click on down-arrow	move topic text up one line
Click outside text panel	bring up history menu
Click on hot-spot/list line	selects the hot-spot/ list line
Click on maximize/restore icon (top right-hand corner)	maximizes/restores topic window
Double-click on hot-spot /list line	activate the hot-spot/ list line

Double-click on word in main   search for a topic with
panel (not list topic)   that name

Descriptions of HYHELP Menu Functions

This section describes the menu functions available from the
HYHELP menus.

Append-to-file

Select the Append-to-file function to append any or all of the
current topic to the end of the text file PASTE.TXT. If no text has
been marked, the whole of the topic is copied to the file.

The text selected is formatted to 76 characters wide before being
copied. This function is available from the output menu, available
by selecting output from the main menu.

Back

Selecting the Back function causes the previously displayed topic
to be re-displayed. If you select the function repeatedly without
selecting any other topics in between, the topics so far displayed
in this session are displayed again in reverse order. Up to 40
topics can be displayed in this way.

Bookmarks

A bookmark is a user-defined index item identifying a specific
point in a specific topic. In the same way you would use a real
bookmark to mark a place in a book, you use these bookmarks to
mark places in the information.

When the bookmark function is selected a list of all the bookmarks
you have defined is displayed in a pop-up window. The bookmark menu is also displayed. From this menu you can go to, add,
delete or rename any bookmark.

Bookmarks are listed in alphabetic order, just like an index. Each bookmark is a user defined name relating to a point within a particular topic. Select a bookmark by moving to it using the cursor movement keys, **Page-Up, Page-Down**, **Home** and **End** keys, or click on it. The selected bookmark is highlighted.

Go to a bookmark (activate it) by double-clicking on it or by selecting it and pressing **Enter** or the Goto function on the menu. When activated, the topic relating to the bookmark is displayed positioned at the point the bookmark was defined.

Press **Escape** or click the mouse outside the main panel area to leave the bookmark menu without activating any function.

From the bookmark menu you can also add, rename or delete a bookmark. These are described below.

Adding a bookmark

Having entered the bookmark menu, a bookmark can be defined at the current position in the current topic. Select the Add function. The title of the topic is placed in the field in the menu. You can use this as the name of the bookmark, or replace it with a different name.

Having typed the desired name for the bookmark, press **Enter**. This adds the given bookmark to the list and returns to the main menu.

Deleting a bookmark

If you no longer have a need for a bookmark, you can delete it from the list. Select bookmark to be deleted from the list and then select the Delete function. The bookmark is removed from the list.

Renaming a bookmark

An existing bookmark can be given a different name at any time. Select the bookmark to be renamed by moving to it using the cursor movement keys, **Page-Up, Page-Down, Home** and **End** keys, or click on it. The selected bookmark is highlighted.

Select the Rename function, type the new name for the bookmark and press **Enter**. The selected bookmark is renamed and the new name placed in the list at its new alphabetical position.

Browse Forward and Browse Backward

The browse functions allow the topics in the current on-line information file to be displayed in the sequence they were stored in the file, or, for .HNF format files, in a sequence selected by the creator of the file - a browse chain. If no browse chain has been defined then you see the next/previous topic in the file.

Select Browse ->> to see the next topic and Browse <<- to see the previous topic in the chain.

The sequence in which topics are displayed when using browse depends entirely on the structure of the file and cannot be described in detail here.

Contents

When the Contents function is selected, a list of the contents are displayed where available.

The general contents for an .HNF format file is displayed as a list of entries in a pop-up window. Entries are in the order that the topics are stored in the file and each entry is the title of a topic in the current file. All topics with titles appear in the contents list.

To select an entry use the cursor-up, cursor-down, **Page-Up, Page-Down, Home** or **End** keys or click on it. The selected entry is highlighted.

Activate an entry by double-clicking on it, or by selecting it and pressing **Enter**. When activated, the topic relating to the contents entry is then displayed.

Press **Escape** or click the mouse outside the main panel area to leave the contents list without activating any entry.

On-line Help

The contents in the On-line Reference is displayed and used in a different way. This is described in the section, *On-line Reference*.

Copy-to-file

Select the Copy-to-file function to place any or all of the current topic into the text file PASTE.TXT. If no text has been marked, the whole topic is copied to the file.

The text selected is formatted to 76 characters wide before being copied. This function is available from the output menu, available by selecting output from the main menu.

Help

Pressing **F1=help** causes the HYHELP On-line Help file to be selected and the help topic for this menu to be displayed. The other topics in the HYHELP file can be viewed in the usual way. However, you cannot access any other files.

Press **Escape** to return.

History

Selecting the History function causes a list of topics previously viewed to be displayed in a pop-up window. The list is in time sequence with the most recently visited topic occurring at the top of the list. Each entry in the list is the title of a topic. The list contains the forty most recent entries.

To select an entry use the **cursor-up**, **cursor-down**, **Page-Up, Page-Down, Home** or **End** keys or click on it. The selected entry is highlighted.

Activate an entry by double-clicking on it, or by selecting it and pressing **Enter**. When activated, the topic relating to the contents entry is displayed.

Press **Escape** or click the mouse outside the main panel area to leave the history list without activating any entry.

Home

The Home function, when selected, causes the home topic of the current On-line Help file to be displayed. This can be useful for repositioning yourself at a known point within a file.

Index

If there is an index of the correct form in the current file this function is available. Selecting the Index function displays the index. The general index for a .HNF format file is displayed as a list of entries in a pop-up window. Entries are in alphabetical order and each entry relates to a specific topic in the current file.

To select an entry use the **cursor-up**, **cursor-down**, **Page-Up, Page-Down, Home** or **End** keys or click on it. The selected entry is highlighted. You can also select an entry by pressing a letter key, which moves the cursor to the first item starting with that letter.

Activate an entry by double-clicking on it, or by selecting it and pressing **Enter.** When activated, the topic relating to the index entry is displayed.

Press **Escape** or click the mouse outside the main panel area to leave the index list without activating any function.

Mark

When the output menu is selected, a text cursor appears in the main window. To select a part of the topic to be output, move the text cursor to the first or last line of the block you wish to mark using the cursor up or cursor down keys. Select the Mark-on function, and move the text cursor to the last or first line. The marked area is highlighted.

Selecting one of the output functions causes the selected operation to take place on just the marked area of the topic and the marking to be removed. To remove the marking without any action, select the Mark-off function.

On-line Help

This function is available from the output menu, available by selecting output from the main menu.

Print

The Print function allows a topic or part of a topic to be sent to a printer. If no text has been marked then the whole of the topic is printed.

The text selected is formatted to 76 characters wide before being printed.

This function is available from the output menu, available by selecting output from the main menu.

Search

When the Search function is selected you are requested to enter the name of the topic to be searched for. When you have entered the name press **Enter** to activate the search or **Escape** to leave the search menu.

All the files available to HYHELP, as listed in the files list, are searched, in the order specified, for a topic that has the entered name.

The On-line Reference

The On-line Reference contains items from the printed and on-line manuals that you may wish to access on-line. This includes:

■ COBOL system

Animator
Compiler
Checker
Screens

■ COBOL language

Call-by-name routines
COBOL syntax

■   COBOL messages

Run-time errors
Syntax errors

The following sections will help you to find your way around the information.

Structure

The On-line Reference is organized as a hierarchical structure. All topics can be reached by starting at the top of the hierarchy and moving downwards. Each subject item has a number of topics related to it. These topics are regarded as being at the same level. All items within a particular subject are also grouped at the same level of the hierarchy.

Moving around (navigating) the On-line Reference, or any other on-line information, is very easy. Using hot-spots, browse, index and contents it is easy to move from one topic to another. However, it is also quite easy to become lost. To ensure that you can always find your way back, you should become familiar with the following functions:

■   Contents

■   Index

■   History list

■   Bookmarks

■   Up

Contents

The On-line Reference contents are set up in a different manner to that in a standard .HNF format file. In the On-line Reference a separate topic is displayed for the contents showing only the top-level contents. This topic is displayed when the Contents hot-spot is activated.

Activating a content item hot-spot causes another topic to be displayed which contains either a lower level contents topic for the chosen subject, or a list of topics available for that subject.

Activating the Up hot-spot moves you back up the contents hierarchy.

Index

To select an entry use the **cursor-up**, **cursor-down**, **Page-Up**, **Page-Down, Home** or **End** keys or click on it. The selected entry is highlighted. You can also select an entry by pressing a letter key, which moves the cursor to the first item starting with that letter.

Activate an entry by double-clicking on it, or by selecting it and pressing **Enter.** When activated, the topic relating to the index entry is displayed.

Press **Escape** or click the mouse outside the main panel area to leave the index list without activating any function.

History list

Every topic that you enter is added to the history list. The last 40 topics visited are retained on the list. You can access the list at any time. Assuming you remember the title of a topic, you can select it from the history list and are returned there.

Alternatively, using the Back hot-spot or the Back function from the menu you can move back through the topics in the history list until you find the one you want.

Bookmarks

If you arrive at a topic that you know you want to return to you can easily set a bookmark to that topic. Then, when you wish to return to the topic, simply select the relevant bookmark from the bookmark list.

Up

Using the Up hot-spot within each topic of the On-line Reference you can move up the hierarchy from any point. The hierarchy of the On-line Reference is very shallow. Consequently, using Up returns you to a familiar contents list very quickly.

On-line Help

PART III

REFERENCE

Chapter 9

Language Reference

Overview

This Language Reference provides basic information about CO-BOL language syntax. When editing a program, you can get on-screen information by placing the cursor on a COBOL word and pressing **Alt+1**. The On-line Reference information will display either the function of the word with a syntax diagram of its use or a table of contents from which to select a topic. For fuller detail of the COBOL language, please see *Further References* at the end of this book.

COBOL Syntax

Personal COBOL Program Source

A COBOL program can consist of four divisions:

1. Identification Division - an identification of the program.

2. Environment Division - a description of the equipment to be used to compile and run the program.

3. Data Division - a description of the data to be processed.

4.   Procedure Division - a set of procedures to specify the operations to be performed on the data.

Each division is divided into sections which are further divided into paragraphs, which in turn are made up of sentences.

In ANSI 85 COBOL the Identification Division must be included in every program, but the Environment, Data and Procedure Divisions may be omitted. In Micro Focus COBOL, the Identification Division may also be omitted. Personal COBOL will accept a program that contains only the sections and divisions that are necessary to the program.

Syntax Diagram Conventions

COBOL syntax is shown using diagrams called "railroad tracks", in which the words and phrases comprising a construct are shown joined by lines indicating the order they should be written in. You read these diagrams left-to-right. Each diagram starts with ▶▶ and ends with ▶◀.

Sometimes the track forks to show alternatives and then joins up again. An arrow starting after a word or phrase and pointing back before it, forming a loop, means it can be repeated. The length of a track has no significance.

When a diagram reaches the right-hand side of the page, it is continued further down. A track continued onto a new line ends with ▶, and the new line begins with ▶. If several tracks are are continued they are numbered so you can match up each track with its continuation.

Within the diagrams, COBOL reserved words which are not significant and can be left out without affecting the sense of the statement (noise words) are indicated by a "drop-out" with narrow sides. Reserved words which are optional, but change the sense of the statement when included are shown by a drop-out with wide sides. For example, in the statement:

the word NEW can be left out without affecting the operation. However, omitting the word BACKWARDS will produce a different effect than if it is included.

COBOL Syntax Diagrams

Construct: COBOL Source Program

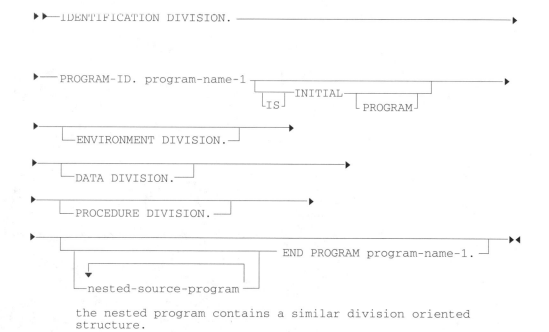

the nested program contains a similar division oriented
structure.

Construct: Identification Division

Function: Identifies the program and contains documentry information about it.

Syntax:

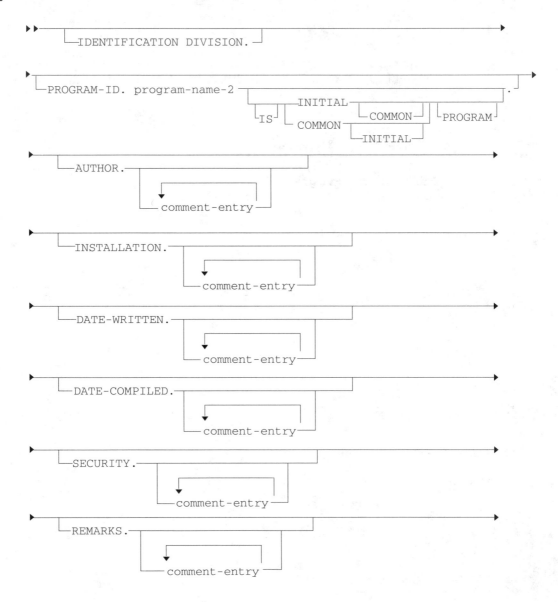

Construct: Environment Division

Function: Links names used in the program to external objects and selects options of the COBOL environment.

Syntax:

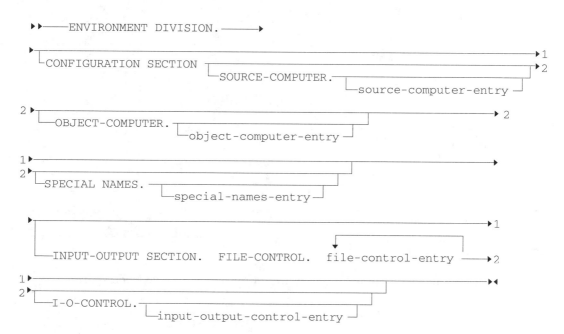

Construct: Source-computer Paragraph

Function: Describes the computer where the program is to be compiled, and enables debugging code.

Syntax:

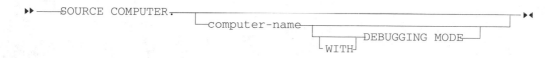

Construct: Object-computer Paragraph

Function: Describes the computer where the program is to run, and selects some options of the COBOL environment.

Syntax:

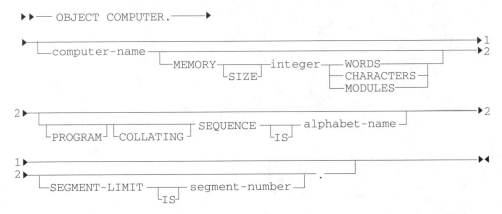

Construct: Special-names Paragraph

Function: Links names used in the program to external switches, and selects some options of the COBOL environment.

Syntax:

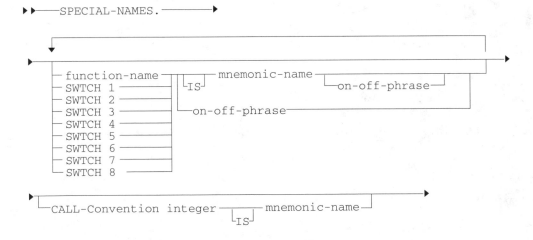

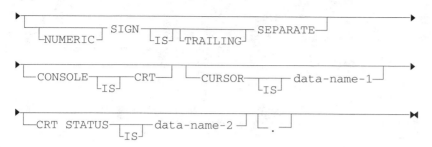

where on-off phrase is:

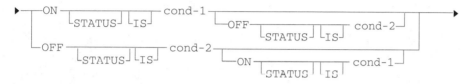

Construct: Input-Output Section

Function: Gives details of files and specifies file handling options.

Syntax:

Construct: File-control Entry (SELECT)

Function: Assigns names to files, for use in the program, and describes the files.

Syntax: Sequential.

```
▶▶ ──SELECT──┬──────────────┬──file-name-1──────▶
             ├─NOT OPTIONAL─┤
             └─OPTIONAL─────┘

▶──ASSIGN─┬────┬──▶
          └─TO─┘
```

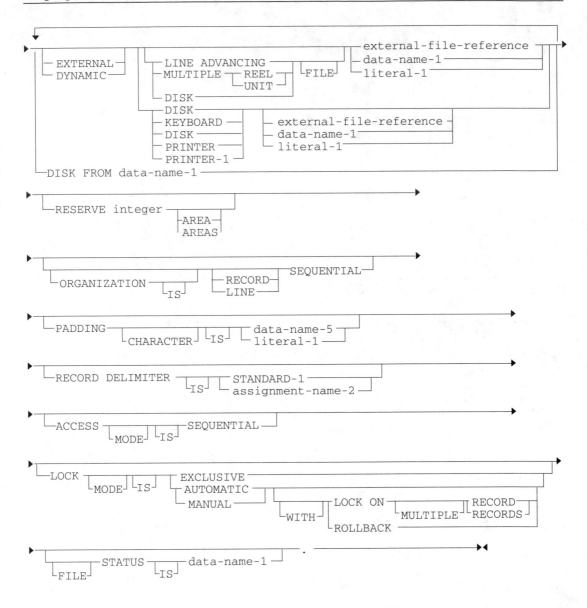

Construct: File-control Entry (SELECT)

Function: Assigns names to files, for use in the program, and describes the files.

Syntax: Relative.

Construct: File-control Entry (SELECT)

Function: Assigns names to files, for use in the program, and describes the files.

Syntax: Indexed.

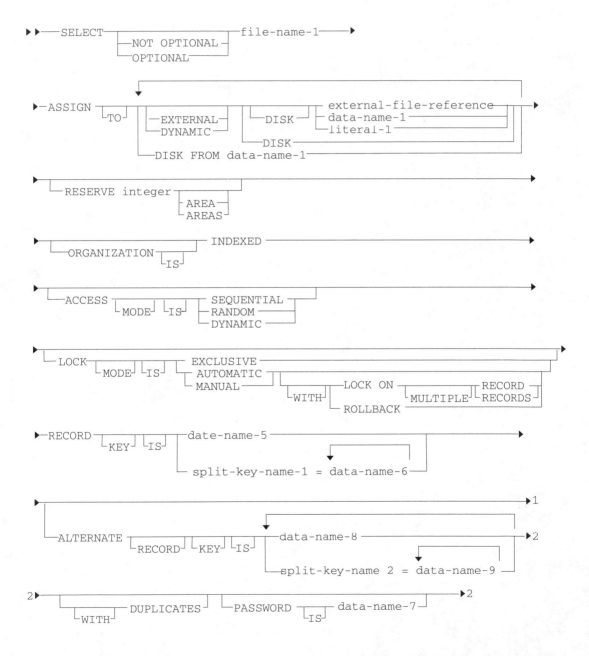

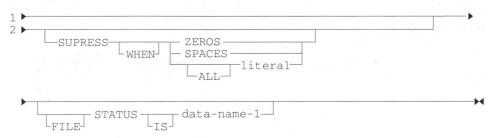

Construct: File-control Entry (SELECT)

Function: Assigns names to files, for use in the program, and describes the files.

Syntax: Sort-merge.

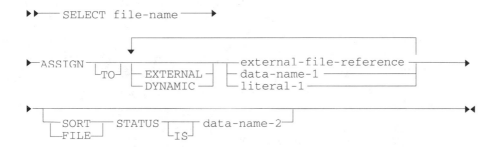

Construct: I-O-Control Paragraph

Function: Specifies file-handling options.

Syntax:

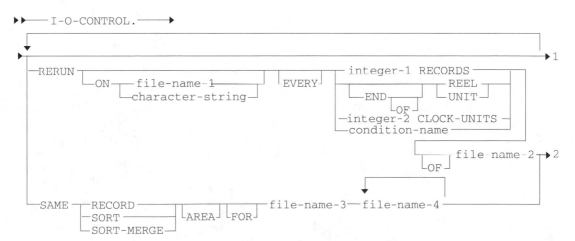

Construct: Data Division

Function: Defines the data that the program is to accept as input, work on internally, or produce as output.

Syntax:

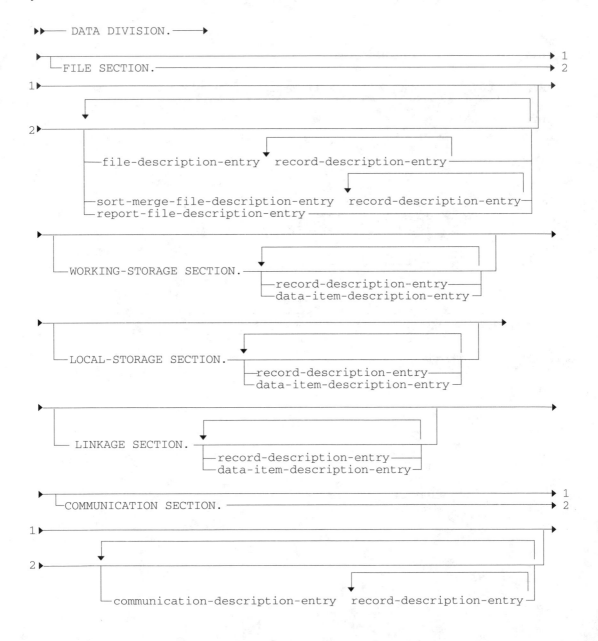

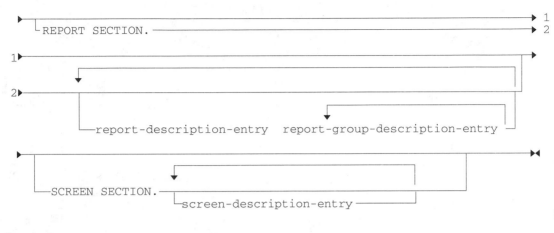

Construct: File Description Entry (FD)

See also:

Sort-merge file Description Entry.

Function: Gives further details of a file (in addition to the information in the File-control paragraph) and begins the descriptions of its record layouts.

Syntax: Please see the On-line Reference for specific syntax in a given instance.

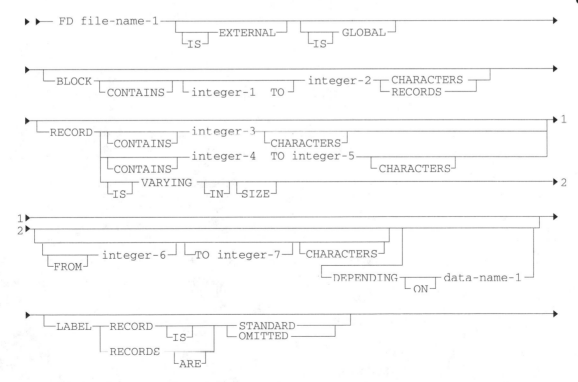

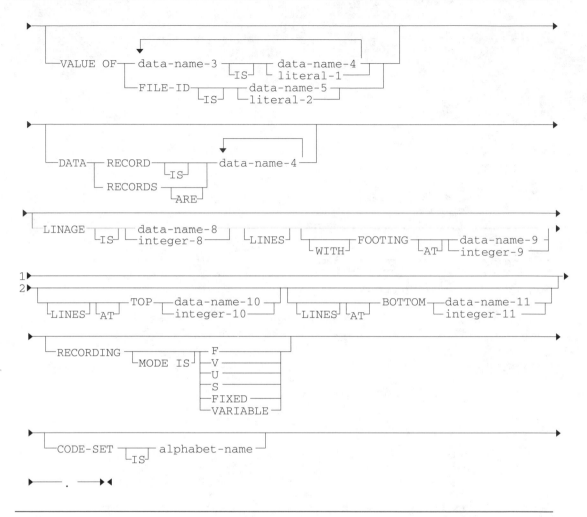

Construct: Sort-Merge File Description Entry (SD)

Function: Gives further details of a Sort-Merge file (in addition to the information in File-control paragraph) and begins the descriptions of its record layouts.

Syntax:

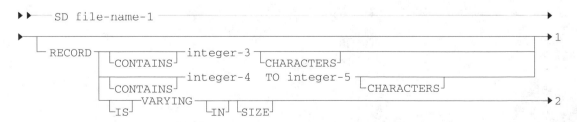

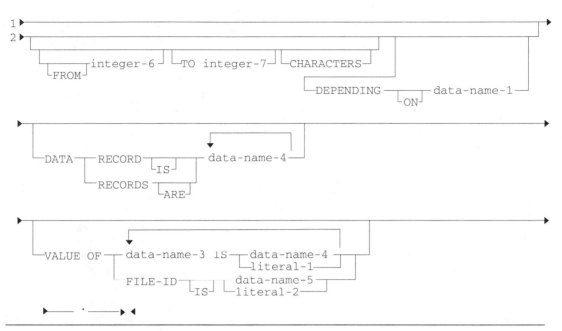

Construct: Data Description Entry

Function: Reserves and names an area of memory for storing an item of data, and describes the data to be stored there.

Syntax:

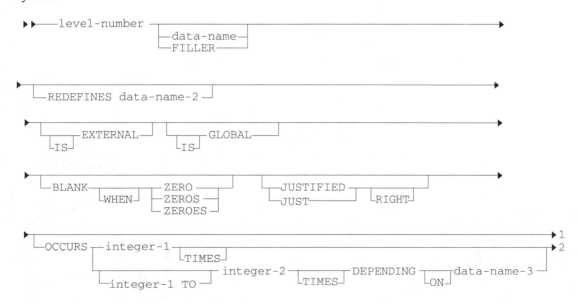

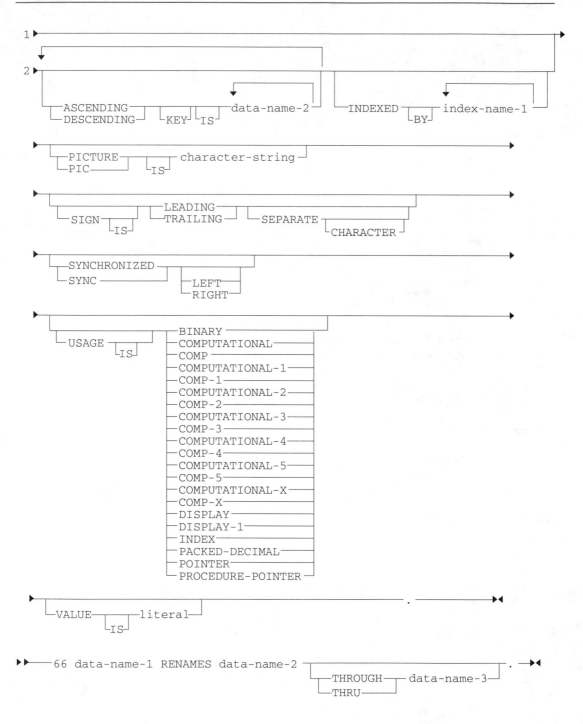

```
1 ▶─────────────────────────────────────────────────────────────────▶

2 ▶───────────────────────────────────────────────────────────────────
      ┌─ASCENDING──┐   ┌─KEY─┐ ┌─IS─┐ ─data-name-2─    ─INDEXED─ ┌─BY─┐ ─index-name-1─
      └─DESCENDING─┘

  ▶──────────────────────────────────────────────────────────────────▶
      ┌─PICTURE─┐ ┌─IS─┐ character-string
      └─PIC─────┘

  ▶──────────────────────────────────────────────────────────────────▶
      ┌─SIGN─ ┌─IS─┐   ┌─LEADING──┐  ─SEPARATE─
                       └─TRAILING─┘            └─CHARACTER─┘

  ▶──────────────────────────────────────────────────────────────────▶
      ┌─SYNCHRONIZED─┐
      └─SYNC─────────┘   ┌─LEFT──┐
                         └─RIGHT─┘

  ▶──────────────────────────────────────────────────────────────────▶
      ─USAGE─ ┌─IS─┐  ┌─BINARY────────────────┐
                     ─COMPUTATIONAL──
                     ─COMP──
                     ─COMPUTATIONAL-1──
                     ─COMP-1──
                     ─COMPUTATIONAL-2──
                     ─COMP-2──
                     ─COMPUTATIONAL-3──
                     ─COMP-3──
                     ─COMPUTATIONAL-4──
                     ─COMP-4──
                     ─COMPUTATIONAL-5──
                     ─COMP-5──
                     ─COMPUTATIONAL-X──
                     ─COMP-X──
                     ─DISPLAY──
                     ─DISPLAY-1──
                     ─INDEX──
                     ─PACKED-DECIMAL──
                     ─POINTER──
                     └─PROCEDURE-POINTER──┘

  ▶──────────────────────────────────── . ─────────────────▶◀
      ─VALUE─ ┌─IS─┐ ─literal─

▶▶──66 data-name-1 RENAMES data-name-2 ──────────────────── . ──▶◀
                                          ┌─THROUGH─┐ ─data-name-3─
                                          └─THRU────┘
```

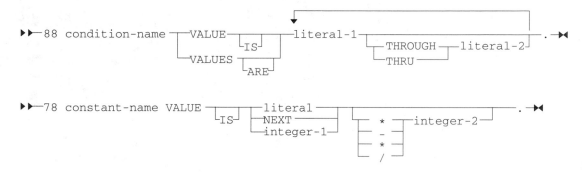

Construct: Screen Description Entry

Function: Reserves and names an area of the screen for displaying or accepting an item of data, and describes the data to be displayed or accepted there.

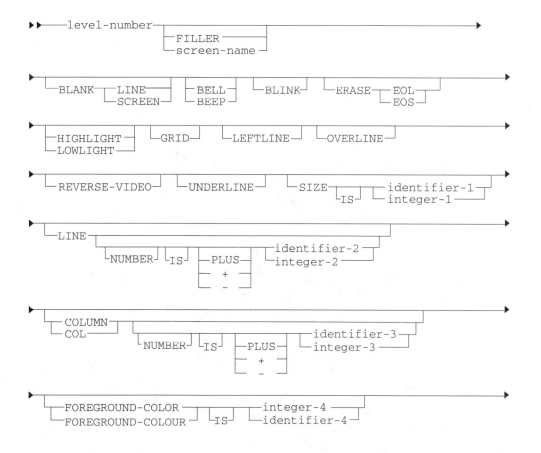

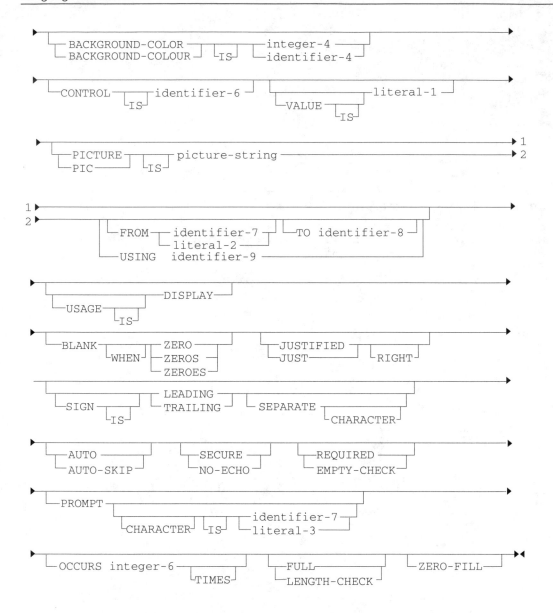

Construct: Procedure Division

Function: Contains the executable statements of the program.

Syntax: Please see the On-line Reference for specific syntax in a given instance.

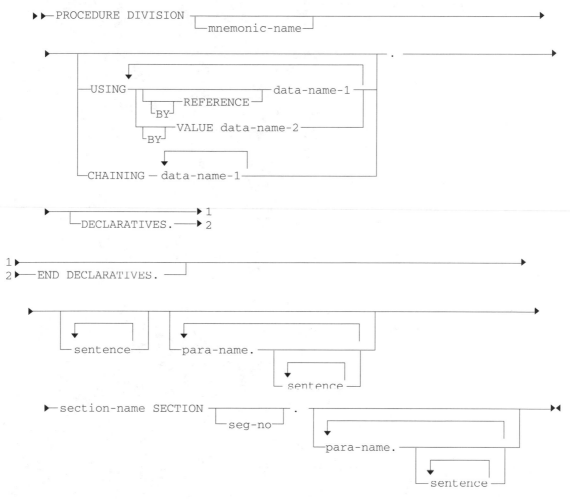

Language Reference

Construct: ACCEPT

Function: Gets data from a physical device, such as the keyboard, or from the operating system.

Syntax 1: Line at a time.

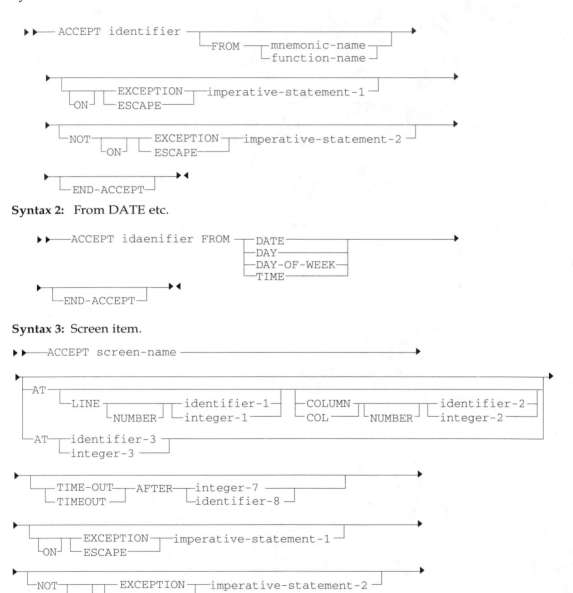

Syntax 2: From DATE etc.

Syntax 3: Screen item.

Syntax 4: Full screen.

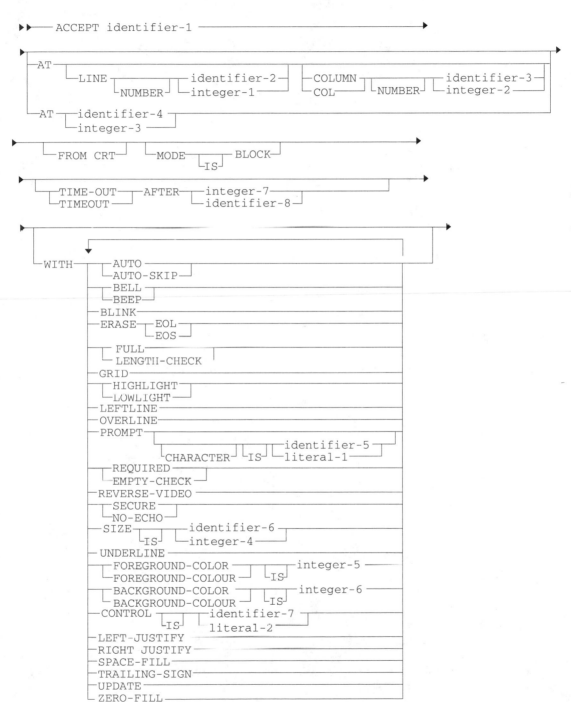

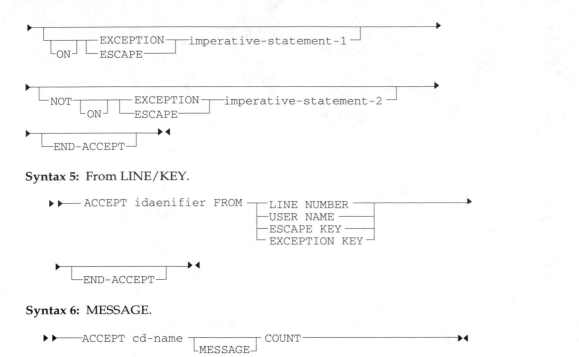

Syntax 5: From LINE/KEY.

```
▶▶── ACCEPT idaenifier FROM ──┬── LINE NUMBER ────┬──────────▶
                              ├── USER NAME ───────┤
                              ├── ESCAPE KEY ──────┤
                              └── EXCEPTION KEY ────┘
```

```
▶──────────────────────▶◀
       └── END-ACCEPT ──┘
```

Syntax 6: MESSAGE.

```
▶▶── ACCEPT cd-name ──┬──────────┬── COUNT ──────────────────▶◀
                      └──MESSAGE──┘
```

Verb: ADD

Function: Adds two or more numeric operands and stores the result.

Syntax 1: Simple.

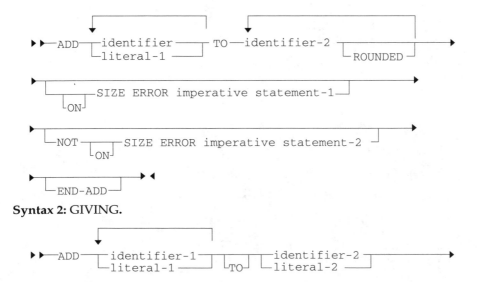

```
▶──────▶◀
  └── END-ADD ──┘
```

Syntax 2: GIVING.

```
▶▶── ADD ──┬── identifier-1 ──┬──┬──────┬── identifier-2 ──┬──▶
           └── literal-1 ─────┘  └─ TO ─┘  └── literal-2 ──┘
```

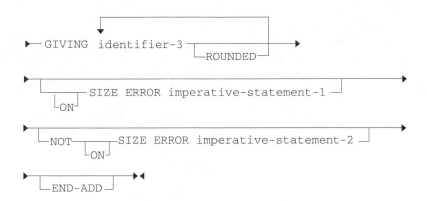

Syntax 3: CORRESPONDING.

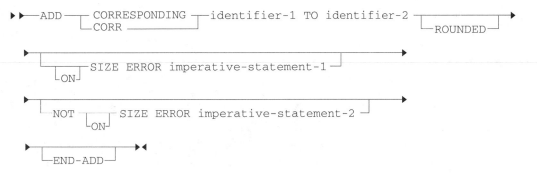

Language Reference

Verb: ALTER

Function: Modifies a predetermined sequence of operations.

Syntax:

Verb: CALL

Function: Transfers control to another program in the run unit, with automatic return of control when that program finishes.

Syntax 1: OVERFLOW.

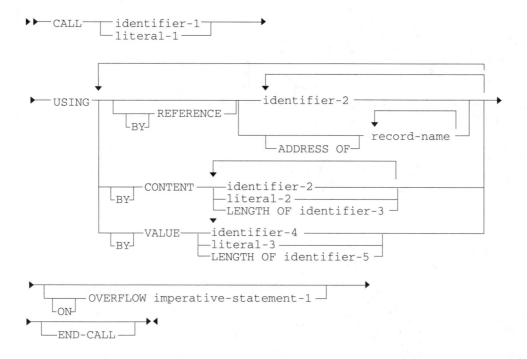

Syntax: EXCEPTION.

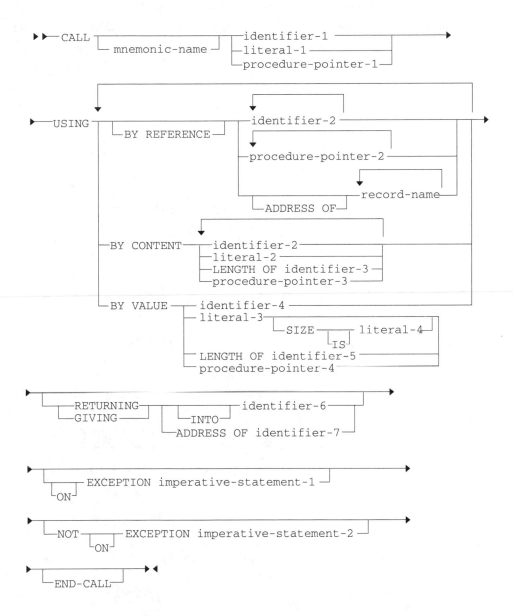

Verb: CANCEL

Function: Ensures that the next time the program referenced is called it will be in its initial state.

Syntax:

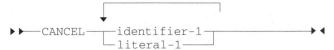

Verb: CHAIN

Function: Transfers control to another program in the run-unit, with no subsequent return of control.

Syntax:

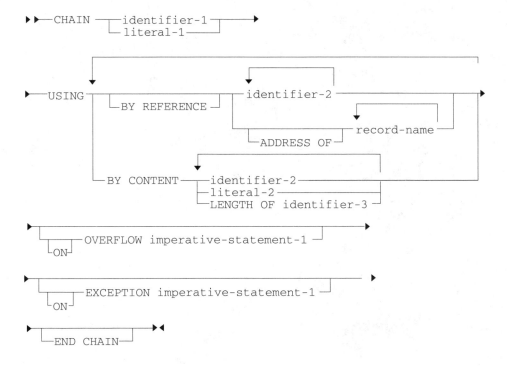

Construct: Class Condition

Function: Tests class of data item.

Syntax:

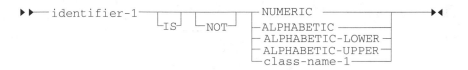

Verb: CLOSE

Function: Terminates the processing of files.

Syntax:

Verb: COMPUTE

Function: Evaluates an arithmetic expression and stores the result.

Syntax:

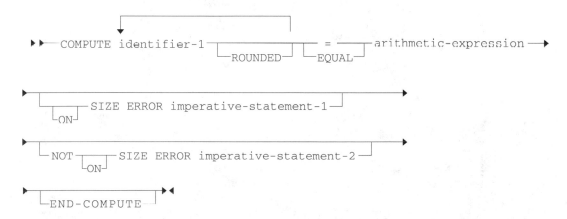

Verb: CONTINUE

Function: No effect. Used where no operation is wanted but COBOL syntax requires a verb.

Syntax:

```
►►── CONTINUE ───►◄
```

Construct: COPY Statement

Function: Include separate text files with optional string replacement.

Syntax:

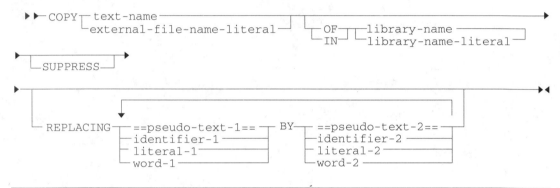

```
►►─COPY─┬─text-name─────────────────────┬──────────────────────────────►
        └─external-file-name-literal────┘    ┌─OF─┬──┬─library-name──────────┬─
                                             └─IN─┘  └─library-name-literal──┘

►──┬──────────┬──►
   └─SUPPRESS─┘

►──┬────────────────────────────────────────────────────────────────►◄
   │                          ┌──────────────────────────┐
   └─REPLACING─┬─==pseudo-text-1==─┬─ BY ─┬─==pseudo-text-2==─┬─
               ├─identifier-1──────┤      ├─identifier-2──────┤
               ├─literal-1─────────┤      ├─literal-2─────────┤
               └─word-1────────────┘      └─word-2────────────┘
```

Verb: DELETE

Function: Deletes a record from a relative or indexed file, or deletes files from the devices they are on.

Syntax 1: RECORD.

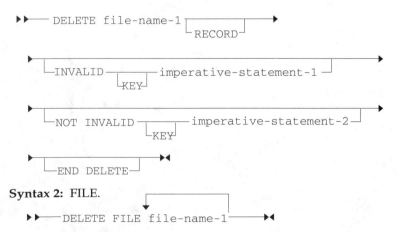

```
►►── DELETE file-name-1 ─┬──────────┬──►
                         └─RECORD───┘

►──┬──────────────────────────────────────────┬──►
   └─INVALID─┬──────┬── imperative-statement-1─┘
             └─KEY──┘

►──┬──────────────────────────────────────────────┬──►
   └─NOT INVALID ─┬──────┬── imperative-statement-2─┘
                  └─KEY──┘

►──┬────────────────┬──►◄
   └─END DELETE─────┘
```

Syntax 2: FILE.

```
►►────DELETE FILE file-name-1────►◄
```

Verb: DISPLAY

Function: Sends data to a physical device, such as the screen..

Syntax 1: Line at a time.

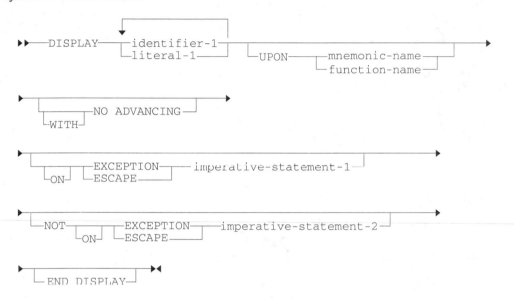

Syntax 2: Screen item.

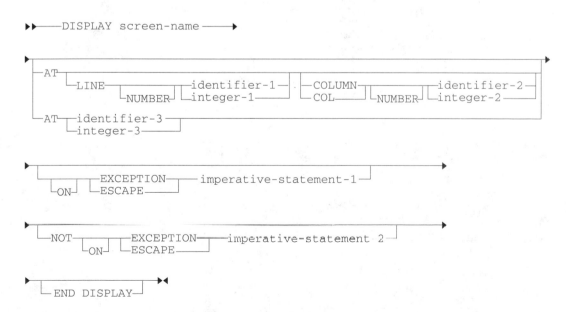

Syntax 3: Full screen.

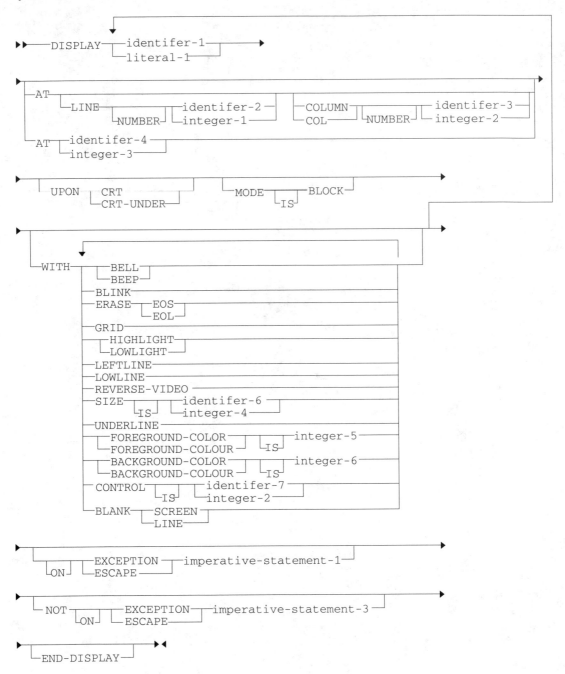

Verb: DIVIDE

Function: Divides one numeric data item into another and stores the quotient and remainder.

Syntax 1: Simple.

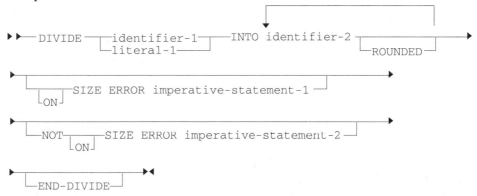

Syntax 2: INTO GIVING.

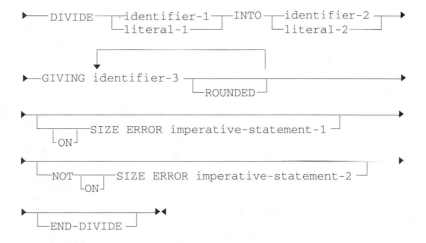

Syntax 3: BY GIVING.

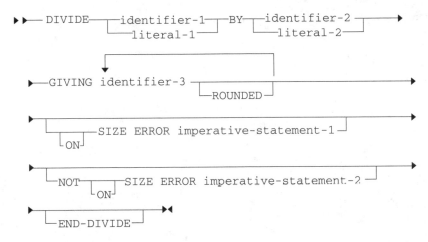

Syntax 4: INTO REMAINDER.

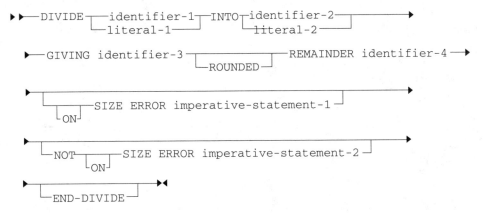

Syntax 5: BY REMAINDER.

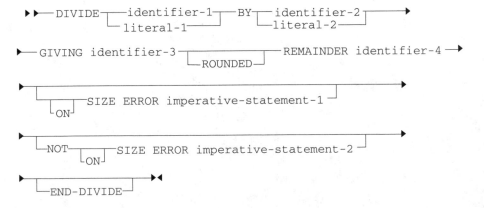

Verb: ENTER

Function: Allows the use of another language in a COBOL program.

General Rule: This statement is treated as for documentation purposes only and is not executed.

Syntax:

Verb: EVALUATE

Function: Tests multiple conditions and executes a different branch depending on the result.

Syntax:

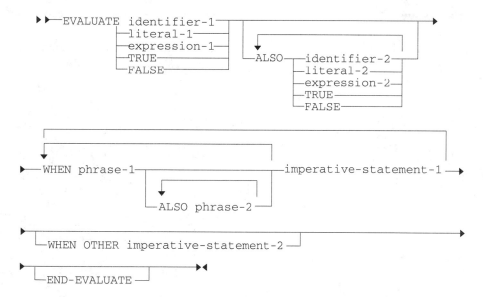

where phrase-1 is:

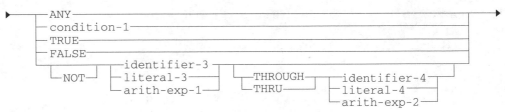

and phrase-2 is:

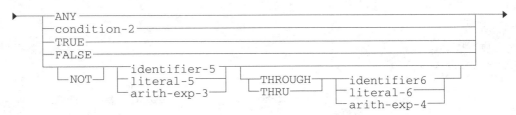

Verb: EXAMINE

Function: Replaces or counts the occurrences of a given character in a data item.

Syntax 1:

```
▶▶──── EXAMINE identifier-1 TALLYING ────▶
    ▶──── UNTIL FIRST ──┬── literal-1 ───────────────────────────────▶
       ── ALL ─────────┘            └── REPLACING BY literal-2 ──┘
       ── LEADING ──────
```

Syntax 2:

```
▶▶──── EXAMINE identifier-1 REPLACING ────▶

    ▶──── ALL ─────────┬── literal-1 BY literal-2 ──────▶◀
       ── LEADING ─────
       ── FIRST ───────
       ── UNTIL FIRST ─┘
```

Verb: **EXHIBIT**

Function: Displays data items, optionally preceded by their identifiers, and literals. The display can be conditional.

Syntax:

Verb: **EXIT**

Function: Marks the end of a procedure or cycle of an in-line perform, causing the indicated level of procedure (PERFORM CYCLE, PERFORM, PARAGRAPH, SECTION or PROGRAM) to be terminated at that point.

Syntax 1: PROGRAM.

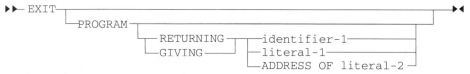

Syntax 2: PERFORM.

Syntax 3: PARAGRAPH.

Language Reference

Verb: GO TO

Function: Transfers control elsewhere in the Procedure Division.

Syntax 1:

Syntax 2:

Verb: GOBACK

Function: Transfers control to the calling program, or to the operating system if the program was not called.

Syntax:

Verb: IF

Function: Tests a condition and executes a different branch depending on the result.

Syntax:

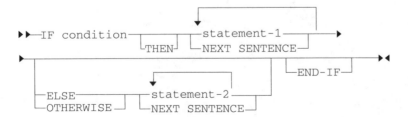

Verb: INITIALIZE

Function: Assigns values to all data items of a specified type that are subordinate to a specified data item.

Syntax:

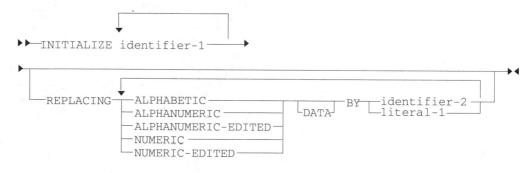

Verb: INSPECT

Function: Counts, replaces, or converts occurrences of a character or group of characters in a data item.

Syntax 1: TALLYING.

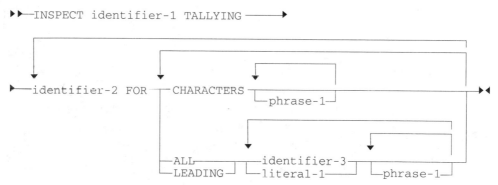

where phrase-1 is:

Syntax 2: REPLACING.

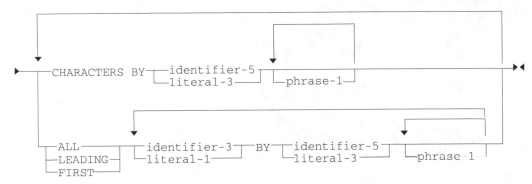

where phrase-1 is:

Syntax 3: TALLYING REPLACING.

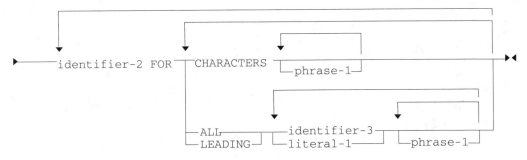

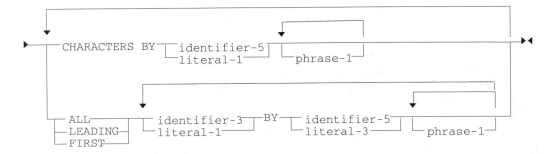

where phrase-1 is:

Syntax 4: CONVERTING.

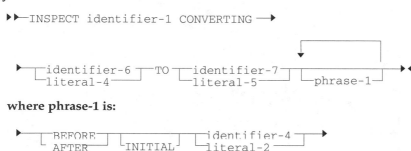

where phrase-1 is:

Verb: **MERGE**

Function: Combines two or more identically sequenced files on a set of specified keys, and passes the records, in merge order, to an output procedure or output file.

Syntax:

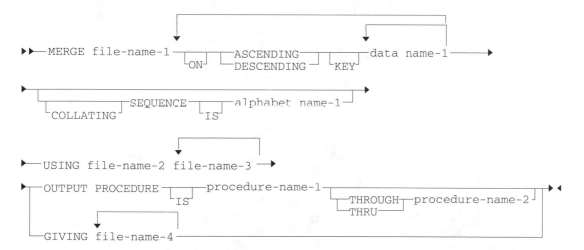

Verb: MOVE

Function: Copies data from one data item to others, in accordance with editing rules.

Syntax 1: Simple.

Syntax 2: Corresponding.

Verb: MULTIPLY

Function: Multiplies numeric data items and stores the result.

Syntax 1: Simple.

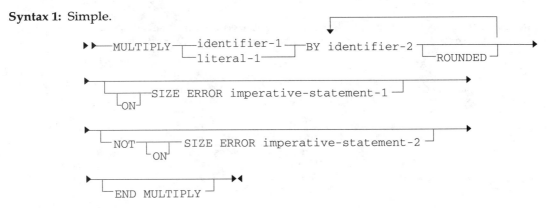

Syntax 2: Giving.

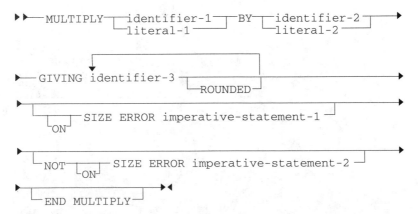

Verb: ON

Function: Causes a group of statements to be executed periodically.

Syntax:

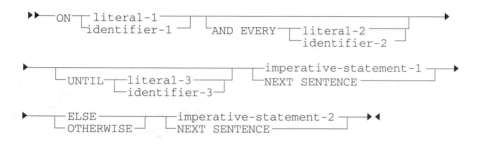

Verb: OPEN

Function: Initiates the processing of files. It checks and/or writes labels and does other related tasks.

Syntax 1: Sequential.

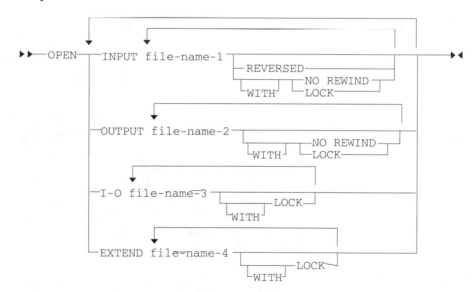

Syntax 2: Relative and indexed.

Verb: PERFORM

Function: Causes a group of statements to be executed repeatedly. If the statements are a procedure, this statement repeatedly transfers control to that procedure, with automatic return of control each time the procedure finishes.

Syntax 1: Simple.

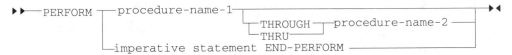

Syntax 2: TIMES.

where phrase is:

```
  ┌─identifier-1─┬─TIMES──────────────────────────►
  └─integer-1───┘
```

Syntax 3: UNTIL.

where phrase is:

```
                          ┌────────────────────┐
────────────────────────────UNTIL condition 1 ──►
     ┌─────TEST─┬─BEFORE─┐
     │ WITH     └─AFTER──┘
```

Syntax 4: VARYING.

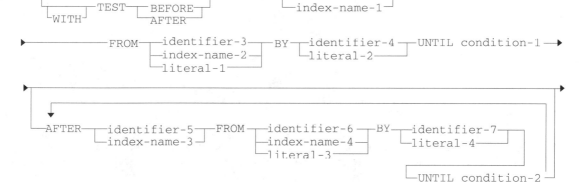

where phrase is:

Construct: Pointer Condition

Function: Compares pointer items.

Syntax:

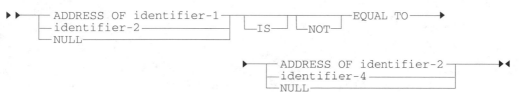

Construct: Qualification

Function: Identifies which item is meant out of several with the same name.

Syntax 1: Data division names.

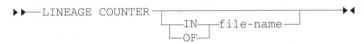

Syntax 2: LINAGE.

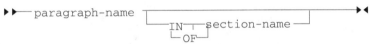

Syntax 3: Procedure division names.

Syntax 4: COPY Library.

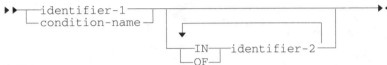

Verb: READ

Function: Gets a record from a file. In sequential access this will be the next or previous record; in random access, it will be a specified record.

Syntax 1: Sequential.

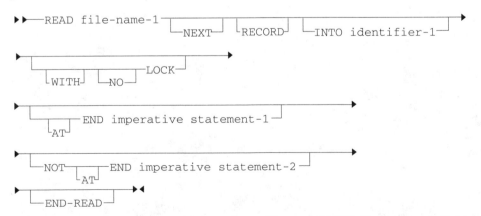

Syntax 2: NEXT/PREVIOUS.

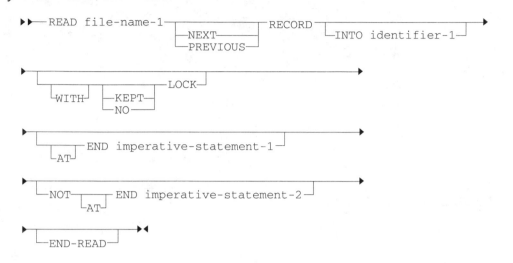

Syntax 3: Relative key.

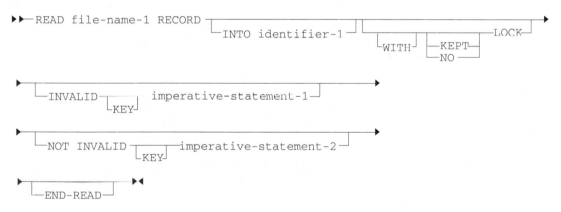

Syntax 4: Record key.

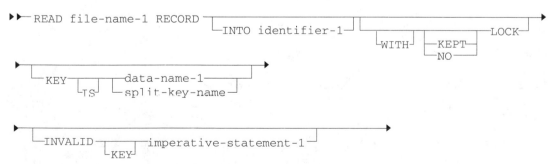

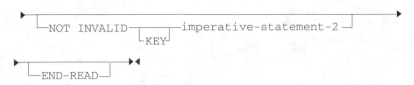

Verb: READY

Function: Enter trace mode.

Syntax:

```
▶▶─READY-TRACE───────────────────────────────▶◀
```

CONSTRUCT: Relation Condition

Function: Comparision between data items.

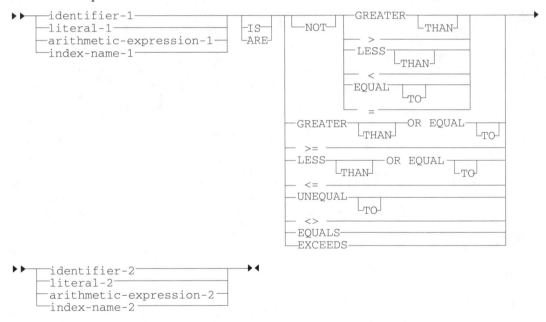

Verb: RELEASE

Function: Passes records to the initial phase of a sort operation.

Syntax:

```
▶▶───RELEASE record-name ─────────────────────▶◀
                       └─FROM identifier-1─┘
```

Construct: REPLACE Statement

Function: Replace text in source lines.

Syntax:

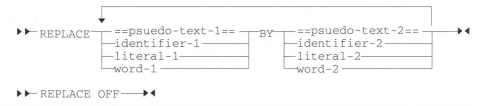

Verb: RESET

Function: End trace mode.

Syntax:

▶▶─ RESET TRACE ─────────────────────▶◀

Verb: RETURN

Function: Gets records from the final phase of a sort operation or merged records during a merge operation.

Syntax:

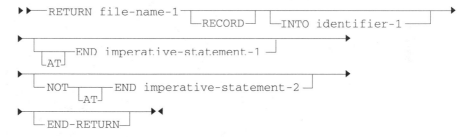

Verb: REWRITE

Function: Replaces an existing record in a file with an updated copy of the same record.

Syntax: Please see the On-line Reference for specific syntax in a given instance.

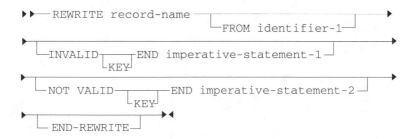

Verb: **SEARCH**

Function: Searches a table for an element satisfying a given condition and sets the associated index-name to point to it.

Syntax 1: Simple.

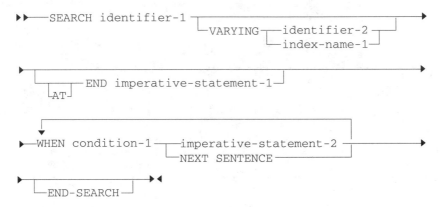

Syntax 2: All.

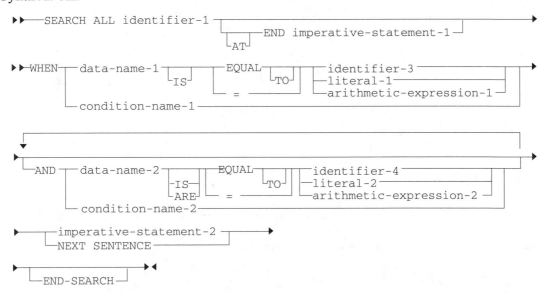

Verb: SET

Function: Assigns a value to an item of a type used for program control rather than data storage; that is index name, condition-name, switch, or data item of USAGE INDEX, POINTER or PROCEDURE-POINTER>

Syntax 1: Index.

Syntax 2: Index UP/DOWN.

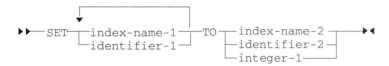

Syntax 3: Condition-name.

Syntax 4: Switch.

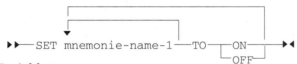

Syntax 5: Address.

Syntax 6: Pointer UP/DOWN.

Syntax 7: Procedure pointer.

Construct: Sign Condition

Function: Tests sign of data item.

Syntax:

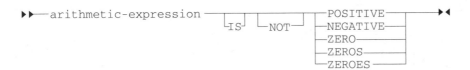

Verb: SORT

Function: Sorts records into order on a set of specified keys. These records can come from a file or from a table, or be created by an input procedure.

Syntax 1:

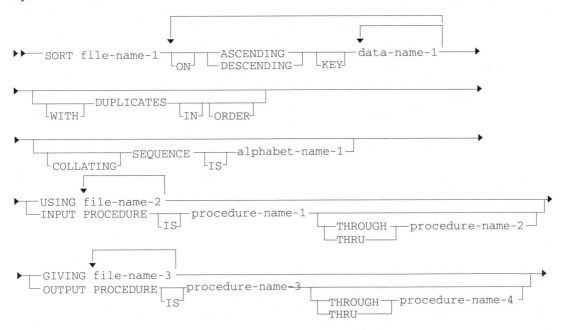

Syntax 2: Table.

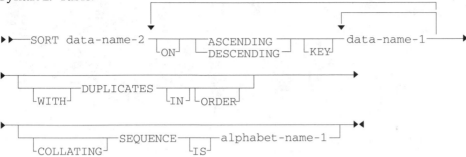

Verb: START

Function: Positions a relative or indexed file for subsequent retrieval of records.

Syntax 1: Relative.

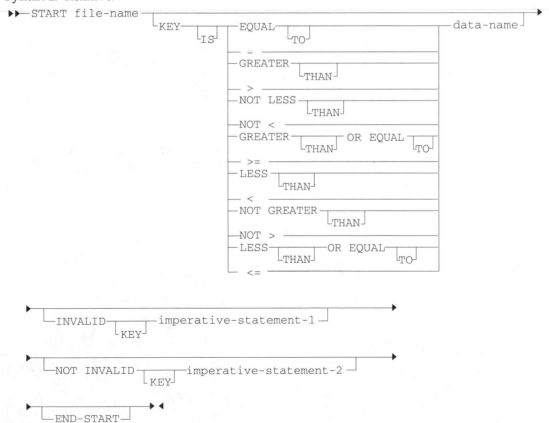

Syntax 2: Indexed.

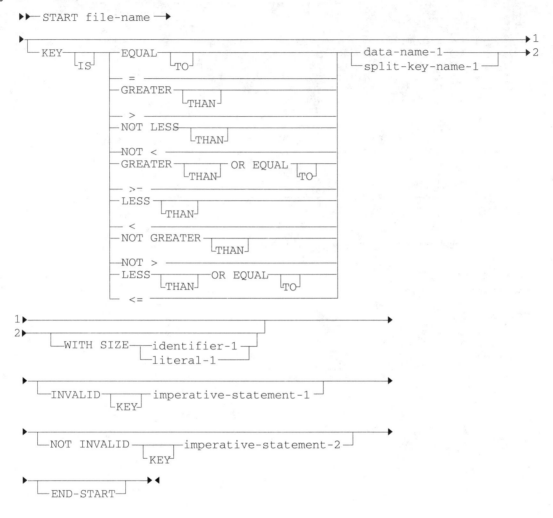

Verb: STOP

Function: Suspends execution of the program, either permanently or temporarily.

Syntax:

Verb: STRING

Function: Concatenates the partial or complete contents of two or more data items and stores the result.

Syntax:

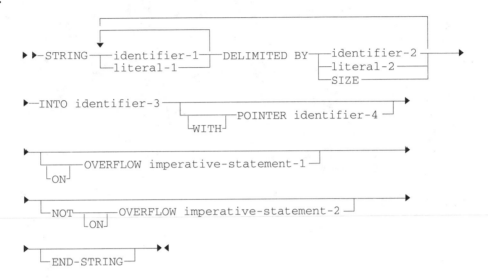

Verb: SUBTRACT

Function: Subtracts one or more numeric data items from another and stores the result.

Syntax 1: Simple.

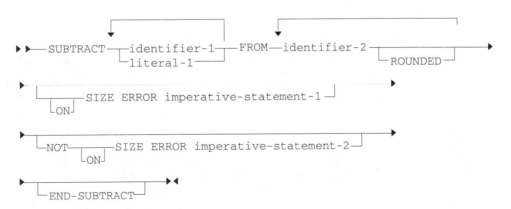

Syntax 2: GIVING.

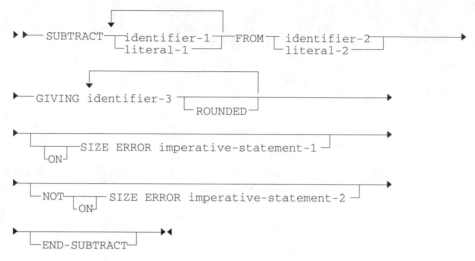

Syntax 3: CORRESPONDING.

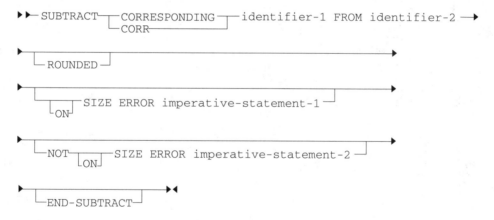

Construct: Subscripting

Function: Identifies which element of a table is meant.

Syntax:

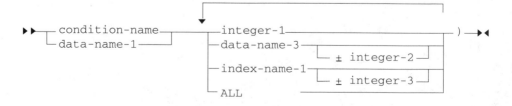

Verb: **UNSTRING**

Function: Splits the contents of a data item into separate character strings and stores them.

Syntax:

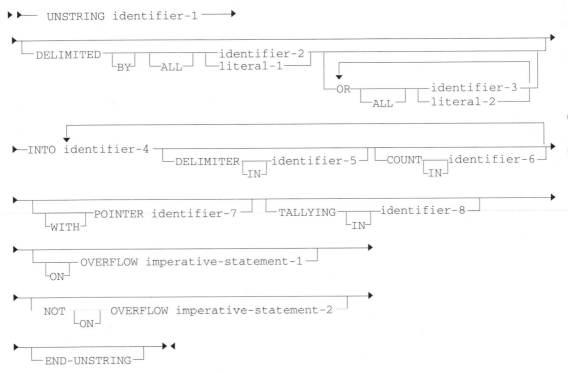

Verb: USE

Function: Causes the section it introduces to be executed whenever specified circumstances arise. Control may transfer itself to that section from any point in the Procedure Division, with automatic return of control when the section finishes. This statement introduces sections in the Declaratives that handle file errors, etc.; the section it introduces is executed only if the file in error has a file status item.

Syntax 1: ERROR/EXCEPTION.

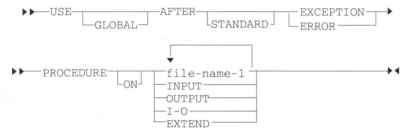

Syntax 2: Reporting.

▶▶──USE────────────BEFORE REPORTING identifier-1──▶◀
        └─GLOBAL─┘

Syntax 3: DEBUGGING.

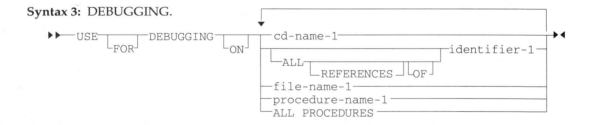

Verb: WRITE

Function: Sends a record to a file. For a sequential file this statement can also position lines vertically on the page.

Syntax 1: ADVANCING.

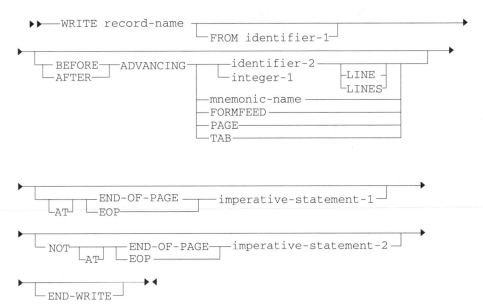

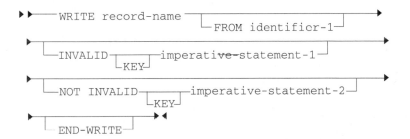

Syntax 2: INVALID KEY.

Chapter 10

COBOL Library Routines

The Personal COBOL System includes a built-in library of routines
which programs can use. The library routines are available using
the COBOL CALL statement, and generally supply features that
are not provided by the COBOL language. The library routines
with names that begin "CBL" are in all current Micro Focus
COBOL products.

Library Routines

Overview

The library routines supplied with the run-time system in this
product supply features not provided by COBOL syntax, such as
operating system functions.

In some cases, the call-by-name and call-by-number routines are
inter-changeable. For each call-by-number routine there may be a
corresponding call-by-name routine. There are also many additional call-by-name routines. These routines may have functionality not found in the corresponding call-by-number routines. You
are encouraged to use call-by-name routines rather than call-by-
number routines where possible.

Call-by-Name Routines

To use a library routine, use the name of the required routine in a
CALL statement with parameters as shown in the description of
the routine.

Routines by Category

Routines by Category is intended to help find routines for particular purposes. Functions are listed by name and organized into categories (with a very brief description of the purpose of each). The section *Descriptions of Routines* contains complete descriptions of the routines, listed in alphabetical order.

The categories of call-by-name routines are:

■ Byte-Stream Files

■ Closedown Procedure

■ File-names

■ Files

■ Keyboard

■ Logic Operators

■ Mouse

■ Printer

■ Screen

■ Text

The routines in each category are listed below. Details common to all the routines in a category are also shown.

Byte-Stream Files

CBL_CLOSE_FILE	Closes a file
CBL_CREATE_FILE	Create byte-stream file
CBL_OPEN_FILE	Open byte-stream file
CBL_READ_FILE	Read byte-stream file
CBL_WRITE_FILE	Write byte-stream file

The Micro Focus byte-stream file routines allow you to read and write data files without the need to adhere to COBOL record definitions.

For all these routines, if the routine is successful the RETURN-CODE register will be set to zero. If the routine fails, the RE-TURN-CODE register will contain a file status value indicating the failure. This file status will always be the standard ANSI '74 file status value. If no ANSI '74 file status is defined for the error, a standard Micro Focus error status will be returned (9/*nnn* where *nnn* is the RTS error number).

Closedown Procedure

PC_EXIT_PROC   Register closedown procedure

File-names

CBL_JOIN_FILENAME   Join parts of file-name
CBL_SPLIT_FILENAME   Divide file-name into parts

These routines enable you to parse a file-name into its component strings and to join strings together to form a file-name. They can be used together to replace components of a file-name, such as the extension. They can handle both null-terminated and space-terminated file-names.

A file-name is split up into device, base-name and extension. For example, in the following file-name:

d:\dir1\dir2\file.dat

The device is *d:\dir1\dir2*, the base-name is *file*, and the extension is *dat*. The maximum length of the file name string is 65 characters.

Files

CBL_CHANGE_DIR   Change current directory
CBL_CHECK_FILE_EXIST   Check if file exists

CBL_COPY_FILE	Copy file
CBL_CREATE_DIR	Create directory
CBL_DELETE_DIR	Delete directory
CBL_DELETE_FILE	Delete file
CBL_READ_DIR	Read current directory
CBL_RENAME_FILE	Rename file
PC_FIND_DRIVES	Find valid drives
PC_LOCATE_FILE	Locate file/expand path
PC_READ_DRIVE	Read current drive
PC_SET_DRIVE	Set current drive

Keyboard

CBL_GET_KBD_STATUS	Test for character at keyboard
CBL_READ_KBD_CHAR	Read character from keyboard (no echo)

Logic Operators

CBL_AND	Logical AND
CBL_EQ	Logical EQuivalence
CBL_IMP	Logical IMPlies
CBL_NOT	Logical NOT
CBL_OR	Logical OR
CBL_XOR	Logical eXclusive OR

These routines carry out logic operations on bits. Apart from CBL_NOT, all these operations have two operands.

In the two-operand routines, interchanging the two operands, source and target, does not change the result except in CBL_IMP. However, the result is always stored in the second operand, target.

If *length* is longer than either data item, bytes following that data item will be used, up to the length specified. This could overwrite program data.

The parameter *length* can be replaced by the syntax:

length of *source*

or

length of *target*

assuming all the bytes of the data item are to be used.

Mouse

CBL_GET_MOUSE_MASK	Get mouse event mask
CBL_GET_MOUSE_POSITION	Get mouse screen coordinates
CBL_GET_MOUSE_STATUS	Get number of events in queue
CBL_HIDE_MOUSE	Hide mouse pointer
CBL_INIT_MOUSE	Initialize mouse support
CBL_READ_MOUSE_EVENT	Read mouse event queue
CBL_SET_MOUSE_MASK	Set mouse event mask
CBL_SET_MOUSE_POSITION	Set mouse screen coordinates
CBL_SHOW_MOUSE	Draw mouse pointer
CBL_TERM_MOUSE	Terminate mouse support
PC_GET_MOUSE_SHAPE	Get mouse pointer shape
PC_SET_MOUSE_HIDE_AREA	Set mouse hide area
PC_SET_MOUSE_SHAPE	Set mouse pointer shape

Using the Routines

The mouse is useful for applications that require users to select from a list of options or move objects around on the screen.

To use these routines, you must have loaded a suitable mouse driver.

You must hide the mouse during the execution of any ANSI ACCEPT or DISPLAY statement that operates on the area of the screen where the mouse pointer is located.

The attributes referred to in the descriptions of routines are screen attributes, not user attributes. The top left-hand corner of the screen is row 0, column 0.

Mouse Events

Whenever the mouse is moved or a button on the mouse is pressed or released, the mouse hardware causes an interrupt. The mouse device driver takes control and, depending on a mask you have set, either saves it in a queue or ignores it. This prevents events being lost if a subsequent interrupt occurs before the application has read the event. With the mouse routines, you can read the event queue and determine how many events are in the queue.

When an event is generated, a description of it is stored in a data structure called the event-data. If the mask allows (see below), this is added to the queue. The layout of *event-data* is:

```
event-type   PIC X(2) COMP-X.
event-time   PIC X(4) COMP-X.
event-row    PIC X(2) COMP-X.
event-col    PIC X(2) COMP-X.
```

where:

event-type is the action (that is, change of state) that took place:

> bit 3 set   = button 3 pressed
> bit 2 set   = button 2 pressed
> bit 1 set   = button 1 pressed
> bit 0 set   = mouse moved
> (other bits are reserved.)

A button release is indicated by the bit for that button changing from 1 to 0. For example, if the mouse moves and button 1 is pressed at the same time, *event-type* contains 3.

event-time   is the time elapsed between when the event took place and some arbitrary but fixed starting time.

event-row   gives the row position of the mouse when the event took place.

event-col   gives the column position of the mouse when the event took place.

The Event Mask

The event mask, which the programmer supplies, tells the system which kinds of event should be queued and which ignored. It has the same structure as *event-type*. An event is queued only if it happens while the corresponding mask bit is on, or while another state is on whose mask bit is on. When an event-data is queued, the bit for each state is set correctly; that is, the mask does not mask them out.

For example, the operator moving the mouse will generate an event if either the mask bit for "mouse moved" is off or the operator is holding down a button and the mask bit for that button is off.

Printer

PC_TEST_PRINTER	Test printer status

Screen

CBL_CLEAR_SCR	Clear screen
CBL_GET_CSR_POS	Get cursor position
CBL_GET_SCR_SIZE	Get screen size
CBL_READ_SCR_ATTRS	Read attribute string
CBL_READ_SCR_CHARS	Read character string
CBL_READ_SCR_CHATTRS	Read character & attribute strings
CBL_SET_CSR_POS	Set cursor position
CBL_SWAP_SCR_CHATTRS	Swap character & attribute
CBL_WRITE_SCR_ATTRS	Write attribute string
CBL_WRITE_SCR_CHARS	Write character string
CBL_WRITE_SCR_CHARS_ATTR	Write character string with attribute
CBL_WRITE_SCR_CHATTRS	Write character & attribute strings
CBL_WRITE_SCR_TTY	Write characters TTY-style
CBL_WRITE_SCR_N_ATTR	Repeat write attribute
CBL_WRITE_SCR_N_CHAR	Repeat write character
CBL_WRITE_SCR_N_CHATTR	Repeat write character & attributes

Text

CBL_TOLOWER   Convert a string to lower case

CBL_TOUPPER   Convert a string to upper case

Descriptions of Routines

Descriptions for all of the call-by-name routines appear alphabetically.

Key

Each description contains the routine name and function and the entries (as appropriate) noted below.

Syntax:

Shows the CALL statement you could use to call the routine. The parameters you have to define are listed in the USING clause.

The optional RETURNING clause is also shown. Every routine returns a value showing the result of the operation. Unless otherwise indicated, zero indicates success, nonzero indicates failure. This value is left in the data item specified in the RETURNING clause - in this manual, *status-code*. If this clause is omitted, the value is left in the special register RETURN-CODE.

Parameters:

Describes any parameters shown in the RETURNING and USING clause. A parameter enclosed in brackets, for example, [parameter1] is optional and may not be needed for all forms of the routine.

Description:

Provides any additional information necessary for the successful use of the routine.

Parameters on Entry:

Indicates which of the parameters shown are passed on entry.

Parameters on Exit:

Indicates which of the parameters shown are returned on exit.

CBL_AND

Does a logical AND between the bits of two data items.

Syntax:

```
CALL "CBL_AND" USING source
                     target
               BY VALUE length
               RETURNING status-code
```

Parameters:

source	Any data item.
target	Any data item.
length	Numeric literal or PIC X(4) COMP-5.
status-code	See the section *Key*.

Description:

The routine starts at the left-hand end of source and target and ANDs the bits together, storing the result in target. The truth table for this is:

source	target	result
0	0	0
0	1	0
1	0	0
1	1	1

Parameters on Entry:

source	One of the data items to AND.
target	The other data item to AND.
length	The number of bytes of source and target to AND. Positions in target beyond this are unchanged.

Parameters on Exit:

target	The result.

CBL_CHANGE_DIR

Changes the current directory.

Syntax:

```
CALL "CBL_CHANGE_DIR" USING path-name
                      RETURNING status-code
```

Parameters:

path-name	PIC X(n).
status-code	See the section *Key*.

Parameters on Entry:

path-name	Relative or absolute path-name terminated by space or null (x"00"). This must be no longer than the number of characters allowed by your operating system and must be valid from the directory that is current when the routine is called.

Parameters on Exit:

None

CBL_CHECK_FILE_EXIST

Checks whether a file exists and returns details if it does.

Syntax:

```
CALL "CBL_CHECK_FILE_EXIST" USING file-name
                                  file-details
                           RETURNING status-code
```

Parameters:

file-name	PIC X(n).
file-details	Group item defined as:
file-size	PIC X(8) COMP-X.
file-date	
day	PIC X COMP-X.
month	PIC X COMP-X.
year	PIC X(2) COMP-X.
file-time	
hours	PIC X COMP-X.
minutes	PIC X COMP-X.
seconds	PIC X COMP-X.
hundredths	PIC X COMP-X.
status-code	See the section *Key*.

Parameters on Entry:

file-name	The file to look for. The name can contain a path-name, and is terminated by a space. If no path is given, the current directory is assumed.

Parameters on Exit:

file-size	The size of the file in bytes.
file-date	The date the file was created.
file-time	The time the file was created.

CBL_CLEAR_SCR

Clears the whole screen to a specified character and attribute.

Syntax:

```
CALL "CBL_CLEAR_SCR" USING character
                           attribute
                     RETURNING status-code
```

Parameters:

character	PIC X.
attribute	PIC X.
status-code	See the section *Key*.

Parameters on Entry:

character	The character to write.
attribute	The attribute to write. See the chapter *IBM Display Attributes* for details on attributes.

Parameters on Exit:

None

CBL_CLOSE_FILE

Closes a file opened for byte-stream operations.

Syntax:

```
CALL "CBL_CLOSE_FILE" USING file-handle
                      RETURNING status-code
```

Parameters:

file-handle	PIC X(4).
status-code	See the section *Key*.

Description:

Any byte-stream file open when a STOP RUN is executed is automatically closed.

Parameters on Entry:

file-handle	The file handle returned when the file was opened.

Parameters on Exit:

None

CBL_CREATE_DIR

Creates a subdirectory. All the directories in the given path, except the last, must already exist.

Syntax:

```
CALL "CBL_CREATE_DIR" USING path-name
                      RETURNING status-code
```

Library Routines

Parameters:

path-name	PIC X(n).
status-code	See the section *Key*.

Parameters on Entry:

path-name Relative or absolute path-name terminated by space or null (x"00").

Parameters on Exit:

None

CBL_CREATE_FILE

Creates a new file for byte-stream operations.

Syntax:

```
CALL "CBL_CREATE_FILE" USING file-name
                             access-mode
                             deny-mode
                             device
                             file-handle
                       RETURNING status-code
```

Parameters:

file-name	PIC X(n).
access-mode	PIC X COMP-X.
deny-mode	PIC X COMP-X.
device	PIC X COMP-X.
file-handle	PIC X(4).
status-code	See the section *Key*.

Parameters on Entry:

file-name	Space- or null-terminated file-name of the file to be opened.
access-mode	Defines access mode: 1= read only 2= write only (deny-mode must be 0) 3= read/write
deny-mode	Defines deny mode: Controls access to the file by other programs. 0= deny both read and write (exclusive) 1= deny write 2= deny read 3= deny neither read nor write
device	Reserved for future use (must be 0)

Parameters on Exit:

file-handle	Returns a file handle for a successful open.

CBL_DELETE_DIR

Deletes a directory. A directory will only be deleted if it is empty.

Syntax:

```
CALL "CBL_DELETE_DIR" USING path-name
                      RETURNING status-code
```

Parameters:

path-name	PIC X(n).
status-code	See the section *Key*.

Parameters on Entry:

path-name	Relative or absolute path-name terminated by space or null (x"00").

Parameters on Exit:

None

CBL_DELETE_FILE

Deletes a file

Syntax:

```
CALL "CBL_DELETE_FILE" USING file-name
                       RETURNING status-code
```

Parameters:

file-name   PIC X(n).
status-code   See the section *Key*.

Parameters on Entry:

file-name   The file to delete. The name can contain a
                   path-name, and is terminated by a space. If
                   no path is given, the current directory is
                   assumed.

Parameters on Exit:

None

CBL_EQ

Does a logical EQUIVALENCE between the bits of two data items.

Syntax:

```
CALL "CBL_EQ" USING source
                    target
              BY VALUE length
              RETURNING status-code
```

Parameters:

source	Any data item.
target	Any data item
length	Numeric literal or PIC X(4) COMP-5.
status-code	See the section *Key*.

Description:

The routine starts at the left-hand end of source and target and EQUIVALENCEs the bits together, storing the result in target. The truth table for this is:

source	target	result
0	0	1
0	1	0
1	0	0
1	1	1

Parameters on Entry:

source	One of the data items to EQUIVALENCE.
target	The other data item to EQUIVALENCE.
length	The number of bytes of source and target to EQUIVALENCE. Positions in target beyond this length are unchanged.

Library Routines

Parameters on Exit:

    target   The result.

CBL_GET_CSR_POS

Returns the cursor position.

Syntax:

```
CALL "CBL_GET_CSR_POS" USING screen-position
                       RETURNING status-code
```

Parameters:

screen-position	Group item defined as:
row-number	PIC X COMP-X.
column-number	PIC X COMP-X.
status-code	See the section *Key*.

Parameters on Entry:

None

Parameters on Exit:

screen-position   The screen position of the cursor. The top left corner is row 0, column 0. If the cursor is invisible, row-number and column-number are both set to 255.

CBL_GET_KBD_STATUS

Checks whether there is a character waiting to be read from the keyboard.

Syntax:

```
CALL "CBL_GET_KBD_STATUS" USING key-status
                          RETURNING status-code
```

Parameters:

key-status	PIC X COMP-X.
status-code	See the section *Key*.

Parameters on Entry:

None

Parameters on Exit:

key-status	0 = no character available 1 = character available

CBL_GET_MOUSE_MASK

Returns the mouse event mask.

Syntax:

```
CALL "CBL_GET_MOUSE_MASK" USING mouse-handle
                          event-mask
                          RETURNING status-code
```

Parameters:

mouse-handle	PIC X(4) COMP-X.
event-mask	PIC X(2) COMP-X.
status-code	See the section *Key*.

Description:

See *Mouse* in *Routines by Category* earlier in this section.

Parameters on Entry:

mouse-handle   Mouse identifier, obtained by earlier call to CBL_INIT_MOUSE.

Parameters on Exit:

event-mask   See *Mouse* in the section *Routines by Category* earlier in this section.

CBL_GET_MOUSE_POSITION

Returns the screen position of the mouse pointer.

Syntax:

```
CALL "CBL_GET_MOUSE_POSITION" USING mouse-handle
                                    mouse-position
                         RETURNING status-code
```

Parameters:

mouse-handle	PIC X(4) COMP-X.
mouse-position	Group item defined as:
mouse-row	PIC X(2) COMP-X.
mouse-col	PIC X(2) COMP-X.
status-code	See the section *Key*.

Description:

See *Mouse* in *Routines by Category* earlier in this section.

Parameters on Entry:

mouse-handle   Mouse identifier, obtained by earlier call to
CBL_INIT_MOUSE.

Parameters on Exit:

mouse-position   The screen position of the mouse pointer.

CBL_GET_MOUSE_STATUS

Finds out the number of events in the queue.

Syntax:

```
CALL "CBL_GET_MOUSE_STATUS" USING mouse-handle
                                  queued-events
                       RETURNING status-code
```

Parameters:

mouse-handle	PIC X(4) COMP-X.
queued-events	PIC X(2) COMP-X.
status-code	See the section *Key.*

Description:

See *Mouse* in *Routines by Category* earlier in this section.

Parameters on Entry:

mouse-handle   Mouse identifier, obtained by earlier call to
CBL_INIT_MOUSE.

Parameters on Exit:

queued-events   The number of events in the queue.

CBL_GET_SCR_SIZE

Returns information on the size of the screen.

Syntax:

```
CALL "CBL_GET_SCR_SIZE" USING depth
                              width
                        RETURNING status-code
```

Parameters:

depth   PIC X COMP-X.
width   PIC X COMP-X.
status-code   See the section *Key*.

Parameters on Entry:

None

Parameters on Exit:

depth   Number of lines.
width   Number of columns.

CBL_HIDE_MOUSE

Makes the mouse pointer invisible.

Syntax:

```
CALL "CBL_HIDE_MOUSE" USING mouse-handle
                      RETURNING status-code
```

Parameters:

mouse-handle   PIC X(4) COMP-X
status-code   See the section *Key*.

Description:

After this routine has been called, mouse events still take place, but the mouse pointer is not displayed.

See also *Mouse* in *Routines by Category* earlier in this section.

Parameters on Entry:

mouse-handle   Mouse identifier, obtained by earlier call to CBL_INIT_MOUSE.

Parameters on Exit:

None

CBL_IMP

Does a logical IMPLIES between the bits of two data items.

Syntax:

```
CALL "CBL_IMP" USING source
                     target
               BY VALUE length
               RETURNING status-code
```

Parameters:

source	Any data item.
target	Any data item.
length	Numeric literal or PIC X(4) COMP-5.
status-code	See the section *Key*.

Description:

The routine starts at the left-hand end of source and target and IMPLIES the bits together, storing the result in target. The truth table for this is:

source	target	result
0	0	1
0	1	1
1	0	0
1	1	1

Parameters on Entry:

source	One of the data items to IMPLIES.
target	The other data item to IMPLIES.
length	The number of bytes of source and target to IMPLIES. Positions in target beyond this are unchanged.

Parameters on Exit:

    target   The result.

CBL_INIT_MOUSE

Initializes mouse support. This routine must be called before other mouse routines can be called.

Syntax:

```
CALL "CBL_INIT_MOUSE" USING mouse-handle
                            mouse-buttons
                      RETURNING status-code
```

Parameters:

mouse-handle	PIC X(4) COMP-X
mouse-buttons	PIC X(2) COMP-X
status-code	See the section *Key*.

Description:

See Mouse in *Routines by Category* earlier in this section.

Parameters on Entry:

None

Parameters on Exit:

mouse-handle	Mouse identifier. You pass this to any mouse routines you call subsequently.
mouse-buttons	The number of buttons on the mouse.

Library Routines

CBL_JOIN_FILENAME

Forms a file-name by joining together its component parts; that is, the device-name, base-name path and extension.

Syntax:

```
CALL "CBL_JOIN_FILENAME" USING split-join-params
                               join-buffer
                               device-buffer
                               basename-buffer
                               extension-buffer
                         RETURNING status-code
```

Parameters:

split-join-params	Group item defined as:
param-length	PIC X(2) COMP-X.
split-join-flag1	PIC X COMP-X.
split-join-flag2	PIC X COMP-X.
device-offset	PIC X(2) COMP-X.
device-length	PIC X(2) COMP-X.
basename-offset	PIC X(2) COMP-X.
basename-length	PIC X(2) COMP-X
extension-offset	PIC X(2) COMP-X.
extension-length	PIC X(2) COMP-X
total-length	PIC X(2) COMP-X.
split-buf-len	PIC X(2) COMP-X.
join-buf-len	PIC X(2) COMP-X.
first-path-*component-length*	PIC X(2) COMP-X.
join-buffer	PIC X(n).
device-buffer	PIC X(n)
basename-buffer	PIC X(n).
extension-buffer	PIC X(n).
status-code	See the section *Key*.

Description:

The new file-name is formed by concatenating:

■ the first *device-length* bytes (starting from device-offset) of *device-buffer*

■ the first *basename-length* bytes (starting from basename-offset) of *basename-buffer*

■ the first *extension-length* bytes (starting from extension-offset) of *extension-buffer*

and is placed in *join-buffer* with length *total-length*.

This routine can be made to fold to upper case by setting the least significant bit (bit 0) of *split-join-flag1*. If this bit is not set, the case will be preserved.

This routine can accept either null-terminated or space-terminated strings. Setting the second least significant bit (bit 1) of *split-join-flag1* results in the routine expecting null-terminated strings. If this bit is not set, space-terminated strings are expected.

The device, base-name, and extension fields can be shorter than the lengths specified by *device-length*, *basename-length*, and *extension-length* respectively, if they are terminated with either a space or a null, depending on the setting of bit 1 of *split-join-flag1*.

device-buffer, *basename-buffer*, *extension-buffer*, and *join-buffer* do not have to be four distinct buffers. This means that this routine can be used with CBL_SPLIT_FILENAME to replace one component of a file-name.

If *device-buffer* is not empty and does not have a trailing "\" or "/" or colon, and *basename-buffer* is not empty, the routine inserts a "\" between the device and base-name in *join-buffer*.

If extension is ".", the string returned in *join-buffer* has an extension of spaces; that is, the file-name has a trailing dot.

If *total-length* is less than *join-buf-len*, the characters after the end of the file-name are nulls or spaces depending on bit 1 of *split-join-flag1*.

If device consists of a valid drive letter, but no colon, the routine adds one. It does not do this for a device (for example, LPT1) that does not need one. You cannot join a device (for example, LPT1, as opposed to a drive letter) to a non-empty base-name.

See also *File-names* in *Routines by Category* earlier in this section and the description of CBL_SPLIT_FILENAME.

Parameters on Entry:

param-length	Length of *split-join-params* in bytes, including the two bytes for *param-length*. The normal value for *param-length* is 24.
split-join-flag1	bit 1 - if set, specifies that the strings are null-terminated, otherwise they are space-terminated.
	bit 0 - if set, specifies that the new file-name will be folded to upper case, otherwise the original case will be preserved.
device-offset	Offset of the start of the device in *device-buffer* (indexed from one).
device-length	Length of device if not space- or null-terminated.
basename-offset	Offset of the start of the basename in *basename-buffer* (indexed from one).
basename-length	Length of base-name if not space- or null-terminated.
extension-offset	Offset of the start of the extension in *extension-buffer* (indexed from one).
extension-length	Length of extension if not space- or null-terminated.
device-buffer	Device-name.
basename-buffer	Base-name.

extension-buffer   Extension.

join-buf-len   Length of join-buffer.

Parameters on Exit:

total-length   Total number of characters in the file-name.
join-buffer   The joined-up file-name.
status-code   Return status:
                        0 = success
                        1 = file-name too big for *join-buffer*
                        4 = illegal file-name

CBL_NOT

Does a logical NOT on the bits of a data item

Syntax:

```
CALL "CBL_NOT" USING target
               BY VALUE length
               RETURNING status-code
```

Parameters:

target   Any data item.
length   Numeric literal or PIC X(4) COMP-5.
status-code   See the section *Key*.

Description:

The routine starts at the left-hand end of target and inverts bits.
The truth table for this is:

before	after
0	1
1	0

Library Routines

See also *Logic Operators* in *Routines by Category* earlier in this section.

Parameters on Entry:

target   The data to operate on.

Parameters on Exit:

target   The data with the bits inverted.
length   The number of bytes of target to change.
                                       Positions beyond this are unchanged.

CBL_OPEN_FILE

Opens an existing file for byte-stream operations.

Syntax:

```
CALL "CBL_OPEN_FILE" USING file-name
                           access-mode
                           deny-mode
                           device
                           file-handle
                    RETURNING status-code
```

Parameters:

file-name   PIC X(n).
access-mode   PIC X COMP-X
deny-mode   PIC X COMP-X.
device   PIC X COMP-X.
file-handle   PIC X(4).status-code
status-code   See the section *Key*.

Description:

See *Byte-stream Files* in *Routines by Category* earlier in this section.

Parameters on Entry:

file-name	Space- or null-terminated file-name of the file to be opened.
access-mode	Defines access mode: 1 = read only 2 = write only (deny-mode must be 0) 3 = read/write
deny-mode	Defines deny mode: controls access to the file by other programs. 0 = deny both read and write (exclusive) 1 = deny write 2 = deny read 3 = deny neither read nor write
device	Reserved for future use (must be 0).

Parameters on Exit:

file-handle	Returns a file handle for a successful open.

CBL_OR

Does a logical OR between the bits of two data items.

Syntax:

```
CALL "CBL_OR" USING source
                    target
              BY VALUE length
              RETURNING status-code
```

Parameters:

source	Any data item.
target	Any data item.
length	Numeric literal or PIC X(4) COMP-5.
status-code	See the section *Key*.

Library Routines

Description:

The routine starts at the left-hand end of source and target and ORs the bits together, storing the result in target. The truth table for this is:

source	target	result
0	0	0
0	1	1
1	0	1
1	1	1

See also *Logic Operators* in *Routines by Category* earlier in this section.

Parameters on Entry:

source	One of the data items to OR.
target	The other data item to OR.
length	The number of bytes of source and target to OR.Positions in target beyond this are unchanged.

Parameters on Exit:

target	The result.

CBL_READ_DIR

Returns the current directory or path.

Syntax:

```
CALL "CBL_READ_DIR" USING path-name
                          path-name-length
                    RETURNING status-code
```

Parameters:

path-name	PIC X(n).
path-name-length	PIC X COMP-X.
status-code	See the section *Key*.

Parameters on Entry:

path-name-length   Length of path-name to be used. If this is too small for the path-name, the routine fails.

Parameters on Exit:

path-name   Relative or absolute path-name terminated by space or null (x"00").

CBL_READ_FILE

Reads bytes from a file.

Syntax:

```
CALL "CBL_READ_FILE" USING file-handle
                           file-offset
                           byte-count
                           flags
                           buffer
                    RETURNING status-code
```

Parameters:

file-handle	PIC X(4).
file-offset	PIC X(8) COMP-X.
byte-count	PIC X(4) COMP-X.
flags	PIC X COMP-X.
buffer	PIC X(n)
status-code	See the section *Key*.

Description:

See also *Byte-Stream Files* in *Routines by Category* earlier in this section.

Parameters on Entry:

file-handle	The file handle returned when the file was opened.
file-offset	The offset in file at which to read. This field is currently limited to a maximum value of x"00FFFFFFFF".
byte-count	The number of bytes to read. This field is currently limited to a maximum value of x"00FFFF".
flags	This parameter can take the following values: 0 = for standard read 128 = to have the current file size returned in the *file-offset* field

Parameters on Exit:

file-offset	Contains the current file size on return if the flags parameter is set to 128 on entry.
buffer	The buffer into which the bytes are read. It is your responsibility to ensure that the buffer is large enough to hold the number of bytes to be read. The buffer parameter is allowed to cross a 64K segment boundary.

CBL_READ_KBD_CHAR

Waits until a character is typed and then reads it with no echo.

Syntax:

```
CALL "CBL_READ_KBD_CHAR" USING char
                         RETURNING status-code
```

Parameters:

char	PIC X.
status-code	See the section *Key*.

Parameters on Entry:

None

Parameters on Exit:

char	The character that was typed, in ASCII.

CBL_READ_MOUSE_EVENT

Reads the mouse event queue and returns information about an event.

Syntax:

```
CALL "CBL_READ_MOUSE_EVENT" USING mouse-handle
                                  event-data
                                  read-type
                     RETURNING status-code
```

Parameters:

mouse-handle	PIC X(4) COMP-X.
event-data	See *Mouse* in *Routines by Category* earlier in this section.
read-type	PIC X COMP-X.
status-code	See the section *Key*.

Library Routines

Description:

If there are no events in the event queue, the return from this routine depends on the value of *read-type*. If *read-type* is zero, the routine returns immediately with all zero values in *event-data*. If *read-type* has a value of one, return is delayed until an event has been queued.

See also *Mouse* in *Routines by Category* earlier in this section.

Parameters on Entry:

mouse-handle	Mouse identifier, obtained by earlier call to CBL_INIT_MOUSE.
read-type	Indicates what to do if there are no events in the queue: 0 = return immediately 1 = wait for an event, then return.

Parameters on Exit:

event-data	See *Mouse* in *Routines by Category* earlier in this section.

CBL_READ_SCR_ATTRS

Reads a string of attributes from the screen.

Syntax:

```
CALL "CBL_READ_SCR_ATTRS" USING screen-position
                          attribute-buffer
                          string-length
                    RETURNING status-code
```

Parameters:

screen-position	Group item defined as:
row-number	PIC X COMP-X.
column-number	PIC X COMP-X.
attribute-buffer	PIC X(n).
string-length	PIC X(2) COMP-X.
status-code	See the section *Key*.

Parameters on Entry:

screen-position	The screen position to start reading at. The top left corner is row 0, column 0.
string-length	The length of the string to read.

Parameters on Exit

attribute-buffer	The attributes read from the screen. This data item must be at least as long as specified by string-length; positions in it beyond that length are unchanged.
string-length	If the end of the screen is reached, the length read is returned in here.

CBL_READ_SCR_CHARS

Reads a string of characters from the screen.

Syntax:

```
CALL "CBL_READ_SCR_CHARS" USING screen-position
                                character-buffer
                                string-length
                          RETURNING status-code
```

Parameters:

screen-position	Group item defined as:
row-number	PIC X COMP-X
column-number	PIC X COMP-X.
character-buffer	PIC X(n).
string-length	PIC X(2) COMP-X.
status-code	See the section *Key*.

Parameters on Entry:

screen-position	The screen position at which to start reading. The top left corner is row 0, column 0.
string-length	The length of the string to read.

Parameters on Exit:

character-buffer	The characters read from the screen. This data item must be at least as long as specified by *string-length*; positions in it beyond that length are unchanged.
string-length	If the end of the screen is reached, the length read is returned in here.

CBL_READ_SCR_CHATTRS

Reads a string of characters and their attributes from the screen.

Syntax:

```
CALL "CBL_READ_SCR_CHATTRS" USING screen-position
                                  character-buffer
                                  attribute-buffer
                                  string-length
                           RETURNING status-code
```

Parameters:

screen-position	Group item defined as:
row-number	PIC X COMP-X.
column-number	PIC X COMP-X.
character-buffer	PIC X(n).
attribute-buffer	PIC X(n).
string-length	PIC X(2) COMP-X.
status-code	See the section *Key*.

Parameters on Entry:

screen-position The screen position at which to start reading.The top left corner is row 0, column 0.

string-length The length of the string to read.

Parameters on Exit:

character-buffer The characters read from the screen. This data item must be at least as long as specified by *string-length*; positions in it beyond that length are unchanged.

attribute-buffer The attributes read from the screen. This data item must be at least as long as specified by *string-length*; positions in it beyond that length are unchanged.

string-length If the end of the screen is reached, the length read (in cells, that is, character-attribute pairs) is returned in here.

CBL_RENAME_FILE

Changes the name of a file.

Syntax:

```
CALL "CBL_RENAME_FILE" USING old-file-name
                             new-file-name
                       RETURNING status-code
```

Library Routines

Parameters:

old-file-name	PIC X(n)
new-file-name	PIC X(n).
status-code	See the section *Key*.

Parameters on Entry:

old-file-name	The file to rename. The name can contain a *path-name*, and is terminated by a space. If no path is given, the current directory is assumed.
new-file-name	The new name, terminated by a space. If *old-file-name* contains a path-name, this must contain the same path-name.

Parameters on Exit:

None

CBL_SET_CSR_POS

Moves the curso.r

Syntax:

```
CALL "CBL_SET_CSR_POS" USING screen-position
                       RETURNING status-code
```

Parameters:

screen-position	Group item defined as:
row-number	PIC X COMP-X.
column-number	PIC X COMP-X.
status-code	See the section *Key*.

Parameters on Entry:

screen-position   The screen position at which to put the
cursor. The top left corner is row 0, column 0.
To make the cursor invisible, set row-number
and column-number to 255. Any other legal
on-screen values make the cursor visible.

Parameters on Exit:

None

CBL_SET_MOUSE_MASK

Sets the mouse event mask.

Syntax:

```
CALL "CBL_SET_MOUSE_MASK" USING mouse-handle
                                event-mask
                          RETURNING status-code
```

Parameters:

mouse-handle   PIC X(4) COMP-X.
event-mask   PIC X(2) COMP-X.
status-code   See the section *Key*.

Description:

CBL_GET_MOUSE_MASK should be called first to find out which
events are enabled.

See also *Mouse* in *Routines by Category* earlier in this section.

Parameters on Entry:

mouse-handle	Mouse identifier, obtained by earlier call to CBL_INIT_MOUSE.
event-mask	See *Mouse* in *Routines by Category* earlier in this section.

Parameters on Exit:

None

CBL_SET_MOUSE_POSITION

Moves the mouse pointer.

Syntax:

```
CALL "CBL_SET_MOUSE_POSITION" USING mouse-handle
                                    mouse-position
                          RETURNING status-code
```

Parameters:

mouse-handle	PIC X(4) COMP-X.
mouse-position	Group item defined as:
mouse-row	PIC X(2) COMP-X.
mouse-col	PIC X(2) COMP-X.
status-code	See the section *Key*.

Description:

See *Mouse* in *Routines by Category* earlier in this section.

Parameters on Entry:

mouse-handle	Mouse identifier, obtained by earlier call to CBL_INIT_MOUSE.
mouse-position	The screen position to move the mouse pointer to.

Parameters on Exit:

None

CBL_SHOW_MOUSE

Makes the mouse pointer visible.

Syntax:

```
CALL "CBL_SHOW_MOUSE" USING mouse-handle
                      RETURNING status-code
```

Parameters:

mouse-handle	PIC X(4) COMP-X
status-code	See the section *Key*.

Description:

When the mouse support has been initialized by the CBL_INIT_MOUSE call, the pointer is not displayed until this routine is called. After this call the system displays the mouse pointer until a routine to hide the mouse or terminate mouse support is called. This routine cancels any collision area defined earlier by PC_SET_MOUSE_HIDE_AREA.

See also *Mouse* in *Routines by Category* earlier in this section.

Library Routines

Parameters on Entry:

mouse-handle	Mouse identifier, obtained by earlier call to CBL_INIT_MOUSE.

Parameters on Exit:

None

CBL_SPLIT_FILENAME

Splits a file-name into its component parts; that is, the device-name, base-name and extension.

Syntax:

```
CALL "CBL_SPLIT_FILENAME" USING  split-join-params
                                 split-buffer
                          RETURNING status-code
```

Parameters:

split-join-params	Group item defined as:
param-length	PIC X(2) COMP-X.
split-join-flag1	PIC X COMP-X.
split-join-flag2	PIC X COMP-X.
device-offset	PIC X(2) COMP-X
device-length	PIC X(2) COMP-X.
basename-offset	PIC X(2) COMP-X.
basename-length	PIC X(2) COMP-X.
extension-offset	PIC X(2) COMP-X.
extension-length	PIC X(2) COMP-X.
total-length	PIC X(2) COMP-X.
split-buf-len	PIC X(2) COMP-X.
join-buf-len	PIC X(2) COMP-X.
first-path-	
component-length	PIC X(2) COMP-X.
split-buffer	PIC X(n)
status-code	See the section *Key*.

Description:

This routine can be made to fold to upper case by setting the least significant bit (bit 0) of *split-join-flag1*. If this bit is not set, the case will be preserved.

This routine can accept either null-terminated or space-terminated strings. Setting the second least significant bit (bit 1) of *split-join-flag1* results in the routine expecting null-terminated strings. If this bit is not set, space-terminated strings are expected.

If there are two or more dots in the file-name (not counting dots in the device or *path-name)*, the extension returned consists of the characters between the last dot and the end of the file-name. The base-name contains everything up to, but not including, the last dot.

To make a distinction between file-names with no extension and file-names with spaces extension (that is, base-names whose last character is a dot), if the extension is spaces *extension-length* is 1 and *extension-offset* points to the last dot.

See also *File-names* in *Routines by Category* earlier in this section and the description for CBL_JOIN_FILENAME.

Parameters on Entry:

param-length	Length of *split-join-params* in bytes, including the two bytes for *param-length*. The normal value for *param-length* is 24.
split-join-flag1	bit 1 - if set, specifies that the file-name is null-terminated, otherwise it is space-terminated.
	bit 0 - if set, specifies that the new strings will be folded to upper case, otherwise the original case will be preserved.
split-buf-len	Length of *split-buffer*.
split-buffer	The string to split.

Library Routines

Parameters on Exit:

split-join-flag2	bit 1 - set if there is a wildcard in the device. bit 0 - set if there is a wildcard in base-name or extension.
device-offset	Start of device-name in *split-buffer*, from one.
device-length	Length of *device-name*; zero if there is none. This includes any following colon.
basename-offset	Start of *base-name* in split-buffer, from one.
basename-length	Length of *base-name*; zero if there is none. This does not include the following dot.
extension-offset	Start of extension in *split-buffer*, from one.
extension-length	Length of extension; zero if there is none. This does not include the preceding dot.
total-length	Total number of characters in the string.
first-path-component-length	Number of characters up to and including the first \ or / or colon; if *split-buffer* contains none of these, this field = *device-length*.
split-buffer	Unchanged unless bit 1 of *split-join-flag1* is set, when it is folded to upper case.
status-code	0 = success
	4 = illegal file-name

CBL_SWAP_SCR_CHATTRS

Swaps a string of characters and their attributes with a string from the screen.

Syntax:

```
CALL "CBL_SWAP_SCR_CHATTRS" USING screen-position
                                  character-buffer
                                  attribute-buffer
                                  string-length
                           RETURNING status-code
```

Parameters:

screen-position	Group item defined as:
row-number	PIC X COMP-X.
column-number	PIC X COMP-X.
character-buffer	PIC X(n).
attribute-buffer	PIC X(n).
string-length	PIC X(2) COMP-X.
status-code	See the section *Key*.

Parameters on Entry:

screen-position	The screen position at which to start writing. The top left corner is row 0, column 0.
character-buffer	The characters to write.
attribute-buffer	The attributes to write.
string-length	The length of the string to write. If this would go off the end of the screen, the write finishes at the end of the screen.

Parameters on Exit:

character-buffer	The characters read from the screen. This *data item* must be at least as long as specified by *string-length*; positions in it beyond that length are unchanged.
attribute-buffer	The attributes read from the screen. This *data item* must be at least as long as specified by *string-length*; positions in it beyond that length are unchanged.
string-length	If the end of the screen is reached the length swapped (in cells, that is, character-attribute pairs) is returned in here.

Library Routines

CBL_TERM_MOUSE

Terminates mouse support, releasing internal resources.

Syntax:

```
CALL "CBL_TERM_MOUSE" USING mouse-handle
                      RETURNING status-code
```

Parameters:

mouse-handle	PIC X(4) COMP-X
status-code	See the section *Key*.

Description:

The routine releases internal resources allocated by
CBL_INIT_MOUSE. After this routine, mouse-handle is no longer
valid and calling any mouse routine other than
CBL_INIT_MOUSE will result in an error.

See also *Mouse* in *Routines by Category* earlier in this section.

Parameters on Entry:

mouse-handle	Mouse identifier, obtained by earlier call to CBL_INIT_MOUSE.

Parameters on Exit:

None

CBL_TOLOWER

Converts a string of letters to lower case.

Syntax:

```
CALL "CBL_TOLOWER" USING string
                   BY VALUE length
                   RETURNING status-code
```

Parameters:

string	PIC X(n).
length	PIC X(4)COMP-5
status-code	See the section *Key*.

Description:

The routine starts at the left-hand end of string and converts letters to lower case (also called folding to lower case).

Parameters on Entry:

string	The string to convert
length	The number of bytes of string to change; positions beyond this are unchanged.

Parameters on Exit:

string	The converted string.

Library Routines

CBL_TOUPPER

Converts a string of letters to upper case.

Syntax:

```
CALL "CBL_TOUPPER" USING string
                   BY VALUE length
                   RETURNING status-code
```

Parameters:

string	PIC X(n)
length	PIC X(4) COMP-5.
status-code	See the section *Key*.

Description:

The routine starts at the left-hand end of string and converts letters to upper case (also called folding to upper case).

Parameters on Entry:

string	The string to convert.
length	The number of bytes of string to change; positions beyond this are unchanged.

Parameters on Exit:

string	The converted string.

CBL_WRITE_FILE

Writes bytes to a file.

Syntax:

```
CALL "CBL_WRITE_FILE" USING file-handle
                            file-offset
                            byte-count
                            flags
                            buffer
                      RETURNING status-code
```

Parameters:

file-handle	PIC X(4).
file-offset	PIC X(8) COMP-X.
byte-count	PIC X(4) COMP-X.
flags	PIC X COMP-X.
buffer	PIC X(n).
status-code	See the section *Key*.

Description:

See *Byte-stream Files* in *Routines by Category* earlier in this section.

Parameters on Entry:

file-handle	The file handle returned when the file was opened.
file-offset	The offset in file at which to write. This field is currently limited to a maximum value of x"00FFFFFFFF".
byte-count	The number of bytes to write. This field is currently limited to a maximum value of x"00FFFF". Putting a value of zero in this field will cause the file to be truncated or extended to the size specified in the file-offset field.

Library Routines

flags	This parameter can take the following value: 0 = for standard write
buffer	The buffer from which the bytes are written. It is your responsibility to ensure that the buffer is large enough to hold the number of bytes to be written. The buffer parameter is allowed to cross a 64 Kilobyte segment boundary.

Parameters on Exit:

None

CBL_WRITE_SCR_ATTRS

Writes a string of attributes to the screen.

Syntax:

```
CALL "CBL_WRITE_SCR_ATTRS" USING screen-position
                                 attribute-buffer
                                 string-length
                           RETURNING status-code
```

Parameters:

screen-position	Group item defined as:
row-number	PIC X COMP-X.
column-number	PIC X COMP-X.
attribute-buffer	PIC X(n).
string-length	PIC X(2) COMP-X.
status-code	See the section *Key*.

Parameters on Entry:

screen-position	The screen position at which to start writing. The top left corner is row 0, column 0.

attribute-buffer	The attributes to write.
string-length	The length of the string to write. If this would go off the end of the screen, the write finishes at the end of the screen.

Parameters on Exit:

None

CBL_WRITE_SCR_CHARS

Writes a string of characters to the screen.

Syntax:

```
CALL "CBL_WRITE_SCR_CHARS" USING screen-position
                                 character-buffer
                                 string-length
                          RETURNING status-code
```

Parameters:

screen-position	Group item defined as:
row-number	PIC X COMP-X
column-number	PIC X COMP-X.
character-buffer	PIC X(n).
string-length	PIC X(2) COMP-X.
status-code	See the section *Key*.

Parameters on Entry:

screen-position	The screen position at which to start writing. The top left corner is row 0, column 0.
character-buffer	The characters to write.
string-length	The length of the string to write. If this would go off the end of the screen, the write finishes at the end of the screen.

Parameters on Exit:

None

CBL_WRITE_SCR_CHARS_ATTR

Writes a string of characters to the screen, giving them all the same attribute.

Syntax:

```
CALL "CBL_WRITE_SCR_CHARS_ATTR" USING screen-position
                                      character-buffer
                                      string-length
                                      attribute
                               RETURNING status-code
```

Parameters:

screen-position	Group item defined as:
row-number	PIC X COMP-X.
column-number	PIC X COMP-X.
character-buffer	PIC X(n).
attribute	PIC X.
string-length	PIC X(2) COMP-X.
status-code	See the section *Key*.

Parameters on Entry:

screen-position	The screen position at which to start writing. The top left corner is row 0, column 0.
character-buffer	The characters to write.
attribute	The attribute to write.
string-length	The length of the string to write.

Parameters on Exit:

None

CBL_WRITE_SCR_CHATTRS

Writes a string of characters and their attributes to the screen.

Syntax:

```
CALL "CBL_WRITE_SCR_CHATTRS" USING screen-position
                                   character-buffer
                                   attribute-buffer
                                   string-length
                            RETURNING status-code
```

Parameters:

screen-position	Group item defined as:
row-number	PIC X COMP-X.
column-number	PIC X COMP-X.
character-buffer	PIC X(n).
attribute-buffer	PIC X(n).
string-length	PIC X(2) COMP-X.
status-code	See the section *Key*.

Parameters on Entry:

screen-position	The screen position at which to start writing. The top left corner is row 0, column 0.
character-buffer	The characters to write.
attribute-buffer	The attributes to write.
string-length	The length of the string to write. If this would go off the end of the screen, the write finishes at the end of the screen.

Parameters on Exit:

None

CBL_WRITE_SCR_N_ATTR

Writes a specified attribute to a string of positions on the screen.

Syntax:

```
CALL "CBL_WRITE_SCR_N_ATTR" USING screen-position
                                  attribute
                                  fill-length
                           RETURNING status-code
```

Parameters:

screen-position	Group item defined as:
row-number	PIC X COMP-X.
column-number	PIC X COMP-X.
attribute	PIC X.
fill-length	PIC X(2) COMP-X.
status-code	See the section *Key*.

Parameters on Entry:

screen-position	The screen position at which to start writing. The top left corner is row 0, column 0.
attribute	The attribute to write.
string-length	The number of screen positions to write the attribute to. If this would go off the end of the screen, the write finishes at the end of the screen.

Parameters on Exit:

None

CBL_WRITE_SCR_N_CHAR

Writes a specified character to a string of positions on the screen.

Syntax:

```
CALL "CBL_WRITE_SCR_N_CHAR" USING screen-position
                                  character
                                  fill-length
                           RETURNING status-code
```

Parameters:

screen-position	Group item defined as:
row-number	PIC X COMP-X.
column-number	PIC X COMP-X.
character	PIC X.
fill-length	PIC X(2) COMP-X.
status-code	See the section *Key*.

Parameters on Entry:

screen-position	The screen position at which to start writing. The top left corner is row 0, column 0.
character	The character to write.
string-length	The number of screen positions to write the character to. If this would go off the end of the screen, the write finishes at the end of the screen.

Parameters on Exit:

None

CBL_WRITE_SCR_N_CHATTR

Writes a specified character and attribute to a string of positions on the screen.

Syntax:

```
CALL "CBL_WRITE_SCR_N_CHATTR" USING screen-position
                                    character
                                    attribute
                                    fill-length
                              RETURNING status-code
```

Parameters:

screen-position	Group item defined as:
row-number	PIC X COMP-X
column-number	PIC X COMP-X.
character	PIC X.
attribute	PIC X.
fill-length	PIC X(2) COMP-X.
status-code	See the section *Key*.

Parameters on Entry:

screen-position	The screen position at which to start writing. The top left corner is row 0, column 0.
character	The character to write.
attribute	The attribute to write.
string-length	The number of screen positions to write the character-attribute pair to. If this would go off the end of the screen, the write finishes at the end of the screen.

Parameters on Exit:

None

CBL_WRITE_SCR_TTY

Writes a string of characters to the screen starting at the current position and scrolling.

Syntax:

```
CALL "CBL_WRITE_SCR_TTY" USING character-buffer
                               string-length
                         RETURNING status-code
```

Parameters:

character-buffer	IC X(n)
string-length	PIC X(2) COMP-X
status-code	See the section *Key*.

Parameters on Entry:

character-buffer	The characters to write.
string-length	The length of the string to write. If this goes off the edge of the screen, the screen is scrolled up a line and the write continues on the bottom line.

Parameters on Exit:

None

CBL_XOR

Does a logical XOR between the bits of two data items.

Syntax:

```
CALL "CBL_XOR" USING source
                     target
               BY VALUE length
               RETURNING status-code
```

Parameters:

source	Any data item.
target	Any data item.
length	Numeric literal or PIC X(4) COMP-5.
status-code	See the section *Key*.

Description:

The routine starts at the left-hand end of source and target and exclusive-ORs the bits together, storing the result in target. The truth table for this is:

source	target	result
0	0	0
0	1	1
1	0	1
1	1	0

See also *Logic Operators in Routines by Category* earlier in this section.

Parameters on Entry:

source	One of the data items to exclusive-OR.
target	The other data item to exclusive-OR.
length	The number of bytes of *source* and *target* to

exclusive-OR. Positions in *target* beyond this
are unchanged.

Parameters on Exit:

target   The result.

PC_EXIT_PROC

Posts or removes a closedown procedure to be invoked automatically when the application terminates.

Syntax:

```
CALL "PC_EXIT_PROC" USING install-flag
                          install-address
                    RETURNING status-code
```

Parameters:

install-flag   PIC X COMP-X.
install-address   USAGE PROCEDURE-POINTER
status-code   See the section *Key*.

Description:

The routine sets RETURN-CODE to zero for success, nonzero for
failure. The procedure will be executed whether the application
finishes normally (with a STOP RUN) or abnormally (with a
Ctrl+Brk, RTS error, etc). You can install several closedown procedures for an application by repeated calls of this routine.

A closedown procedure can be written in any language. If it is in
COBOL, *install-address* must be the address of an entry point.
You can obtain this address using the statement:

set *install-address* to entry *entry-name*

A closedown procedure in COBOL can include any legal COBOL, including CALL statements. The closedown procedure will terminate when the main program in the procedure does an EXIT PROGRAM/GOBACK or when a STOP RUN statement is executed.

A closedown procedure in any other language must preserve the i86 machine code BP register and direction flag, and terminate with a far return (RETF) instruction; that is, it must be a far procedure.

Parameters on Entry:

install-flag   Indicates the operation to be performed:
0 = install closedown procedure
1 = de-install closedown procedure

install-address   Address of closedown procedure.

Parameters on Exit:

None

PC_GET_MOUSE_SHAPE

Returns information about the shape of the mouse pointer.

Syntax:

```
CALL "PC_GET_MOUSE_SHAPE" USING mouse-handle
                                reserved-item
                                mouse-ptr-shape
                          RETURNING status-code
```

Parameters:

mouse-handle	PIC X(4) COMP-X.
reserved-item	PIC X(10).
mouse-ptr-shape	Group item defined as:

char_AND_mask	PIC X COMP-X.
attr_AND_mask	PIC X COMP-X.
char_XOR_mask	PIC X COMP-X.
attr_XOR_mask	PIC X COMP-X.
status-code	See the section *Key*.

Description:

The masks in *mouse-ptr-shape* are bit maps that, applied to a screen position, would superimpose the mouse shape upon it. The pointer shape is formed by PC_SET_MOUSE_SHAPE by ANDing the screen character at the mouse position with char_AND_mask, XORing the result with char_XOR_mask, and then displaying the result on the screen. The attribute is formed similarly.

To call this routine you must have previously called PC_SET_MOUSE_SHAPE with the same *mouse-handle*. The data item *reserved-item* must be as preserved from that call.

See also *Mouse* in *Routines by Category* earlier in this section.

Parameters on Entry:

mouse-handle	Mouse identifier, obtained by earlier call to CBL_INIT_MOUSE.
reserved-item	Reserved for future use.

Parameters on Exit:

mouse-ptr-shape	The bit maps that would create the pointer's current shape.

Library Routines

PC_LOCATE_FILE

This routine has two uses. It can be used to expand an environment variable in a file specification, where the environment variable contains a list of several paths. It can also determine whether an OPEN INPUT using a particular file specification will find the file in a library or as a separate disk file.

Syntax:

```
CALL "PC_LOCATE_FILE" USING user-file-spec
                            user-mode
                            actual-file-spec
                            exist-flag
                            path-flag
                      RETURNING status-code
```

Parameters:

user-file-spec	PIC X(n).
user-mode	PIC X COMP-X.
actual-file-spec	Group item defined as:
buffer-len	PIC X(2) COMP-X.
buffer	PIC X(n).
exist-flag	PIC X COMP-X.
path-flag	PIC X COMP-X.
status-code	See the section *Key*.

Parameters on Entry:

user-file-spec	Contains the file name specification; this can include an embedded environment variable or library name. For example:
	standard file-name
	  device\file-name.ext
	embedded environment variable:
	  $envname\file-name.ext
	embedded library name:
	  device\library-name.LBR\file-name.ext

user-mode	Specifies what to do with *user-file-spec*: 0 = Check whether the file exists in a

library or as a separate disk file.

If *user-file-spec* includes an embedded library-name, that library is opened (if it exists)and searched for the file. The library is left open afterwards.

If *user-file-spec* includes an embedded environment variable, the file will be searched for along each path specified in that variable. If it is found, *actual-file-spec* on exit contains the file specification with the environment variable expanded to the successful path.

Otherwise, *actual-file-spec* on exit contains the file specification with the environment variable expanded to the first path it contained.

1 = If *user-file-spec* includes an environment variable, *actual-file-spec* on exit contains the file specification with the environment variable expanded to the first path it contained. The file is not searched for.

2 = If *user-file-spec* includes an environment variable, *actual-file-spec* on exit contains the file specification with the environment variable expanded to the next path it contained. The file is not searched for. This option should only be used after a successful call with *user-mode* = 1 or 2. See path-flag below.

path flag

If *user-mode* = 2, this data item should contain the value that was returned in this item from the previous *user-mode* = 1 or 2 call.

Parameters on Exit:

buffer-len	Size of following buffer.
buffer	Buffer to contain the resolved file specification, as described under user-mode.
exist-flag	If *user-mode* = 0, this data item on exit shows whether the file specified in user-file-spec exists.

Library Routines

	0 = file not found or not searched for
	1 = file was found in a library that was already open
	2 = file was found in a library specified in *user-file-spec*
	3 = file was found as a separate disk file
	If *user-mode* is not 0, then this data item is always 0 on exit.
path-flag	Shows whether *user-file-spec* contained an embedded environment variable that has been expanded in *actual-file-spec* as follows:
	0 = actual-file-spec does not include an expanded environment variable
	1 = *actual-file-spec* contains an expanded environment variable
status-code	Return status:
	0 = success
	1 = the environment variable does not exist
	4 = resulting file-name is illegal
	255 = other error

PC_READ_DRIVE

Returns the current default drive letter.

Syntax:

```
CALL "PC_READ_DRIVE" USING drive
                     RETURNING status-code
```

Parameters:

drive	PIC X.
status-code	See the section *Key*.

Parameters on Entry:

None

Parameters on Exit:

drive   Drive letter, upper- or lower-case.

PC_SET_DRIVE

Sets the default drive letter.

Syntax:

```
CALL "PC_SET_DRIVE" USING drive
                    RETURNING status-code
```

Parameters:

drive   PIC X.
status-code   See the section *Key*.

Parameters on Entry:

drive   Drive letter, upper- or lower-case.

Parameters on Exit:

None

PC_SET_MOUSE_HIDE_AREA

Defines an area ("collision area") where the mouse is to be invisible.

Syntax:

```
CALL "PC_SET_MOUSE_HIDE_AREA" USING mouse-handle
                              collision-area
                    RETURNING status-code
```

Library Routines

Parameters:

mouse-handle	PIC X(4) COMP-X.
collision-area	Group item defined as:
top-row	PIC X(2) COMP-X.
left-col	PIC X(2) COMP-X.
bottom-row	PIC X(2) COMP-X.
right-col	PIC X(2) COMP-X.
status-code	See the section *Key*.

Parameters on Entry:

mouse-handle	Mouse identifier, obtained by earlier call to CBL_INIT_MOUSE.
collision-area	Defines the collision area. Whenever the pointer is in this area, it is hidden. A value of zeros in this item makes the whole screen a collision area. There can be only one collision area at any one time.

Parameters on Exit:

None

PC_SET_MOUSE_SHAPE

Sets the shape of the mouse pointer.

Syntax:

```
CALL "PC_SET_MOUSE_SHAPE" USING mouse-handle
                                reserved-item
                                mouse-ptr-shape
                          RETURNING status-code
```

Parameters:

mouse-handle	PIC X(4) COMP-X.
reserved-item	PIC X(10).

mouse-ptr-shape	Group item defined as:
char_AND_mask	PIC X COMP-X.
attr_AND_mask	PIC X COMP-X.
char_XOR_mask	PIC X COMP-X.
attr_XOR_mask	PIC X COMP-X.
status-code	See the Section *Key*.

Description:

The masks in *mouse-ptr-shape* are bit maps that, applied to a screen position, would superimpose the mouse shape upon it. The pointer shape is formed by PC_SET_MOUSE_SHAPE by ANDing the screen character at the mouse position with *char_AND_mask*, XORing the result with *char_XOR_mask*, and then displaying the result on the screen. The attribute is formed similarly.

See also *Mouse* in *Routines by Category* earlier in this section.

Parameters on Entry:

mouse-handle	Mouse identifier, obtained by earlier call to CBL_INIT_MOUSE.
reserved-item	Reserved for future use
mouse-ptr-shape	The bit maps to create the pointer's desired shape.

Parameters on Exit:

None

PC_TEST_PRINTER

Returns information about the status of a printer.

Syntax:

```
CALL "PC_TEST_PRINTER" USING printer-no
                             printer-status
                       RETURNING status-code
```

Library Routines

Parameters:

printer-no	PIC X COMP-X.
printer-status	PIC X COMP-X.
status-code	See the section *Key*.

Parameters on Entry:

printer-no   Number of the printer to check; must be 0, 1, or 2.

Parameters on Exit:

printer-status   A combination of the following values:
128 (x"80") = not busy
64 (x"40") = acknowledge
32 (x"20") = out of paper
16 (x"10") = selected
8 (x"08")   = I/O error
4 (x"04")   = spare
2 (x"02")   = spare
1 (x"01")   = timeout

Note: These values reflect the status set by the IBM graphics printer. Other printers may return different values.

Call-by-Number Routines

To use a library routine, use the number of the required routine in a COBOL CALL statement.

Routines Available

There are call-by-number routines available to perform the following functions:

84	execute a DOS interrupt
85	examine a one-byte location
86	set a one-byte location
88	output one byte to a hardware port
91	set/read switches and miscellaneous
91/35	run program with given command line
94	examine a two-byte location
95	input one byte from a hardware port
96	input two bytes from a hardware port
97	output two bytes to a hardware port
E5	sound beep
F4	pack data into a byte
F5	unpack data into byte

Note: Some of these routines have options allowing many different functions to be performed.

Descriptions of Routines

Descriptions for all of the call-by-number routines appear in numerical order according to their hex numbers. Each routine is shown in a CALL statement that you could use to call it. The parameters it needs are shown in the USING clause.

Execute a DOS Interrupt

```
CALL x"84" USING interrupt-number, flag, AX-parameter,
     BX-parameter, CX-parameter, DX-parameter
```

where:

interrupt-number   is a PIC X COMP-X field containing the value of the DOS interrupt number.

flag   is a PIC X COMP-X field containing 8 bits set to a 0 or a 1 depending on what is to be placed in the registers AX, BX, CX, and DX.

Library Routines

AX-, BX-, CX-, and DX-parameters are group items, each consisting of two PIC X COMP-X data items, corresponding to the high and low halves of a 16-bit register. They contain values to be addressed by a register if the corresponding flag bit equals 0 or the value to be placed in the register if the flag bit equals 1.

This routine can be used only for interrupts that accept parameters through the AX, BX, CX, and DX registers. Any interrupt which requires support outside of this constraint, such as control of DS and ES or adjustments to the stack after the interrupt, should be accessed using assembler subprogramming.

The Flag Byte

The least significant 4 bits of the flag byte control the contents of AX, BX, CX, and DX on entry. If the least significant bit is set, AX is loaded with the 16-bit value in the AX parameter. If the least significant bit is not set, then DS:AX addresses the AX parameter. The most significant 4 bits of the flag byte control the contents of AX, BX, CX, and DX on exit. If the most significant bit is set, the value returned in DX by the interrupt is placed in the DX parameter.

On entry to the interrupt call, DS=ES=program address space.

Example

The following example uses the DOS FCB interface to open a file.

```
* dos interrupt number=21h
01 msdos          pic x comp-x value h"21".

* the contents of the parameter funct are to be placed in and
* taken from AX before and after the interrupt.
01 flag           pic x comp-x value h"11".

01 funct.
      02 funct-ah  pic x comp-x.
      02 funct-al  pic x comp-x.
```

```
01 fcb.
    02 filler    pic x value x"00".
    02 filler    pic x(8) value "myfile".
    02 filler    pic x(3) value "dat".
    02 filler    pic x(25).

01 null-param    pic x.

    move 15 to funct-ah
* ah = dos function, open fcb
    call x"84" using msdos, flag, funct,
            null-param, null-param, fcb.


* al = result
    if funct-al is not = 0
            go to file-not-found
    end-if.
```

Read from One- or Two-byte Location

CALL $\begin{Bmatrix} \text{x"85"} \\ \text{x"94"} \end{Bmatrix}$ USING *segment, offset, data-value*

where:

segment   is a PIC 9(5) field containing the segment you want
               to examine.

offset   is a PIC 9(5) field containing the offset within
               the segment.

data-value   is a PIC X field for x"85", or PIC XX for x"94", to
               contain the value returned.

CALL x"85" returns a one-byte value; CALL x"94" returns a two-byte value. The contents found at the location you specify are copied into your program in the field data-value.

Library Routines

Write to One- or Two-byte Location

CALL $\left\{ \begin{array}{c} \text{x"86"} \\ \text{x"95"} \end{array} \right\}$ USING *segment, offset, data-value*

where:

segment   is a PIC 9(5) field containing the segment to which you want to write.

offset   is a PIC 9(5) field containing the offset within the segment.

data-value   is a PIC X field for CALL x"86", or a PIC XX field for CALL x"95", containing the data you want to write.

CALL x"86" writes to a one-byte location; CALL x"95" writes to a two-byte location. The data in data-value is copied to the location you specify.

Read from Hardware Port

CALL $\left\{ \begin{array}{c} \text{x"87"} \\ \text{x"96"} \end{array} \right\}$ USING *port, data-value*

where:

port   is a PIC 9(5) field containing the port from which to input.

data-value   is a PIC X field for CALL x"87", or PIC XX for CALL x"96", which contains the value returned.

CALL x"87" returns a one-byte value; CALL x"96" returns a two-byte value.

Write to Hardware Port

CALL $\left\{ \begin{array}{c} \text{x"88"} \\ \text{x"97"} \end{array} \right\}$ USING *port, data-value*

where:

port   is a PIC 9(5) field containing the hardware port to which you want to wrte.

data-value   is a PIC X field for CALL x"88" , or PIC XX for CALL x"97", which contains the value you want to write.

CALL x"88" writes a one-byte value; CALL x"97 writes to a two-byte value. The port is output from your program.

Interprogram Function Calls

    CALL   x"91"   USING result, function-num, parameter

where:

result   is a PIC X COMP-X field that contains zero if the call is successful, or non-zro if not successful. The numberreturned for non-success ful calls varies accordin to function-num.

function-num   is a PIC COMP-X field that contains one of the values listed below, depending on which function you want.

The format of *parameter* depends on the function.

function-num can contain:

11	to set the COBOL program switches
12	to read the COBOL program switches
13	to et the run-time switches
4	to read the run-time switches
15	to check if a program exists
16	to get the number of linkage parameters
35	to call program under DOS ("4B"call)
46	to enable insertion of null characters
47	to disable insertion of null characters
48	to enable tab insertion
49	to disable tab insertion

Library Routines

Function 11

Sets the COBOL program switches. *parameter* is a group item consisting of two ata items:

- a PIC X COMP-X OCCURS 8 data item that represents switches 0 to 7, inclusive. A 1 in the first element of this item sets switch 0, a 1 in the second element sets switch 1, and so on.

- a PIC X COMP-X data item that contains 1 to set the standard ANSI Debug module on, 0 to switch it off.

To update one switch without affecting the others, you should read the switches with Function 12, update parameter, and then call this function.

Function 12

Reads the COBOL program switches. *parameter* is a group item consisting of two data items:

- a PIC X COMP-X OCCURS 8 data item that represents switches 0 to 7, inclusive, as for Function 11.

- a PIC X COMP-X data item that shows whether the standard ANSI Debug module is enabled as described in Function 11.

Function 13

Sets the run-time switches. *parameter* is a PIC X COMP-X OCCURS 26 field representing run-time switches A to Z, inclusive. The value in the first byte of this item is put into run-time switch A, the second byte into switch B, and so on.

The individual bits in each byte correspond to the digit that can follow a switch-name. For example, to set +S0 and +S5 you set bits 0 and 5 by passing 1 + 32 = 33 in the "S" byte.

Function 14

Reads the run-time switches. *parameter* is a PIC X COMP-X OCCURS 26 field representing run-time switches A to Z, inclusive, as for Function 13.

Function 15

Checks to see if a program exists. You pass the program name and its length in *parameter*. When the routine exits, *result* is zero if the program is found, non-zero otherwise. *parameter* is a group item consisting of two data items:

- a PIC X COMP-X data item specifying the length in bytes of the data item containing the file-name.

- a PIC X data item of variable length containing the file-name; this data item must be at least 65 bytes long. If the file is found, the routine updates this data item, replacing the file-name that you gave by the full file-name.

If the program file is found, you must then call the program, using the file-name returned.

This call must not be used to check for the existence of data files; use CBL_CHECK_FILE_EXIST instead.

Function 16

Shows how many of the parameters in the CALL statement of the calling program have been transferred to the called subprogram. *parameter* is a PIC X COMP-X field that shows how many parameters have been transferred.

This function can only be used if the program is called from a COBOL program.

Function 35

Performs an EXEC call (like the DOS 4B call) to the program file whose name appears in the parameter field. The command line

Library Routines

can be set up using the DISPLAY...UPON COMMAND-LINE syntax (see *Language Reference* chapter for details). The result field is zero if the EXEC call was successful, nonzero otherwise. If the reason for failure is an operating system error and has a number less than 255, that number is returned. Otherwise 255 is returned. *parameter* is a group item consisting of two data items:

- a PIC X COMP-X field that specifies the number of characters in the file-name. If this field is set to 0, then whatever has been previously written to the command line, using DISPLAY..UPON COMMAND-LINE, is executed.

- a PIC X field of variable length that contains the file-name of the program file.

Note: If you wish to execute batch (.BAT) or command (.CMD) files with this routine, you must use DISPLAY..UPON COMMAND-LINE.

Example

The following example shows how you can perform a "DIR/W" using function 35:

```
working-storage section.
01 command-lin-string  pic x(80) value "dir/w".
01 result              pic x comp-x.
01 func                pic x comp-x value 35.
01 command-lin.
      03 command-lin-length  pic x comp-x value zero.


procedure division.
main.
      display command-lin-string upon command-line
      call x"91" using result, func, command-lin
      if result = zeros
            display "call worked".
else
            display "call failed".

stop run.
```

Function 46

Enables insertion of a null character x"00" before data characters whose value is less than x"1B" in line sequential files. If you wish to include non-ASCII data in a file then you must enable null insertion. This function allows you to enable null insertion for individual files regardless of the setting of the run-time switch N. parameter is the file-identifier specified in the File Description (FD), and must refer to a line sequential file which is currently open. For example:

```
fd payroll-file
    ...
    call x"91" using result, func-num,
                payroll-file
```

Function 47

Disables insertion of a null character x"00" before data characters whose value is less than x"1B" in line sequential files. This function allows you to disable null insertion for individual files regardless of the setting of the run-time switch N. *parameter* is the file-identifier specified in the File Description (FD) and must refer to a line sequential file which is currently open (see Function 46 above for an example). This function cannot be used if the file is declared as EXTERNAL.

Function 48

Enables insertion of tab characters in line sequential files. On input all tab characters are expanded to the correct number of spaces, while on output to disk, multiple spaces before a tab stop position are contracted to a tab character. This function allows you to enable tab insertion for individual files regardless of the setting of the run-time switch T. *parameter* is the file-identifier specified in the File Description (FD) and must refer to a line sequential file which is currently open. See Function 46 above for an example.

Library Routines

Function 49

Disables insertion of tab characters in line sequential files. On input all tab characters are expanded to the correct number of spaces; on output to disk, spaces are output as spaces. This function allows you to disable tab insertion for individual files regardless of the setting of the run-time switch T. *parameter* is the file-identifier specified in the File Description (FD) and must refer to a line sequential file which is currently open. See Function 46 above for an example.

Control the Screen

```
CALL    x"A7"   USING function-num, parameter
```

where:

function-num   is a PIC X COMP-X field which contains a value indicating the function required:

> 6 reads the current User attribute
> 7 sets the current User attribute
> 16 turns on or off the User attribute

parameter   is a PIC X COMP-X field containing:

(for functions 6 and 7)

> the User attribute

(for function 16)

> 0 to turn the User attribute on
> 1 to turn the User attribute off

The User attribute is initially off for each program.

The User attribute, if turned on, is used when displaying text upon the screen and supersedes any Screen attribute set for the character positions being used in the display.

When using WRITE to CON:, the output always goes directly to the operating system, using ANSI.SYS.

If the User attribute is not enabled, the Screen attribute currently set for that character position is unaltered.

DISPLAY UPON CRT-UNDER forces highlighting if the User attribute is set on.

DISPLAY SPACE UPON CRT clears the screen to the User attribute for each screen position.

Refer to the *IBM Display Attributes* chapter for details on the values and effects of attributes.

Return Screen Type

```
CALL  x"A7" USING function-num, screen-type
```

where:

function-num   is PIC X COMP-X VALUE 25

screen-type   a PIC X COMP-X field which contains bit
                        settings indicating the type of screen as
                        follows:

                        0 unset = monochrome screen
                        1 reserved
                        2 reserved
                        3 set = EGA-type screen
                        4 set = VGA-type screen
                        5 reserved
                        6 reserved
                        7 reserved

Call x"A7" function 25 returns the current screen type as recognized by the run-time system.

Library Routines

Handle Function Keys

CALL x"B0" USING *function-num, parameter*

where:

function-num   is a PIC X COMP-X data item and
                        contains a value
                        which determines the function of the
                        subprogram:

                        0 to set up a function key table
                        2 to test the status of shift-type keys

parameter   varies for the functions as described below:

(for function 0)   is a table of the form:

   PIC X COMP-X

                        the return byte. Contains the table entry
                        matching the key used or zero if no match
                        is made.

   PIC X COMP-X

                        the length of the next item (in bytes).
                        This must contain the value 0 (which
                        terminates the table), 1 or 2.

   PIC X(n)

                        contains the code sequence produced by
                        the required key. n is the length defined
                        in the length parameter above.

   The last two items are repeated once for every key to
   be detected. The table is terminated by a length
   parameter of 0.

(for function 2)   is an eight-byte item of the form:

PIC X

> the return byte, which contains bit
> settings indicating the status of the keys
> (1=key pressed, 0=key not pressed) in the
> following order (bit 7 is the high-order bit
> and bit 0 the low-order bit):

Key	Bit
Ins	7
Caps Lock	6
Num Lock	5
Scroll Lock	4
Alt	3
Ctrl	2
Shift (left key) 1	
Shift (right key)	0

PIC X COMP-X

> must be set to 2 before the call is made.
>
> This item is overwritten by the call, and
> should, therefore, be reset to 2 prior to each
> call.

PIC X(6)

> contents are unimportant

Notes:

- For the last four of the above keys, this program returns a 1 only if the key is actually pressed at the time the program is called; for the other 4 keys, the relevant bit is alternately set and unset each time the key is pressed.

- To make these bit settings more accessible to COBOL, you can use the UNPACK BYTE routine described in this chapter, or the logical operation routines documented in *Library Routines (Call-by-Name)*.

Library Routines

■ Effective use of this function requires that the call is repeated at very frequent intervals.

■ CALL x"B0" is specific to an IBM environment. If you intend to use our application in a non-IBM environment, use CALL x"AF".

■ The function key table used by CALL x"AF" is separate from the function key table used by CALL x"B0". Both can be enabled at the same time with all key sequences in the x"B0" table causing the carriage return x"0D" character to be returned to ADIS.

Example - Detecting Function Keys

An ACCEPT statement normally recognizes as control keys only the keys used in data entry (for example, , , ,) and is terminated by the **Enter** key; any other control key is rejected with a beep.

Other control keys and function keys can be made available by calling library routine x"B0" using function 0.

This routine declares a table of key-code sequences, one for each additional key which is to be recognized. Details of the code sequences sent by each key are available in the *IBM Personal Computer Technical Reference Manual.*

After the routine has been called, an ACCEPT statement is termi-nated by the **Enter** key or by any one of the keys whose code sequence matches an entry in the table. The first byte of the table then contains a number indicaing which entry in the table has been matched; zero indicates that the **Enter** key was used. If the **Enter** key has a entry in the table, then the entry number of tat key is returned rather than zero.

The routine may be called with different tables as often as you require. If the current table is changed (for example, if a key is changed or the length increased), then you don't need to call the routine again.

A table used by a particular program remains enabled for that program until it is superseded by another call to this routine, regardless of how many times this routine is called by other programs in your suite.

Note: You must explicitly set up a table for each program in your suite of programs that uses this facility; passing the table in the Linkage Section is not sufficient.

As long as you know the key-code sent, you can define any key in the table. For example, a table entry with length of 1 and a key-code of PIC X VALUE "C" causes the letter C to end an ACCEPT. You could, therefore, use such a key to "break-out" of an AC-CEPT, perform your own processing, and return to the ACCEPT statement. The effect of this is that you have redefined the effect of that particular key.

The result byte is set both on termination of an ACCEPT and on each call to the routine, CBL_READ_KBD_CHAR, when a key in the defined table has been pressed. When this occurs, the character code, x"0D" is returned to the CBL_READ_KBD_CHAR routine, and the result byte indicates which key in the table has been pressed. This means that, you can use CBL_READ_KBD_CHAR to read any single keystroke, including function keys.

For a complete list of code sequences sent by keys, see the technical reference manual for your personal computer.

The following code is an example of how to use the function key call together with CBL_READ_KBD_CHAR:

```
procedure division.
            .         .

            .         .
* Set up function key list
      call x"B0" using B0-function
            B0-parameter-block
      ...
* Read a character from the keyboard
      call "CBL_READ_KBD_CHAR" using char
      if char = x"0D"
* A key defined in the function key table was
* pressed
      evaluate B0-return-byte
```

Library Routines

```
              when 1
                . . .
              when 2
                . . .
           end-evaluate
            . . .
        else
         if char = x"00"
         * A function key not defined in the table was
* pressed
                   call "CBL_READ_KBD_CHAR" using char
* char contains the key's scan code
             . . .
         else
* char contains a character
         end-if
       end-if.
```

Sound the Beep

```
CALL x"E5"
```

This routine causes a beep of about 1/8 second duration.

Pack Byte

```
CALL  x"F4"  USING byte, array
```

where:

byte   is a PIC X COMP-X field that contains the new byte.

array   is a PIC X COMP-X OCCURS 8 field that contains the
              eight bytes to be packed.

The routine takes the eight fields from *array* and uses the least
significant bit of each byte to form *byte*. The first occurrence in
array becomes the most significant bit of *byte* (bit 7).

Unpack Byte

```
CALL  x"F5"  USING byte, array
```

where:

byte   is a PIC X COMP-X field that contains the byte to be unpacked.

array   is a PIC X COMP-X OCCURS 8 field that contains the unpacked bits.

The routine takes the eight bits of byte and moves them to the corresponding occurrence within array

Chapter 11

ADIS

Overview

ADIS is a run-time support module which provides for Screen
Section and enhanced ACCEPT/DISPLAY syntax. Calls can be
made from the COBOL application to ADIS to configure it at run
time; for example, to enable function keys.

Enhanced ACCEPT/DISPLAY

The enhanced ACCEPT/DISPLAY syntax provides functionality
beyond the standard ANSI ACCEPT syntax, which enables you to
input a data-item or accept the day, date or time into a data-item,
and the ANSI DISPLAY syntax, which allows you to output
literals and the contents of data items.

With the enhanced ACCEPT/DISPLAY syntax supported by
ADIS, you can specify screen position and screen attributes. It also
makes it possible to do either single-field or multiple-field AC-
CEPT operations. For multiple-field ACCEPT operations, FILLER
describes the number of character positions to skip over to the
next field. In a DISPLAY operation, FILLER defines the number of
spaces between literals. All areas defined as FILLER are unaffected by the ACCEPT or DISPLAY operation.

Screen Section

The Screen Section is a section in the Data Division containing one or more screen definitions. A screen definition may contain fields, groups, text and attributes. Fields may have edited picture strings and may also have such features as NO-ECHO, JUSTIFIED RIGHT, BLANK WHEN ZERO, etc. How the screen definitions are ACCEPTed and DISPLAYed in the Procedure Division is handled by ADIS.

Configuration

ADIS can be configured to affect the behavior of ACCEPT and DISPLAY statements at run time. You can configure ADIS by making calls to ADIS from the COBOL application at run-time.

Operation

This section describes how Enhanced ACCEPT and DISPLAY statements are handled at run time when used with:

- Elementary data items

- Group items

- Screen Section items

The term field used in relation to screen handling refers to an area on the screen that corresponds to a single data-item during accept and display operations.

Single Field ACCEPT and DISPLAY Statements

This section describes how ACCEPT and DISPLAY statements in the following format are handled at run-time:

```
display data-item at xxyy ...
accept data-item at xxyy ...
```

where data-item is an elementary item defined in the Data Division of your program and xxyy specifies the position on the screen (xx=line, yy=column) where the DISPLAY or ACCEPT field starts. The length of the field is governed by the length and type of data-item, and the SIZE clause.

DISPLAY Statements

The following sections describe the way that the DISPLAY statement functions.

Format of Displayed Data

When a data item is displayed on the screen, it occupies the same number of characters on the screen as it does bytes in memory.

Examples

Data Item Description	Size on Screen	Comment
X(5)	5 characters	
N(5)	10 characters	Each PIC N character occupies 2 bytes in memory
9(5)	5 characters	
99.99	5 characters	
Z(4)9	5 characters	
99V99	4 characters	V is an implied decimal point and so is not displayed on the screen

S9(4)	4 characters	The sign is implied and so is not displayed on the screen
S9(4) SIGN LEADING SEPARATE	5 characters	
9(4) COMP	2 characters	COMP fields are stored in binary; a 9(4) COMP field occupies 2 bytes in memory

As can be seen from the above examples, it is only really sensible to display fields defined as USAGE DISPLAY which do not contain implied signs or decimal points. When the field is displayed, it is copied byte-for-byte from the data item onto the screen at the required position.

Note: ANSI DISPLAY operations do convert non-USAGE DISPLAY numeric items to USAGE DISPLAY before displaying.

Control Sequences in Displayed Data

Control sequences cannot be embedded in the data that is displayed. If you do embed control codes (that is, ASCII codes less than 32) into the data, the IBM graphics character corresponding to that code is displayed. For example, displaying ASCII code 7 results in a diamond character being displayed instead of sounding the bell. (For some products developed for other environments, such characters are replaced by a space.) All highlighting, cursor control, etc., must be done through the syntax provided.

Displaying Highlighted Text

If you use the CRT-UNDER phrase in a DISPLAY statement, the data item is displayed highlighted. Depending on your CRT, use of the CRT-UNDER phrase may cause data items to be displayed underlined or in reverse-video.

ACCEPT Statements

The following sections describe how the ACCEPT statement is executed on different types of fields.

Alphanumeric Fields

The term Alphanumeric Field is used here to cover all alphanumeric, alphabetic and alphanumeric-edited fields. For the purposes of an ACCEPT, an alphanumeric-edited field is treated as an alphanumeric field of the same length. Any insertion symbols such as "/" or "0" are ignored and treated as an X. Therefore, a field defined as PIC XX0XX0XX is treated as if it was specified as PIC X(8).

If the field is defined as alphabetic, only the characters "A" to "Z", "a" to "z" and space are allowed into the field.

The cursor is initially placed at the start of the field.

As data is entered into the field, the cursor is advanced to the next character. The cursor can be moved back over the data in the field using the cursor keys, and editing functions such as backspace, delete, etc. are provided. By default, the **Ins** key is set up to toggle between insert mode and replace mode.

Fixed Format Data Entry

This is also known as formatted mode. It can best be described as "What you see is what you get". As each key is pressed, the field is automatically reformatted to conform to the picture string. Therefore, ADIS tries to ensure that the field always looks on the screen as it is stored in the Data Division, and its size is the same as the size of the data item.

Therefore, as with the DISPLAY statement, it is only really sensible to accept fields that are defined as USAGE DISPLAY with no implied sign or decimal point.

During data entry, characters other than numeric digits, +, - and the decimal point character are rejected. Insertion characters in edited fields are automatically skipped over as the cursor is moved backwards and forwards. Any sign indicator is automatically modified if a "+" or "-" is pressed, regardless of where the cursor is in the field.

Zeros are allowed as insertion characters only as a leading symbol before a decimal point, or as a trailing symbol following a decimal point. For example, PIC 0.9999 and PIC 999.90 are valid, but PIC 0.0009 and PIC 999,000 are not.

Data entry of simple numerics and numeric-edited fields with no zero suppression is similar to that for alphanumeric fields, except that insert mode is not supported in numeric and numeric-edited fields. If the decimal point character is pressed in a simple numeric field, the digits are right justified. For example, a field defined as PIC 9(5) which initially contains zeros is accepted as follows (underlined characters indicate cursor position):

Initial display	0̲0000
Pressing 1 will give	10̲000
Pressing 2 will give	120̲00
Pressing 4 will give	1240̲0
Pressing backspace will give	120̲00
Pressing "." will give	0001̲2

Data entry into zero-suppressed fields is handled differently. The cursor is initially placed on the first character position that is not zero-suppressed. If all the digits before the decimal point are suppressed, the cursor is positioned on the decimal point itself.

While the cursor is to the left of the decimal point (that is, in the integer part of the field), the cursor moves to the right as digits are entered until the decimal point is reached. Any further digits are inserted immediately before the decimal point until all the integer places are filled. The cursor is then automatically moved to the first decimal digit and advances as the decimal digits are entered.

If you wish to enter digits after the decimal point when there are integer places still unfilled, the decimal point (.) must be entered.

For example, assume that a numeric-edited data field is defined as PIC ZZZ99.99 and initially contains zeros, the field will be displayed as follows during the ACCEPT:

Initial display	00.00
Pressing 1 gives	10.00
Pressing 2 gives	12.00
Pressing 3 gives	123.00
Pressing 4 gives	1234.00
Pressing backspace gives	123.00
Pressing 5 gives	1235.00
Pressing 6 gives	12356.00
Pressing 7 gives	12356.70
Pressing 8 gives	12356.78

If you want to enter 123.45 into the same field, the field appears as follows:

Initial display	00.00
Pressing 1 gives	10.00
Pressing 2 gives	12.00
Pressing 3 gives	123.00
Pressing "." gives	123.00
Pressing 4 gives	123.40
Pressing 5 gives	123.45

Fixed format mode is only allowed on numeric-edited data items of length up to 32 characters. If they are longer than 32 characters, they are automatically handled in free-format mode as described below. Fields are also automatically treated as free-format if a SIZE clause is specified in the ACCEPT statement.

Free-format Data Entry

During data entry into a free-format field, the field is treated as an alphanumeric field of the appropriate length. It is only when the user leaves the field that it is reformatted to comply with the picture string. Any characters other than the digits, the sign character and the decimal point character are discarded.

Fields occupy the same number of characters on the screen as they do bytes in memory, with the exception that an additional character is allocated for implied signs and decimal points. Therefore, a data item defined as PIC S99V99 occupies six characters on the screen in free-format mode as opposed to four characters in fixed-format mode.

Data entry is the same as for alphanumeric fields.

If an enhanced ACCEPT statement is being used, the clauses SPACE-FILL, ZERO-FILL, LEFT-JUSTIFY, RIGHT-JUSTIFY and TRAILING-SIGN are applicable only to free-format non-edited fields (and are ignored with fixed-format fields). See the description of the ACCEPT statement in the *Language Reference* chapter for further details of these clauses.

General Notes

These notes concern the accepting of data into fields:

■ If a field is too long to fit on one line on the screen, it is split into separate sub-fields at run-time. Each sub-field fits entirely onto one line. The cursor automatically auto-skips into the next sub-field at the end of one sub-field, regardless of the setting of any auto-skip controls.

For example, if you accept a data item that is PIC X(190) at line 1, column 1 and the screen is only 80 characters wide, the field is broken into three sub-fields, two with 80 characters and one with 30 characters.

■ If a field extends beyond the end of the screen, the action taken depends on the type of field:

■ Alphanumeric fields are truncated to a size that fits on the screen.

■ Numeric and numeric-edited fields are treated as if they were defined as FILLER (that is, not a field) and are ignored.

■ As most terminals scroll upwards as a result of a character appearing in the final character position of the screen (bottom right) it is not possible to use this character position as part of an ACCEPT.

Microsoft COBOL V2.2 Emulation

The style of data entry into numeric and numeric-edited fields in Microsoft's COBOL Version 2.2 is quite different from the style used in this product. The main difference is that decimal points and implied signs are treated as if they were specified as "." and "-". Therefore, a PIC S99V99 field is treated as if it was specified as a -99.99 field during execution of an ACCEPT or DISPLAY statement under Microsoft COBOL V2.2. All ACCEPT and DISPLAY statements behave as if the phrase MODE IS BLOCK has been specified.

The other major difference between the behavior of this COBOL system and Microsoft COBOL V2.2 during execution of a numeric ACCEPT is that Microsoft COBOL V2.2 accepts data from right-to-left and this COBOL accepts data from left-to-right.

Displaying or Accepting Group Items

When displaying or accepting group items, each elementary item within the group is treated as a separate field. If an elementary item is defined as FILLER, it is simply used as a positioning item of the appropriate size (that is, you cannot accept into FILLER items or display FILLER items).

Displaying Group Items

Consider the following group item:

```
01 display-item.
      03 display-item-1        pic x(20).
      03 filler                pic x(35).
      03 display-item-2        pic 9(10).
      03 filler                pic x(105).
      03 display-item-3        pic z(4)9.
```

If the following statement is executed on a screen 80 characters wide:

```
display display-item at 0101
```

`display-item-1` is displayed at row 1, column 1,
`display-item-2` is displayed at row 1, column 56, and
`display-item-3` is displayed at row 3, column 11

All other areas of the screen are unaffected by the DISPLAY.
FILLER items do not cause any data to be displayed on the screen.
Consequently, data already on the screen in the positions defined
by each FILLER is not altered in any way by the DISPLAY.

If a data item is defined as follows :

```
01 data-item.
    03 data-char          pic x occurs 2000.
```

and the following statement is executed:

```
    display data-item at 0101
```

then this is treated as a display of 2000 fields, each defined as PIC
X, which is unlikely to be what you require. To avoid this, either
redefine `data-item` as a PIC X(2000) and display that or use the
MODE IS BLOCK clause described below.

Accepting into Group Items

When accepting into a group item, each field is accepted into as
described for single-field ACCEPT statements earlier in this
section.

Unless you explicitly position the cursor (see *The CURSOR IS
Clause* later in this section), the cursor is initially placed at the start
of the first field.

When the end of a field is reached, the cursor is normally advanced to the beginning of the next field automatically. The keys
set up for next and previous field operations (usually tab and
back-tab) move you between the individual fields. In addition, the
cursor keys move you around the fields.

The MODE IS BLOCK Clause

If the MODE IS BLOCK clause is added to an ACCEPT or DIS-PLAY of a group item, the group item is treated as if it was an elementary item of the total size of the group item.

For example, if the following statement is executed:

```
display display-item at 0101 mode is block.
```

where display-item is as defined in the section *Displaying Group Items*, display-item is treated as if it was an elementary item defined as:

```
01 display-item          pic x(175).
```

Consequently, the contents of the FILLER items are also displayed.

The CURSOR IS Clause

This feature allows you to specify precisely where in a field you want the cursor to be positioned at the start of the ACCEPT operation, and returns where the cursor was left at the end of an ACCEPT operation. If you do not specify a CURSOR IS clause in your program, the cursor is always initially positioned at the start of the first field for every ACCEPT operation.

The CURSOR IS clause is defined in the SPECIAL-NAMES paragraph, as follows :

```
special-names.
    cursor is cursor-position.
```

where cursor-position is a field defined in your Working-Storage section as follows :

```
01 cursor-position.
    03 cursor-row            pic 99.
    03 cursor-column         pic 99.
```

where:

cursor-row
Specifies the row the cursor is positioned on. Valid values are between 1 and the number of lines on the screen.

cursor-column
Specifies the column the cursor is positioned on. Valid values are between 1 and the number of columns on the screen.

Whenever an ACCEPT statement is executed, ADIS attempts to initially position the cursor at the position specified in cursor-position. If the position specified is invalid (that is, either cursor-row or cursor-column does not contain a valid value), the cursor is positioned at the start of the first field on the screen.

If the value in cursor-position is valid, ADIS searches through all of the fields to see if the requested cursor position lies within one of them. If it does, the cursor is positioned at the required point. If it does not, then the cursor is positioned at the start of the first field. Therefore, if you want the cursor to be positioned at the start of the first field, set both cursor-row and cursor-column to 1.

Where the defined position is on a suppressed character or insertion symbol in a numeric edited field, the cursor moves to the first available character to the right. If there is no further data item, the cursor returns to the first data item on the screen.

When the ACCEPT is terminated, if the value in cursor-position at the start of the ACCEPT was valid, the position of the cursor when the terminating key is pressed is returned in cursor-position. Note, however, that this may not be the same position as the current cursor position, since ADIS usually moves the cursor to the end of the field upon termination of an ACCEPT operation to allow relative positioned ACCEPT statements to start at the correct point on the screen.

If the value in cursor-position at the start of the ACCEPT was invalid, then, when the ACCEPT is terminated, the contents of cursor-position are unchanged.

One example of the use of this facility is that in menu-type operations, the operator need only move the cursor to a position on the screen corresponding to the selection required. The operator's choice can be determined by the returned value of cursor-position.

Large Screens

Screens larger than 25 lines can be detected by your COBOL system. On a screen larger than 25 lines the +C switch should be used at run time.

Programs using ANSI ACCEPT/DISPLAY statements, enhanced ACCEPT/DISPLAY syntax, Screen Section and the COBOL system library routines should run correctly on large screens. It is worth noting, however, that if an application is developed for a screen larger than the screen it is run on, then it results in the loss of the extra lines, or, in single field ACCEPT/DISPLAY statements, it results in the screen being scrolled up by one line.

ADIS Run Time Configuration

One of the powerful features of ADIS is that it can be configured to tailor the behavior of ACCEPT and DISPLAY statements. This section describes features of ADIS that are not available via CO-BOL syntax, but can be accessed with the x"AF" COBOL system library routine.

All of these features are accessed by the following call statement:

```
call x"af" using set-bit-pairs parameter-block
```

where the parameters are defined as follows:

```
01 set-bit-pairs              pic 9(2) comp-x value 1.
01 parameter-block.
      03 bit-pair-setting     pic 9(2) comp-x.
      03 filler               pic x value "2".
      03 bit-pair-number      pic 9(2) comp-x.
      03 filler               pic 9(2) comp-x value 1.
```

The values to be set for the fields *bit-pair-setting* and *bit-pair-number* are given in each of the descriptions below.

With all x"AF" calls, if an error occurs, the first parameter is set to the value 255.

The functions available using this facility are as follows:

- Enable/disable pre-display

- Enable/disable display of the ADIS indicators

- Enable/disable display of ADIS error messages

- Enable/disable auto-skip between fields

- Enable/disable input data case conversion

- Enable/disable password concealment

Enable/Disable Pre-display

This allows you to control whether or not the initial contents of fields are pre-displayed before any data entry is allowed when an ACCEPT statement is executed.

Note: The pre-display of fields defined as fixed format numeric or numeric-edited cannot be turned off.

The fields in *parameter-block* should be set as follows:

bit-pair-number must be set to 76.

bit-pair-setting should be set to one of the following values:

0   Only fixed-format numeric and fixed-format numeric-edited fields are pre-displayed.

1   Only numeric fields and fixed-format numeric-edited fields are pre-displayed.

2   A field is pre-displayed as soon as the cursor is moved into it.

3   All of the fields in the ACCEPT are

pre-displayed before any data entry is allowed. The default.

Example

The following code will turn off pre-display of fields for all following ACCEPT operations:

```
move 76 TO bit-pair-number
move 0 TO bit-pair-setting
call x"af" using set-bit-pairs parameter-block
```

Enable/Disable Display of the ADIS Indicators

These routines allow you to enable or disable the display of the indicators that ADIS displays during an ACCEPT to indicate insert/replace mode, autoclear mode or "off end of field". By default, these indicators are displayed.

There are different calls to control each of these indicators, but they all have the same format.

The fields in *parameter-block* should be set as follows:

bit-pair-number should be set to one of the following:

> 56 To control the Insert/Replace mode indicator
> 57 To control the "Off end of field" indicator
> 58 To control the "Autoclear" indicator

bit-pair-setting should be set to one of the following:

> 0   The indicator is displayed if necessary. The default.
>
> 3   The indicator is never displayed.

Example

The following code will disable display of the insert/replace indicator and enable display of the "Off end of field" indicator.

```
move 56 to bit-pair-number
move 3 to bit-pair-setting
call x"AF" using set-bit-pairs parameter-block
move 57 to bit-pair-number
move 0 to bit-pair-setting
call x"AF" using set-bit-pairs parameter-block
```

Enable/Disable Display of ADIS Error Messages

This routine allows you to enable or disable the display of the messages that ADIS may output during execution of an ACCEPT statement. By default, these messages are displayed.

The fields in *parameter-block* should be set as follows:

bit-pair-number must be set to 44.

bit-pair-setting should be set to one of the following values:

0   Error messages are never displayed, but the bell is rung. Invalid data entered into a numeric or numeric- edited field in free-format mode is not reported as an error.

1   Error messages are never displayed, but the bell is rung. Invalid data entered into a numeric or numeric-edited field in free format mode is reported as an error by ringing the bell.

2   Error messages are displayed and the bell is rung if the appropriate error occurs. Invalid data entered into a numeric or numeric-edited field in free-format mode is not reported as an error.

3   Error messages are displayed and the bell is rung if the appropriate error occurs. Invalid data entered into a numeric or numeric-edited field in free-format mode is reported as an error by ringing the bell.

Example

The following code will disable the display of error messages and disable the reporting of invalid data in numeric and numeric-edited fields.

```
move 44 TO bit-pair-number
move 0 TO bit-pair-setting
call x"af" using set-bit-pairs parameter-block
```

Enable/Disable Auto-skip Between Fields

This routine allows you to control circumstances in which auto-skip to a following or preceding field may occur, during execution of an ACCEPT statement.

The fields in *parameter-block* should be set as follows:

> *bit-pair-number* must be set to 81.
>
> *bit-pair-setting* should be set to one of the following values:

1	No auto-skip. An explicit field-tab or cursor key (but not Backspace) must be used to move between fields.
3	Auto-skip enabled. Any cursor movement or a character key will cause auto-skip to the next field if at end of the current field. The default.

Example

The following code will disable auto-skip between fields:

```
move 81 TO bit-pair-number
move 1 TO bit-pair-setting
call x"af" using set-bit-pairs parameter-block
```

Enable/Disable Input Data Case Conversion

This routine allows you to control whether lower-case ASCII characters are automatically converted to upper-case on entry during execution of an ACCEPT statement.

The fields in *parameter-block* should be set as follows:

bit-pair-number must be set to 85.

bit-pair-setting should be set to one of the following values:

   0   No case conversion occurs. (The default.)

   1   Lower case alphabetic input data is converted to upper case on entry.

Example

The following code will enable conversion to upper case of all alphabetic input.

```
move 85 to bit-pair-number
move 1 to bit-pair-setting
call x"af" using set-bit-pairs parameter-block
```

Enable/Disable Password Concealment

This routine allows you to control whether characters input when an ACCEPT statement is executed should be echoed to the screen, or not.

The fields in *parameter-block* should be set as follows:

bit-pair-number must be set to 84.

bit-pair-setting should be set to one of the following values:

   0   Input is echoed to the screen. (The default.)

1   Input is not echoed to the screen for the next ACCEPT statement encountered only.

2   Input is not echoed to the screen for any following ACCEPT statements until it is re-enabled.

Example

The following code will conceal the input for the next ACCEPT statement only:

```
move 84 to bit-pair-number
move 1 to bit pair setting
call x"af" using set-bit-pairs parameter-block
```

Select Timeout Units

This routine allows you to determine whether the timeout value is interpreted as seconds or tenths of a second.

The fields in *parameter-block* should be set as follows:

bit-pair-number must be set to 14.

bit-pair-setting should be set to one of the following values:

0   Units are seconds.

1   Units are tenths of a second.

Timeout Reset Control

This routine allows you to control whether the timer is reset every time a character is entered, or times out after the specified period anyway.

The fields in *parameter-block* should be set as follows:

bit-pair-number must be set to 15.

bit-pair-setting should be set to one of the following values:

0   Timer is never reset. Timeout occurs after the specified time from the start of the accept.

1   The timer is reset each time a character is entered.

Screen Section

The Screen Section provides screen handling facilities for use with ACCEPT and DISPLAY statements. It allows the display of non-scrolling areas of the screen as defined in the screen section. A screen section entry is a *screen description*. It is similar in appearance to a data description but defines a *screen item* or area of the screen rather than an area in memory. Many screen items describe only the layout of fields within a field on the screen, and are never referenced explicitly.

The screen section entry construct, and use of screen-names with ACCEPT and DISPLAY statements, are documented in the *Language Reference* chapter of this book.

Screen Descriptions define areas on the screen. Each entry consists of a level number, an optional screen name, and various optional clauses relating to the positioning of fields as well as to console functions.

The options which can be used in a screen section entry or in a suitable ACCEPT or DISPLAY statement are described below. The following table shows where each option is permitted:

Screen Clauses/ Screen Options/ Data Description Clauses	SCREEN SECTION FIELDS				WITH PHRASE		
	Input	Output	Update	Literal	Accept	Display	Control
AUTO	X		X		X		X
BACKGROUND-COLOR	X	X	X	X	X	X	X
BELL	X	X	X	X	X	X	X
BLANK	X	X	X	X		X	X
BLANK WHEN ZERO	X	X	X				
BLINK	X	X	X	X	X	X	X
COLUMN	X	X	X	X			
ERASE	X	X	X	X	X		
FOREGROUND-COLOR	X	X	X	X	X	X	X
FULL	X		X		X		X
GRID	X	X	X	X	X	X	X
HIGHLIGHT	X	X	X	X	X	X	X
JUSTIFIED	X	X	X				X
LEFT-JUSTIFY					X		
LEFTLINE	X	X	X	X	X	X	X
LINE	X	X	X	X			
LOWLIGHT	X	X	X	X	X	X	
OCCURS	X	X	X				
OVERLINE	X	X	X	X	X	X	X
PROMPT	X		X		X		X
REQUIRED	X		X		X		X
REVERSE-VIDEO	X	X	X	X	X	X	X
RIGHT-JUSTIFY					X		
SECURE	X		X		X		X
SIGN	X	X	X				
SIZE	X	X	X	X	X	X	
SPACE-FILL					X		
TRAILING -SIGN					X		X
UNDERLINE	X	X	X	X	X	X	

ADIS

Screen Section Option Descriptions

In the descriptions which follow, the Format definitions use these conventions:

<u>UNDERLINED</u> words in upper case are required
UPPER CASE words which are not underlined may be written or not as the programmer wishes.
Lower-case words represent names which the programmer will devise.
Words separated by | are alternatives.
Words enclosed between <> are options which may be included but which will change the meaning of the phrase.

The AUTO Clause

The AUTO clause automatically terminates an ACCEPT operation of the screen item when the last character position is keyed. No explicit terminator key is necessary. If AUTO is used at a group level it applies to all subordinate items.

Format: <u>AUTO</u>

The BACKGROUND-COLOR Clause

The BACKGROUND-COLOR clause specifies the background color of the screen item. If the clause is used at a group level it applies to all subordinate items. The color is specified as an integer. The colors and corresponding values are:

0	black
1	blue
2	green
3	cyan
4	red
5	magenta
6	brown or yellow
7	white

The default color is black.

Format: <u>BACKGROUND-COLOR</u> IS integer

The BELL Clause

The BELL clause causes an audible alarm to occur each time the item containing the clause is displayed. BELL may only be used with elementary items.

Format: <u>BELL</u>

The BLANK LINE or SCREEN Clause

During a DISPLAY operation, each subsidiary item within a screen-name is displayed according to source sequence. At an item with BLANK LINE, the screen is cleared to spaces from the beginning of the line to the end of the line. The cursor position is not changed. BLANK LINE may only be used for elementary items. At an item with BLANK SCREEN, the entire screen is cleared to spaces and the cursor repositioned to line 1, column 1.

Format: <u>BLANK</u> <u>LINE</u> | <u>SCREEN</u>

The BLANK WHEN ZERO Clause

The BLANK WHEN ZERO clause causes the blanking of a screen item when its value is zero. This clause is allowed only with fields that are numeric or numeric-edited.

Format: <u>BLANK</u> WHEN <u>ZERO</u>

The BLINK Clause

The BLINK clause causes the screen item to blink when it appears on the screen. If the clause is used at a group level it applies to all suitable subordinate items.

Format: <u>BLINK</u>

The COLUMN Clause

The COLUMN clause specifies the column at which the screen item starts on the screen. COL is an abbreviation for COLUMN. If "+" or "-" is specified then the column number is relative to that at which the preceding screen item ends, otherwise the clause gives an absolute column number, which defaults to 1 if no number is given. If a position is specified which is off the screen, wraparound occurs.

Format: <u>COL</u>UMN <NUMBER IS <+ | -> identifier | integer>

The CONTROL Clause

The CONTROL clause allows attributes associated with a screen section item to be defined at run time. Options which may be used with CONTROL are shown in table 11-1.
If the clause is used at a group level it applies to all suitable subordinate items.

Format: <u>CONTROL</u> is identifier

The ERASE Clause

The ERASE clause clears part of the line or the screen starting at the cursor position. When ERASE EOL is specified, blanking occurs from the start of the screen data element to the end of the line. When ERASE EOS is specified, blanking occurs from the start of the screen data element to the end of the screen. If neither EOS or EOL are specified, only the screen data element is cleared. The ERASE clause can be specified only for elementary items. The clause is ignored in an ACCEPT.

Format: <u>ERASE</u> <u>EOL</u> | <u>EOS</u>

The FOREGROUND-COLOR Clause

The FOREGROUND-COLOR clause specifies the foreground color of the screen item. If the clause is used at a group level it applies to all suitable subordinate items. The color is specified as an integer. The colors and corresponding values are:

0	black
1	blue
2	green
3	cyan
4	red
5	magenta
6	brown or yellow
7	white

The default color is white.

Format: FOREGROUND-COLOR IS integer | identifier

The FULL Clause

The FULL clause specifies that the operator must either leave the item completely empty or fill it entirely with data. If the clause is used at a group level it applies to all suitable subordinate items. The FULL clause is not effective if a function key is used to terminate the ACCEPT.

Format: FULL

The GRID Clause

The GRID clause causes each character of the screen item to have a vertical line on its left-hand side when the item appears on the screen. Each line is within the character position. If the clause is used at a group level it applies to all suitable subordinate items. If this clause is used on a system which does not support characters with vertical left-hand lines it has no effect.

Format: GRID

ADIS

The HIGHLIGHT Clause

The HIGHLIGHT Clause causes the screen item to appear in high intensity mode when it appears on the screen. If the clause is used at a group level it applies to all suitable subordinate items.

Format: HIGHLIGHT

The JUSTIFIED Clause

The JUSTIFIED Clause specifies non-standard positioning of data within a screen item when data is either moved to it or entered into it.

Format: JUSTIFIED RIGHT

The LEFTLINE Clause

The LEFTLINE Clause causes the leftmost character of the screen item to have a vertical line on its left-hand side when the item appears on the screen. Each line is within the character position. If the clause is used at a group level it applies to all suitable subordinate items. On a system which does not support characters with vertical left-hand lines this clause has no effect.

Format: LEFTLINE

The LINE Clause

The LINE Clause specifies the line at which the screen item starts on the screen. If "+" or "-" is specified then the line number is relative to that at which the preceding screen item ends, otherwise the clause gives an absolute line number, which defaults to 1 if no number is given. If a position is specified which is off the screen, the ACCEPT or DISPLAY is truncated.

Format: LINE <NUMBER IS <+ | -> identifier | integer>

The LOWLIGHT Clause

The LOWLIGHT Clause specifies that the field is to appear on the screen with the lowest intensity. LOWLIGHT may be specified only for an elementary screen description entry.

Format: <u>LOWLIGHT</u>

The OCCURS Clause

The OCCURS Clause eliminates the need for separate entries for repeated screen items and supplies information required for the application of subscripts or indices. If OCCURS applies to the screen item, then a receiving item must have the same number of OCCURS; a sending item must have either no OCCURS at all, or the same number of OCCURS, and the DEPENDING phrase must not be used.

Format: <u>OCCURS</u> integer TIMES

The OVERLINE Clause

The OVERLINE Clause causes every character of the screen item to have a horizontal line above it when the item appears on the screen. The line is within the character position. If the clause is used at a group level it applies to all suitable subordinate items. This clause has no effect on a system which does not support overlining.

Format: <u>OVERLINE</u>

The PICTURE Clause

The PICTURE Clause describes the length, general characteristics and editing requirements of a screen item. The FROM, TO and USING phrases identify the source of data for display and the destination of data accepted; USING is equivalent to the TO and FROM phrases both specifying the same identifier. The PICTURE clause is allowed only with elementary items.

Format: PICTURE IS character-string
<u>FROM</u> identifier | literal>
<u>TO</u> identifier>
<u>USING</u> identifier>

The PROMPT Clause

The PROMPT Clause causes the empty character positions in the screen item to be marked on the screen during an ACCEPT operation while the system is ready to accept operator-keyed data into that item. If the clause is used at a group level it applies to all suitable subordinate items.

Format: <u>PROMPT</u> <<u>CHARACTER</u> IS identifier | literal>

The identifier or literal must be a single character.

The PROTECT Clause

The PROTECT Clause specifies that input to an ACCEPT item is to be prevented. It can only be used for an elementary screen description entry.

Format: <u>PROTECT</u>

The REQUIRED Clause

The REQUIRED Clause specifies that the operator must not leave the screen item empty. If the clause is used at a group level it applies to all suitable subordinate items.

Format: <u>REQUIRED</u>

The REVERSE-VIDEO Clause

The REVERSE-VIDEO Clause causes the screen item to be displayed in reverse-video. If the clause is used at a group level it applies to all suitable subordinate items.

Format: <u>REVERSE-VIDEO</u>

The SECURE Clause

The SECURE Clause prevents operator-keyed data from appearing on the screen. SECURE and NO-ECHO are equivalent. For input fields, only spaces and the cursor appear in the screen item; for update fields, the original contents of the field will be displayed but will not be altered. If the clause is used at a group level it applies to all suitable subordinate items.

Format: <u>SECURE</u> | <u>NO-ECHO</u>

The SIGN Clause

The SIGN Clause specifies the position and representation of the operational sign. This clause is allowed only with input, output and update fields whose pictures contain the character 'S'. It is recommended that the SEPARATE option be used when the SIGN clause is used in a screen description; if SEPARATE is not used, a SIGN denoted by 'S' in a PICTURE clause appears as an overpunch (which changes the character shown). SIGN is allowed only with elementary items.

Format: <u>SIGN</u> IS <u>LEADING</u> | <u>TRAILING</u> <<u>SEPARATE</u>>

The SIZE Clause

The SIZE Clause specifies the current size of the screen item. It may only be used with elementary screen items. The identifier must be an unsigned numeric integer and must not be subject to an OCCURS clause.

Format: <u>SIZE</u> IS identifier | integer

The UNDERLINE Clause

The UNDERLINE Clause causes the screen item to be underlined when it appears on the screen. This clause has no effect if the system does not support underline. If the clause is used at a group level it applies to all suitable subordinate items.

Format: <u>UNDERLINE</u>

The VALUE Clause

The VALUE Clause specifies literal information for display on the screen. This clause is allowed only with elementary items that have no PICTURE clause. The literal must be non numeric.

Format: <u>VALUE</u> IS literal

The ZERO-FILL Clause

The ZERO-FILL Clause causes trailing prompt characters to be replaced by zeros instead of spaces. The clause is allowed only with input and update fields that are alphabetic or alphanumeric.

Format: <u>ZERO-FILL</u>

Screen Section ACCEPT and DISPLAY Statements

ACCEPT and DISPLAY operations involving Screen Section items are treated like any other ACCEPT or DISPLAY operation, but with one important difference. Consider the following code:

```
working-storage section.
01 item-a              pic 9(5).
01 item-b              pic 9(10).
01 item-c              pic x(10).

screen section.
01 demo-screen.
     03 blank screen.
     03 line 1 column 1 pic z(4)9 from item-a.
     03 line 3 column 1 pic 9(10) to item-b.
     03 line 5 column 1 pic x(10) using item-c.
```

When this code is compiled, the compiler sets up a work area for each Screen Section 01 level item (record). Therefore, in this example, a work area is set up for demo-screen large enough to hold the data for the three fields.

When the statement

```
display demo-screen
```

is executed, the contents of item-a and item-c are moved from Working-Storage into the work area, and then the data in the work area for these two fields is displayed on the screen.

When the statement

```
accept demo-screen
```

is executed, data is accepted into the work area for Item-B and Item-C and then the data for these two fields is moved from the work area into the Working-Storage.

It is important to note that moves from the Data Division to the work area occur only on execution of a DISPLAY statement, and moves from the work area to the Data Division occur only during execution of an ACCEPT statement. Therefore, if two ACCEPT statements are executed one after another with no intervening DISPLAY statement, the initial contents of the fields at the start of the second accept are that which was put into the work area during the previous accept not the current contents of the Data Division items.

Another implication of this is that a field should not be defined as numeric-edited in both the Data Division section and the Screen Section. This results in numeric-edited to numeric-edited moves being generated by the compiler to move the Data Division item into the work area and back again. The action of such moves is undefined and has unpredictable results. This is the case even if both the Data Division item and the Screen Section item have the same picture.

Hence, if the following lines are coded in your program:

ADIS

```
working-storage section.
01 ws-item                    pic zz9.99 value 1.23

screen section.
01 demo-screen.
     03 pic zz9.99 using ws-item.

procedure division.
     display demo-screen.
```

the result of the DISPLAY is undefined. The items used in the
Data Division as source or target for Screen Section ACCEPT or
DISPLAY statements should always be non-edited fields.

Keyboard Handling Via ADIS

This section describes:

- Types of keys on the keyboard

- CRT STATUS clause

- Termination

- User function keys

- ADIS keys

- Defining in both the user and ADIS key list

- Data key handling

- ADIS-compatible GET SINGLE CHARACTER call

Function Key Handling

This section describes how to use function keys in this COBOL
system. It only describes the portable method that will work on all
environments. There is another method, using the x"B0" routine,

which is not described here as it is machine dependent. If you are using this routine, refer to *Conflict With the x"B0" COBOL System Library Routine* later in this section for details of how this may cause problems with certain configurations.

Types of Keys on the Keyboard

In general, the keys on the keyboard can be split into two groups - data keys and function keys.

Data Keys

The data keys are those that generate characters that are in the extended ASCII character set, that is, those with ASCII codes in the range 32 to 255. During an ACCEPT operation, pressing one of these keys will simply place the character into the field. However, it is possible to disable a key completely or make it terminate the accept operation (similar to the action of a function key). This is covered later in this section.

There is a complication in that the ASCII codes in the range 0 to 31 can be considered as either data keys or function keys. For most purposes, they are treated as function keys and are disabled as data keys.

Function Keys

The most general definition of a function key is any key you would not find on a typewriter keyboard. This definition includes explicit function keys on the keyboard (usually labeled **F1**, **F2**, etc.) and such keys as **Escape**, the **cursor** keys, **tab**, **rubout**, etc. The return or enter key **Enter** is also treated as a function key, but with special considerations, described later.

In your COBOL system, these keys are divided into two groups - the ADIS keys and the User function keys.

ADIS Keys

This is the term given to those keys that are used by the Accept/
Display module (ADIS) during the execution of an ACCEPT
statement. This includes the **cursor** keys, **tab**, **backspace**, **delete**
and **return**.

Normally, these keys will operate as defined during an ACCEPT.
For example, the **cursor-left** key will move the cursor to the left,
backspace will erase the previous character, and so on. With the
exception of the **return** key, they will not normally terminate the
ACCEPT. However, you can make these keys terminate the
ACCEPT if required. This is described later in this section.

User Function Keys

These keys are so called because the programmer decides what
they will be used for when the application is written. There is no
predefined action assigned to these keys. The user function keys
generally include the keys labeled **F1**, **F2**, etc. and the **Escape** key
as well as any other special keys that are on the keyboard.

The CRT STATUS Clause

If you decide that you want your application to use function keys,
it is highly likely that you will want to be able to determine exactly which key has been pressed. To do this you need to include
the CRT STATUS clause in the Special-Names paragraph of your
program. For example:

```
special-names.
    crt status is key-status.
```

where key-status is a three-byte data item that should be defined
in the Working-Storage section of your program. It has the following definition:

```
01 key-status.
    03 key-type          pic x.
    03 key-code-1        pic 9(2) comp-x.
    03 key-code-2        pic 9(2) comp-x.
```

Whenever an ACCEPT statement is executed, *key-status* will be set to indicate how the ACCEPT was terminated. The exact usage of the individual fields in *key-status* is described later. However, in general they have the following uses:

key-type   Indicates how the ACCEPT was terminated. The values returned are as follows :

> "0" - Normal termination of the ACCEPT
> "1" - Termination by a USER function key
> "2" - Termination by an ADIS key
> "3" - Termination by an 8 bit data key
> "4" - Termination by a 16 bit data key
> "9" - Error

These different values are described fully later in this section.

key-code-1   Indicates the number of the key that terminated the ACCEPT. The exact meaning of this number depends on the value returned in key-type.

key-code-2   If key-type and key-code-1 are zero, key-code-2 contains the raw keyboard code for the key that terminated the ACCEPT operation. Where a sequence of keystrokes rather than a single key has been configured to perform a single function, only the code for the first keystroke is returned.

If key-type is 4, key-code-2 will contain the second byte of the character which caused the ACCEPT to terminate.

Otherwise, the contents of key-code-2 are undefined.

Normal Termination of an ACCEPT

There are two cases of normal termination of an ACCEPT. They both return a value of "0" in *key-type*:

■ The most common way of terminating an ACCEPT is by pressing the return key. This will return a value of 48 (the ASCII code for "0") in *key-code-1*.

■ It is possible to configure ADIS so that an auto-skip in the last field on the screen will terminate the ACCEPT (use ADISCF to do this). This is also classed as a normal termination, but it returns a value of 1 in *key-code-1*.

Example

```
accept data-item at 0101
if key-type = "0"
    if key-code-1 = 48
        display "terminated by return key"
    else
        display "terminated by auto-skip last field"
    end-if
end-if.
```

Using the User Function Keys

There are up to 128 user function keys. Some come already configured, but you can use KEYBCF to configure the keys as needed. The defaults supplied with your COBOL system differ on different operating environments, but the following keys are standard:

PC Keystrokes	User Function Key Number
Escape	0
F1	1
F2	2
F3	3
F4	4
F5	5
F6	6
F7	7
F8	8
F9	9
F10	10

Your keyboard may not have these keys, but if they are there they should be configured as above. Additionally, on the IBM-PC family, the following user function keys are defined:

Shift+F1 - F10	11 - 20
Ctrl+F1 - F10	21 - 30
Alt+F1 - F10	31 - 40
Alt+1 - 9	41 - 49
Alt+0	50
Alt+-	51
Alt+=	52
PgUp	53
PgDn	54
Ctrl+PgUp	55
Ctrl+PgDn	56
Alt+A - Z	65 - 90

The following are available only on the extended PC keyboard.

F11	91
F12	92
Shift+F11	93
Shift+F12	94
Ctrl+F11	95
Ctrl+F12	96
Alt+F11	97
Alt+F12	98

Enabling and Disabling the User Function Keys

Before any of the user function keys can be used, they must be enabled. If a user key is enabled, it will terminate the ACCEPT operation when pressed. If the key is disabled, the key will be rejected and the bell rung.

By default, the user function keys are disabled. Micro Focus COBOL on UNIX has the user function keys enabled by default. Therefore, if you want to write programs that work in both environments, include code to enable the keys you want and disable all others.

The following call is used to selectively enable and disable the user function keys:

```
call x"af" using set-bit-pairs user-key-control
```

where:

```
01 set-bit-pairs              pic 9(2) comp-x value 1.
01 user-key-control.
     03 user-key-setting      pic 9(2) comp-x.
     03 filler                pic x value "1".
     03 first-user-key        pic 9(2) comp-x.
     03 number-of-keys        pic 9(2) comp-x.
```

The fields of *user-key-control* are used as follows:

user-key-setting	Set to 0 to disable keys or 1 to enable keys
first-user-key	The number of the first key to be enabled or disabled
number-of-keys	The number of consecutive keys to enable or disable

Function keys are enabled or disabled until explicitly changed by another call to x"AF" or until the application terminates. Calls to enable or disable function keys are additive. For example, if you call x"AF" to enable Function Key **F1** and then make a second call to enable **F10**, both keys are enabled.

Example

If you want to enable the Escape key and keys **F1** ... **F10**, but you want to ensure that all other user function keys are disabled, then the following code will do this:

```
* Enable 11 keys starting from key 0 (escape key)
      move 1 to user-key-setting
      move 0 to first-user-key
      move 11 to number-of-keys
      call x"af" using set-bit-pairs user-key-control
* Disable 117 keys starting from key 11
```

```
      move 0 to user-key-setting
      move 11 to first-user-key
      move 117 to number-of-keys
      call x"af" using set-bit-pairs user-key-control.
* Enable F1 and F10.
      move 1 to user-key-setting
* Enable F1.
      move 1 to first-user-key
      move 1 to number-of-keys
      call x"af" using set-bit-pairs user-key-control
* Enable F10
      move 10 to first-user-key
      call x"af" using set-bit-pairs user-key-control
```

Detecting the User Function Keys

If you press an enabled user function key during an ACCEPT operation, the ACCEPT will be terminated and the fields in *key-status* will be set as follows:

key-type	"1"
key-code-1	Set to the number of the user key that was pressed
key-code-2	Undefined

Example

```
accept data-item at 0101
if key-type = "1"
     evaluate key-code-1
           when 0 display "escape was pressed"
           when 1 display "f1 was pressed"
           when 10 display "f10 was pressed"
     end-evaluate
end-if.
```

The User Function Keys and Validation Clauses

Normally, if a validation clause, such as FULL or REQUIRED, is specified in an ACCEPT statement, that clause must be satisfied before you can leave the field. For example, when the statement:

```
accept data-item with required
```

is executed, you will not be allowed to terminate the ACCEPT unless something has been entered into the field.

However, if an enabled user function key is pressed during an ACCEPT, it is regarded as an "exception" and will terminate the ACCEPT even if the validation clause has not been satisfied.

Using the ADIS Keys

As noted earlier, the ADIS keys are those keys that perform functions within an ACCEPT such as cursor movement, delete character, backspace, etc. However, it is possible to make these keys terminate the ACCEPT.

First, the distinction has to be made between the keys that perform the functions and the functions themselves, because there is actually a "soft" mapping between the keys and the functions they perform. This means that the programmer can change the function that one of the ADIS keys performs.

The Functions Performed by the ADIS Keys

The functions 0 to 27 are simple functions. Those in the range 55 to 62 are complex functions which may perform different actions depending on some state. For example, those functions provided for RM compatibility have a different action depending on whether or not the UPDATE clause was specified in the ACCEPT statement.

The ADIS Keys

There are 28 ADIS keys. Each of these is "mapped" onto a function, so that when a key is pressed, it performs the function it has been mapped to. What can often be confusing is that the ADIS keys themselves are given names. This name is used to distinguish the different keys, but may not necessarily describe the function the key actually performs. The following list gives the names of the keys and how to obtain them on the IBM PC keyboard.

Key Number	Key Name	Keystroke
0	Terminate accept	None
1	Terminate program	Ctrl+K
2	Carriage return	Enter
3	Cursor left	Cursor Left
4	Cursor right	Cursor Right
5	Cursor up	Cursor Up
6	Cursor down	Cursor Down
7	Home	Home
8	Tab	Tab
9	Back tab	Back tab
10	End	End
11	Next field	None
12	Previous field	None
13	Change case	Ctrl+F
14	Erase character	Backspace
15	Retype character	Ctrl+Y
16	Insert character	Ctrl+O
17	Delete character	Del
18	Restore character	Ctrl+R
19	Clear to end of field	Ctrl+Z
20	Clear field	Ctrl+X
21	Clear to end of screen	Ctrl+End
22	Clear screen	Ctrl+Home
23	Set insert mode	Ins
24	Set replace mode	None
25	Reset field	Ctrl+A
26	Start of field	None
27	Move to Mouse position	None

The keystrokes listed are the defaults shipped with your COBOL system on the IBM-PC.

Note: The carriage return (CR) key is referred to here as the **Enter** key. On the IBM PC keyboard, the CR key is labeled. On some keyboards, there is a CR key and an **Enter** key. In this case, the ADIS key "Carriage Return" should be set up as CR and the ADIS key "Terminate Accept" should be set up as **Enter**.

Mapping the ADIS Keys to the Functions

In general, the ADIS keys are mapped onto the function of the same name. Therefore, the **cursor-left** key will move the cursor to the left, the **backspace** key will erase a character and so on. However, there are some keys that are by default mapped onto different functions:

Key	Function
Carriage Return	Terminate Accept (function 0)
Tab	Next Field (function 11)
Back Tab	Previous Field (function 12)
Set Insert Mode	Insert Toggle (function 58)

Therefore, when you press the **Enter** key on the IBM PC, it will terminate the ACCEPT and when you press the **Ins** key it will toggle between insert mode and replace mode.

At this stage, the idea of mapping keys may seem an unnecessary complication. Where it becomes really useful is in the emulation of other dialects of COBOL. For example, in Microsoft COBOL V2.2, the **Enter** key moves to the next field rather than terminating the ACCEPT. This is easy to emulate by simply changing the mapping for key 2 (Carriage Return) from 0 (Terminate Accept) to 11 (Next Field).

If a key is mapped on to a value of 255, that key will not perform any function during an ACCEPT operation.

Special Mappings

All of the standard functions described above always perform the same function, regardless of context. For example, the "Move to next field" function will always attempt to move to the next field.

However, there are some functions that behave differently depending on the context. These functions are summarized here:

Function Number	Function Name
58	Insert Toggle
59	Replace Toggle
60	Forwards Tab
61	Backwards Tab
62	Restore

For example, the "Set Insert Mode" key (key number 23) is normally mapped to function 58 (Insert Toggle). This means that repeated pressing of the Ins key toggles between Insert and Replace mode.

Changing the Mappings from a Program

You can change the key mappings from an application program using the call:

```
call x"af" using set-map-byte adis-key-mapping
```

where:

```
01 set-map-byte                    pic 9(2) comp-x value 3.
01 adis-key-mapping.
   03 adis-mapping-byte            pic 9(2) comp-x.
   03 adis-key-number             pic 9(2) comp-x.
```

adis-key-number should be set to the number of the key you wish to change. *adis-mapping-byte* should be set to the number of the function you wish the key to be mapped to.

Example

The following code will change the action of the Backspace key (key number 14) to simply move the cursor to the left (function 3), and change the tab key (key number 8) to perform the tab function (function 8).

```
* Change mapping of cursor left key
      move 14 to adis-key-number
      move 3 to adis-mapping-byte
      call x"af" using set-map-byte adis-key-mapping
* Change mapping of the tab key
      move 8 to adis-key-number
      move 8 to adis-mapping-byte
      call x"af" using set-map-byte adis-key-mapping.
```

Conflict With X"B0" COBOL System Library Routine

The x"B0" COBOL system library routine is an alternative method of defining function keys. It is only supported on the COBOL products tailored to the IBM PC family. For further details of this call, refer to the *Library Routines* chapter. However, we recommend that you use the method of detecting function keys defined in this section rather than the X"B0" routine.

In general, you can use the x"B0" routine to define function keys which will terminate an ACCEPT. However, there is one limitation. If you use x"B0", the carriage return key must be mapped on to the "Terminate Accept" function. This is the default for this product. If you change the mapping of carriage return then any key set up by the X"B0" call will not terminate the ACCEPT. Instead, it will perform the function that carriage return has been mapped onto.

Enabling/Disabling the ADIS Keys

By default, all of the ADIS keys are enabled to perform their defined functions during an ACCEPT. However, it is possible to disable the keys or make them act as function keys instead. The call to do this is as follows:

```
call x"af" using set-bit-pairs adis-key-control
```

where:

```
01 set-bit-pairs           pic 9(2) comp-x value 1.
01 adis-key-control.
   03 adis-key-setting      pic 9(2) comp-x.
   03 filler               pic x value "2".
   03 first-adis-key        pic 9(2) comp-x.
   03 number-of-adis-keys   pic 9(2) comp-x.
```

The fields of *adis-key-control* are used as follows:

adis-key-setting   Defines the action of the keys affected, as follows:

0   The keys are disabled. If the key is pressed during an ACCEPT, the key will be rejected.

1   The key will act like a function key. If pressed during an ACCEPT, it will terminate the ACCEPT (see below).

2   The key will do its normal action during an ACCEPT (this is the default value).

3   The key will do its normal action unless it causes the cursor to leave the current field. If this happens, it will act like a function key.

first-adis-key   The number of the first key to be affected.

number-of-adis-keys   The number of consecutive keys to be affected.

Detection of ADIS Keys

If an ADIS key has been set up to act as a function key, it will terminate the ACCEPT operation and key-status will be set up with the following values.

key-type   "2"

key-code-1   Set to the number of the ADIS key that was pressed. Note that this is the number of the

key not the number of the function the key
has been mapped to.

key-code-2   Undefined.

Example

The following code sets up Tab and Backtab to act as function
keys and the cursor left and cursor right keys to act as function
keys if they cause the cursor to leave the field.

```
* Set up tab (key 8) and back-tab (Key 9) to act as
* function keys
     move 1 to adis-key-setting
     move 8 to first-adis-key
     move 2 to number-of-adis-keys
     call x"af" using set-bit-pairs adis-key-control
* Set up cursor left (key 3) and cursor right (key 4)
* to act as function keys ONLY if they cause the cursor
* to leave the field.
     move 3 to adis-key-setting
     move 3 to first-adis-key
     move 2 to number-of-adis-keys
     call x"af" using set-bit-pairs adis-key-control
     accept data-item at 0101

     if key-type = "2"
       evaluate key-code-1
         when 3
            display "cursor left caused the cursor to
-             "leave the field"
         when 4
            display "cursor right caused thecursor to
-             "leave the field"
         when 8
            display "the tab key was pressed"
         when 9
            display "the back tab key was pressed"
      end-evaluate
end-if.
```

Data Key Handling

The data keys are the 256 keys in the extended ASCII character set. Normally, when you press one of these keys during an AC-CEPT, the character is simply put straight into the field. The exception to this is the keys with ASCII codes in the range 0 to 31, that is, the control keys. These are generally disabled.

Controlling the Data Keys

Just like most other keys on the keyboard, it is possible to disable data keys or make them act like function keys, that is, terminate the ACCEPT. To do this, use the following call:

```
call x"af" using set-bit-pairs data-key-control
```

where:

```
01 set-bit-pairs          pic 9(2) comp-x value 1.
01 data-key-control.
   03 data-key-setting    pic 9(2) comp-x.
   03 filler              pic x value "3".
   03 first-data-key      pic x.
   03 number-of-data-keys pic 9(2) comp-x.
```

The fields in data-key-control should be set up as follows:

data-key-setting — Defines the action of the keys affected, as follows:

0 — The key is disabled. If it is pressed, during an ACCEPT, the bell is rung and the key rejected.

1 — The key will act as a function key (see below). It will terminate the ACCEPT.

2 — (The default.) The character will simply be entered into the field.

first-data-key — The first character to be affected.

number-of-data-keys	The number of characters to be affected.

Detecting Data Keys Set Up to Act as Function Keys

If a data key has been set up to act as a function key, it will terminate the ACCEPT when pressed and *key-status* will be set up as follows:

key-type	"3"
key-code-1	Set to the ASCII code of the key that was pressed
key-code-2	Undefined

Example

```
* Set up the characters "A" to "Z" to terminate the
* ACCEPT
    move 1 to data-key-setting
    move "a" to first-data-key
    move 26 to number-of-data-keys
    call x"af" using set-bit-pairs data-key-control
    accept data-item at 0101
    if key-type = "3"
        evaluate key-code-1
          when 65
            display "a pressed"
          when 66
            display "b pressed"
          when 90
            display "z pressed"
        end-evaluate
    end-if.
```

Get Single Character Routine

This routine allows you to get a single key from the keyboard. It uses ADIS itself, so all of the function keys supported by ADIS are supported. The routine only reads the keyboard and so does not echo the key to the screen.

The format of the call is:

```
call x"af" using get-single-char-func key-status
```

where:

```
01 get-single-char-func        pic 9(2) comp-x value 26.

01 key-status.
      03 key-type              pic x.
      03 key-code.
            05 key-code-1       pic 9(2) comp-x.
            05 key-code-2       pic 9(2) comp-x.
```

The values returned in *key-status* are the same as those described previously, except that a value of "0" is never returned in *key-type* by this call. The carriage return key returns a value of "2" in *key-type* and a value of 2 in *key-code-1*.

The values returned in key-status are as follows:

key-type   key-code-1

"1"   Returns the number of the user function pressed.

"2"   Returns the number of the ADIS key pressed. Note that no mapping of keys occurs in this call. Therefore the number returned is the number of the actual key pressed.

"3"   Returns the ASCII code of the 8 bit data key pressed.

"4"   Returns the first byte of the 16 bit data key pressed. The second byte is contained in *key-code-2*. Only applicable on machines that support double-byte characters.

"9"   Error condition. Values are:

        8   Disabled character. The data key pressed is disabled.

9   Invalid keystroke. A function key has been
        pressed that is not defined in either the user
        or ADIS function key list.

Example

```
call x"af" using get-single-char-func key-status
evaluate key-type
   when "1"
*       User function key pressed. Do required
*       action depending on value in key-code-1.
   when "2"
*       ADIS function key pressed. Do required
*       action depending on value in key-code-1.
   when "3"
*       Data key pressed. Do required action
        depending on the ASCII code in key-code-1.
   when "4"
*       Double byte data key pressed. Do required
*       action depending on the 16-bit character in
*       key-code.
   when "9"
*       Invalid or disabled key. Do required action.
end-evaluate.
```

Program Sample

```
***************************************************
* This program is an example of how to write
* programs that make use of function keys.
*
* It is assumed that the Escape key is available,
* but any other function key can be selected by
* either pressing the function key or by pressing
* "/" followed by the first letter of the option.
*
* This program assumes that the Default
* Configuration has been selected using ADISCF.
***************************************************
```

```
special-names.
     cursor is cursor-position
     crt status is key-status.

data division.
working-storage section.

***************************************************
* Parameters to be used for the X"AF" calls.
***************************************************

01 set-bit-pairs                 pic 9(2) comp-x value 1.
01 get-single-character          pic 9(2) comp-x value 26.

01 enable-esc-and-f1.
     03 filler                   pic 9(2) comp-x value 1.
     03 filler                   pic x value "1".
     03 filler                   pic 9(2) comp-x value 0.
     03 filler                   pic 9(2) comp-x value 2.

01 disable-all-other-user-keys.
     03 filler                   pic 9(2) comp-x value 0.
     03 filler                   pic x value "1".
     03 filler                   pic 9(2) comp-x value 2.
     03 filler                   pic 9(2) comp-x value 126.

01 enable-slash-key.
     03 filler                   pic 9(2) comp-x value 1.
     03 filler                   pic x value "3".
     03 filler                   pic x value "/".
     03 filler                   pic 9(2) comp-x value 1.

***************************************************
* Status returned after termination of an ACCEPT.
***************************************************

01 key-status.
     03 key-type                 pic x.
     03 key-code-1               pic 9(2) comp-x.
     03 key-code-1-x             redefines key-code-1 pic x.
     03 key-code-2               pic 9(2) comp-x.
```

```
****************************************************
* Cursor-Position is returned by ADIS containing
* the psition of the cursor when the ACCEPT was
* terminated.
****************************************************

01 cursor-position.
     03 cursor-row                pic 99.
     03 cursor-column             pic 99.


****************************************************
* Work Areas used by the program.
****************************************************

01 work-areas.
     03 wa-name                   pic x(30).
     03 wa-address-line-1         pic x(40).
     03 wa-address-line-2         pic x(40).
     03 wa-address-line-3         pic x(40).
     03 wa-address-line-4         pic x(40).
     03 wa-age                    pic 999.

01 exit-flag                      pic 9(2) comp-x value 0.


****************************************************
* Screen Section.
****************************************************
screen section.

01 main-screen.
     03 blank screen.
     03 line 2 column 27
         value "typical data entry screen".
     03 line 3 column 27
         value "————————".
     03 line 5 column 1 value "name      [".
     03 pic x(30) using wa-name highlight prompt " ".
     03 value "]".
     03 line 7 column 1 value "address   [".
     03 pic x(40) using wa-address-line-1 highlight prompt " ".
     03 value "]".
     03 line 8 column 1 value "          [".
     03 pic x(40) using wa-address-line-2 highlight prompt " ".
     03 value "]".
```

```
      03 line 9 column 1 value "         [".
      03 pic x(40) using wa-address-line-3 highlight prompt " ".
      03 value "]".
      03 line 10 column 1 value "         [".
      03 pic x(40) using wa-address-line-4 highlight prompt " ".
      03 value "]".
      03 line 12 column 1 value "age      [".
      03 pic zz9 using wa-age highlight prompt " ".
      03 value "]".
      03 line 20 column 1 value
         "_____
         "_____".
      03 line 21 column 1 value "f1" highlight.
      03 value "=/help".
      03 column 75 value "esc" highlight.
      03 value "ape".

01 help-screen.
      03 blank screen.
      03 line 1 column 34 value "help screen".
      03 line + 1 column 34 value "——".
      03 line 4 value "escape" highlight.
      03 value "    leave this program.".
      03 line 6 column 1 value "f1 or /h" highlight.
      03 value "   obtains this screen.".
      03 line 8 column 1
         value "use cursor keys to move around ".
      03 value "the fields on the screen".
      03  value "enter will".
      03 line + 1 column 1 value "accept the data ".
      03  value " present new blank form to fill in.".
      03 line 24 column 25
         value "press any key to continue ...".


*****************************************************
* Procedure Division.
*****************************************************
procedure division.
entry-point section.

* First we want to ensure that the keys are enabled as we want
* them. Enable the Escape and F1 keys.
```

```
        call x"af" using set-bit-pairs
                        enable-esc-and-f1
```

* disable every other user function key.

```
        call x"af" using
            set-bit-pairs disable-all-other-user-keys
```

* set up "/" key to act as a function key and terminate
* the accept.

```
        call x"af" using set-bit-pairs
                        enable-slash-key
```

* Now ensure that the cursor position will be returned when an
* ACCEPT is terminated. Setting to row 1, column 1 will ensure
* that the cursor will be initially positioned at the start of
* the first field.

```
        move 1 to cursor-row
        move 1 to cursor-column
```

* Loop until the Escape key is pressed.

```
        perform until exit-flag = 1
                display main-screen
                accept main-screen
                evaluate key-type
                when "0"
```

* Accept terminated normally, i.e., the Enter key was pressed.
* Here, we simply blank out the work areas and restart in the
* first field.

```
                move spaces to work-areas
                move 1 to cursor-row
                move 1 to cursor-column

                when "1"
```

* A user function key has been pressed. This will either be
* Esc or F1 as all others have been disabled.

```
                if key-code-1 = 0
```

* Escape has been pressed, so we wish to leave the program.

```
                move 1 to exit-flag
            else
```

* F1 has been pressed so display the help screen.

```
                perform display-help-screen
            end-if

        when "3"
```

* A data key has terminated the Accept. It must be "/" as no
* other keys have been enabled to do this. Now get the next
* character to see if "H" or "h" has been pressed.

```
            call x"af" using
                get-single-character key-status
            if key-type = "3" and
                (key-code-1-x = "h" or
                key-code-1-x = "h")
              perform display-help-screen
            end-if

        end-evaluate
    end-perform
    stop run.

display-help-screen section.
```

* Display the help screen and then wait for a key to be
pressed.

```
    display help-screen
    call x"af" using
        get-single-character key-status.
```

Mouse Handling Via ADIS

This section descibes how to use a mouse with COBOL programs that use ADIS to handle the scree and keyboard. It shows you how to activate the mouse, and use it in the ADIS ACCEPT.

Using the Mouse

This section describes how to access the mouse for use in screen handling in this COBOL system. By default the mouse is not active so the routines below must be called to allow the mouse to be used. The mouse is only available if the relevant mouse drivers, supplied with the mouse or the operating system, are installed.

Having the mouse pointer enabled during an ADIS ACCEPT statement alows your user to alter the current input field by moving the mouse pointer over another field and pressing the leftmost button on the mouse. This will result in the text cursor being moved to the mouse pointer position.

The leftmost button on the mouse is treated as ADIS key number 27 and bhaves in the same way as all other ADIS keys. The example t the end of this section shows how the action of the leftmost button can be changed so the mouse can be used to terminate an accept operation.

Once the mouse is active (and enabled) the mouse cursor will move on the screen when the mouse is moved. This happens independently of any ADIS operations. ADIS wll take notice of the mouse only when a mouse button is pressed. However the program can determine the position of the mouse at any time using the appropriate routine described below.

Activating/Terminating Use of a Mouse

You control whether a mouse driver is in use or not as follows:

```
call x"af" using use-mouse-function
               usage-parameter
```

where:

```
01 use-mouse-function        pic 9(2) comp-x value 64.
01 usage-parameter           pic 9(2) comp-x.
```

usage-parameter should be set as follows:

0   Terminate the mouse. The mouse pointer is deleted and no further mouse action is possible.

1   Activate the mouse. This activates the mouse driver and draws the mouse pointer.

On return, use-mouse-function contains 255 if no mouse is present.

Example

The following code will activate the mouse:

```
move 1 to usage-parameter
call x"af" using use-mouse-function
          usage-parameter
```

Enabling/Disabling the Mouse

You disable or re-enable the mouse as follows:

```
call x"af" using enable-mouse-function
                 enable-parameter
```

where:

```
01 enable-mouse-function     pic 9(2) comp-x value 66.
01 enable-parameter          pic 9(2) comp-x.
```

enable-parameter should be set as follows:

0   Disable the mouse. The mouse pointer is hidden and all mouse movement and button presses are ignored until the mouse is reactivated.

ADIS

1   Re-enable the mouse. This redraws the
mouse pointer, that is, makes it visible, and
re-enables the ability to detect mouse
movement and button presses.

Example

The following code will disable the mouse:

```
move 0 to enable-parameter
call x"af" using enable-mouse-function
                 enable-parameter
```

Returning Mouse Status and Position

You get the position of the mouse pointer and the status of the
mouse driver as follows:

```
call x"af" using get-mouse-details
                 mouse-details
```

where:

```
01 get-mouse-details        pic 9(2) comp-x value 67.
01 mouse-details.
      03 mouse-x-position    pic 9(4) comp-x.
      03 mouse-y-position    pic 9(4) comp-x.
      03 mouse-status        pic 9(4) comp-x.
```

The status value returned is as defined for the *event-type* field of
the low-level mouse routines in the chapter *Library Routines (Call-by-Name)*.

Example

The following code will display the mouse pointer position:

```
call x"af" using get-mouse-details mouse-details
display "mouse-x-position is" at line 1 column 1
```

```
display mouse-x-position at line 1 column 22
display "mouse-y-position is"at line 2 column 1
display mouse-y-position at line 2 column 22
```

Example of Using a Mouse

The following code sets up the mouse to act as a function key. Pressing the left-hand mouse button will terminate the ACCEPT operation and cause the mouse coordinates to be displayed. The data items are as defined in the details of the routines above.

```
* Activate the mouse
      move 1 to usage-parameter
      call x"af" using use-mouse-function
                  usage-parameter
* Set the mouse (key 27) to act as a function key
      move 3 to adis-key-setting
      move 27 to first-adis-key
      move 2 to number-of-adis-keys
      call x"af" using set-bit-pairs
                        adis-key-control
      accept data-item at 0101
      if key-type = "2" and key-code-1 = 27
            display "the mouse terminated the accept"
            call x"af" using get-mouse-details
                            mouse-details
            display "mouse-x-position is " at line 3 column 1
            display mouse-x-position at line 3 column 22
            display "mouse-y-position is " at line 4 column 1
            display mouse-y-position at line 4 column 22
      end-if
* Terminate the mouse
      move 1 to usage-parameter
      call x"af" using use-mouse-function
                  usage-parameter
```

Chapter 12

COBOL File Handling

One of the many benefits COBOL has to offer as a language is its built-in data file handling capabilities. COBOL uses simple syntax to achieve powerful management of sequential, relative and indexed sequential files.

Overview

This chapter provides information on file handling in Personal COBOL, and relates COBOL file handling to the way files are handled by the operating system. The chapter covers the following topics:

- COBOL data file organizations

- COBOL file naming conventions

- file name extensions used in Personal COBOL

- COBOL data file assignment

- file buffering

- file usage

Operation

COBOL Data File Organizations

Personal COBOL programs can create, update and read files of four different organizations:

- sequential

- line sequential

- relative

- indexed

Sequential

Sequential files are the simplest form of COBOL file. Records are placed in the file in the order they are written, and can only be read back in the same order.

Line Sequential

Line Sequential files are a special type of sequential file. They correspond directly to text files as produced by standard editors. For example, source code files produced using the Personal COBOL Editor are Line Sequential files.

Relative

Every record in a relative file can be accessed directly without having to read through any other records. Each record is identified by a unique ordinal number both when it is written and when it is read back.

Indexed

Indexed files are the most complex form of COBOL file handled directly by the syntax of this COBOL system. Records in an indexed file are identified by a unique user-defined key when written. Each record can contain any number of user-defined keys which can be used to read the record, either directly or in key sequence.

COBOL File Naming Conventions

This COBOL system, and applications created with this system, all use the standard operating system file-name convention:

```
[device:] [[path-name\] file-name [.ext]]
```

where:

device is a system device. It can be a disk drive, the display, a printer, or an RS232 port. If you include `file-name`, `device` must be a disk drive. If you send a listing file to a device, that device cannot be a disk drive. The COBOL system recognizes the following symbolic device names:

A, B, etc.	Disk drive
CON	Console keyboard or screen
AUX COM1	Alternative names for first asynchronous communications adapter port
COM2	Second asynchronous communications port
LPT1 LPT LST PRN	Alternative names for first parallel printer

File Handling

	LPT2 LPT3	Second or third parallel printer
	ERR	Standard Error Output
	NUL	Dummy device - do not create (not available with indexed files)
path-name		is the operating system path containing or to contain the file. If you do not specify a *device* and/or *path-name*, the current drive and/or path is assumed.
file-name		is the name of the disk file. *file-name* can be a maximum of eight characters in length.
.ext		is a period (.) followed by up to three characters giving the file-name extension. You can specify an extension of spaces by putting just the period.

Filename Extensions used in Personal COBOL

The Personal COBOL System uses filename extensions to identify what a file contains. For example, the Editor assumes that files with the extension CBL contain COBOL source code. So when you write a program and save it as a file, the Editor uses the extension CBL for your source code file. If you give your file the name MYPROG the Editor adds the extension CBL, and when the Checker starts it reads the file MYPROG.CBL and compiles the source code from there.

You can use extensions other than CBL for source code files, and the system will handle them correctly provided they do not conflict with the extensions that the system uses itself as listed below. However, we recommend using the extension CBL for source code files.

The Personal COBOL System will create files which have the same base name as your program, but have a different extension. For instance, from your source file MYPROG.CBL the Checker will create MYPROG.INT and MYPROG.IDY, and possibly others. The list below describes the different file name extensions and when the Personal COBOL System may use them. We recommend that you do not use these file extensions for your data files because of the possibility of conflict.

BAK	a backup copy of source code. When the Backup-file option is selected on the Editor's Save-file menu, the Editor renames an existing CBL file to this extension when it would otherwise be overwritten by changed source.
CBL	COBOL source code written by the Editor, used for input to the Checker. Source code can be read from and written to files with different extensions if the extension is specified.
CPY	the Checker and the Editor will both find COPY files with this extension, though the default extension for COPY files written by the Editor is CBL.
IDY	an Animator information file, produced by the Checker and used by Animator.
ILS	Animator query data produced by Animator and used by Animator.
INT	intermediate code, produced by the Checker and used by Animator and by Pcobrun.
LST	a compiled source listing, produced by the Checker when the List-File option is selected on the Checker menu. This text file can contain information about your compiled program, such as a cross-references, and may be examined with the Editor or the View utility.

MSG an error message list, produced by the checker and used by the Editor.

PASTE.TXT text output from the On-line Help System for "pasting" into your source code.

spaces when a file name ends with a period, the extension is considered to be spaces. This is a valid extension for COBOL source code but is not created by default by the Editor.

SRN a screen definition form, created and used by Screens. This is not the source code that Screens can generate to include in your program.

SS a COPY file created by Screens when generating the screen section of a COBOL program skeleton.

WKS a COPY file created by Screens when generating the working-storage section of a COBOL program skeleton.

Data files defined with indexed organization are created as two separate files, the file you named in your COBOL code, and a second file with the same file base name but with the extension IDX. So the COBOL code:

```
select prog-file assign to "MYDATA.DAT"
       organization indexed.
...
open output prog-file
```

would result in two files being created: MYDATA.DAT and MYDATA.IDX. We recommend that you do not use the extension IDX for any of your files. If the extension IDX is used for an organization indexed data file, the system will be unable to create the file and will issue an illegal file-name error.

Files with the following extensions may also be found in the Personal COBOL System, but are not created by it. However, we recommend that you do not use these file extensions for your data files because of the possibility of conflict.

ASM   an assembler source code. The Personal COBOL System does not produce files with this extension, which is used in the Sample programs only.

BIN   a binary executable which can be called from a COBOL program and loaded by the Personal COBOL System. The Personal COBOL System does not produce files with this extension, which is used in the Sample programs only.

CFG   the PCOBOL.CFG configuration file can be edited to change the screen colors used by Personal COBOL. The Personal COBOL System does not produce files with this extension.

DLE   dynamic-load executable. The Personal COBOL System does not produce files with this extension.

EXE   DOS executable. The Personal COBOL System does not produce files with this extension.

HNF   On-line Help and Reference information. The Personal COBOL System does not produce files with this extension.

LBR   many components of Personal COBOL are supplied in library (LBR) files, an efficient way to store executable COBOL programs. (These are not related to the Library Routines.) The Personal COBOL System does not produce files with this extension.

TUT   tutorial text. The Personal COBOL System does not produce files with this extension.

File Handling

COBOL Data-File Assignment

All file processing information is defined within a COBOL program. You define file organization, access method, device assignment and allocation of disk space by the SELECT clause in the Input-Output Section of the Environment Division and with a File Description (FD) entry in the File Section of the Data Division.

The COBOL system offers two types of file assignment facilities: fixed and dynamic. In fixed file assignment the internal file-name is assigned to an external DOS file-name at the time you write your program. In dynamic file assignment the internal user file name is assigned to a file identifier (one that you define). An external DOS file-name can then be stored in the data area associated with this file identifier and can be changed during the run.

Fixed File Assignment

In fixed file assignment, the internal file-name is assigned to an external DOS file-name in the File-Control paragraph of your program. Note that you cannot change the external file-name without recompiling your program.

Environment Division

In the File-Control paragraph the format of the SELECT... ASSIGN TO clause is as follows:

```
select file-name
        assign to external-file-name-literal
            [, external-file-name-literal].
```

where:

file-name	is the internal user file-name and can be any COBOL word you define.
external-file-name-literal	is a file-name in the standard DOS format. It can be the name of a file on disk, optionally including a drive and/or path identifier and

file-name extension, or it can be a device-name. Standard device-names are listed in the section *COBOL File Naming Conventions* earlier in this chapter.

Examples

```
select stockfile assign to "b:warehs.buy".

select printfile assign to "prn:".

select input-file assign to "\data\prog1in".
```

The file-name you specify is then also used in the OPEN statement when the file is needed for use in the program. In Example 1 above you would specify OPEN INPUT STOCKFILE which causes the file WAREHS.BUY to be opened on drive B:.

Dynamic File Assignment

The internal file-name is assigned to a data item. You may choose to define the data name explicitly in the Data Division. If you do, the contents of the data item are used when the file is being opened to specify the file-name to the operating system. In this case, the file-name must be terminated by a space character. If you decide not to define the data item explicitly, the COBOL system supplies an implicit definition of PIC X(65). Then you must re-member to MOVE a value into the data item before using it in any OPEN statement.

Environment Division

In the File-Control paragraph, the format of the SELECT... AS-SIGN TO clause is:

```
select file-name
      assign to dynamic file-identifier
```

File Handling

where:

file-name   is the internal user file-name and can be any COBOL word you define.

file-identifier   is a COBOL data-name.

Examples

```
select stockfile assign dynamic stock-name.

select output-file assign to dynamic real-file-name.
```

Procedure Division

Before the file is opened, you must move the operating system file-name to *file-identifier* specified by the ASSIGN phrase of the SELECT clause:

Example

```
move "b:warehs.buy" to stock-name.
open input stock-file.
    •
    •
    •
close stock-file.
    •
    •
move "c:\data\warehs.sel" to stock-name.
open input stock-file.
    •
    •
close stock-file.
```

You can enter the operating system file-name either by entering the name at the keyboard through an ACCEPT statement or by storing it as variable data. In this way, different external files can be processed by one *file-identifier* during the run of the program. You must move the name of the file to *file-identifier* before the OPEN statement is executed.

Once the OPEN statement has been executed, you can use the *file-identifier* data area for any purpose you require. In the above example, between the two OPEN statements you could use STOCK-NAME to store any data string you need.

File Buffering

All sequentially accessed data files written by the COBOL system are buffered. That is, records are written to a buffer (block) in memory until the block is full, at which time the block is written to disk. This method reduces the number of accesses to disk, consequently speeding up the program.

Similarly when reading records from disk, a block is read from the file into a memory buffer and the next record extracted from the buffer.

When the file is closed, any data that has not already been written to disk is written. The COBOL system then requests that the operating system close the file.

File Usage

Under the COBOL system, the memory required for open files is calculated at the buffer size + 96 bytes for the header record. The buffer size is, by default, 4096 bytes for sequential access files; otherwise it is 512 bytes. If the G run-time switch is turned on, then all files use 512-byte buffers. Screen input and output and direct output to a printer are excluded from this calculation.

However, you should note that:

- Each open indexed sequential file counts as two files.

- Whenever the COBOL system executes a GO TO, PERFORM or CALL statement that causes an overlay to be loaded, another file is used while the overlay or subprogram is being loaded.

File Handling

- When you are using Animator, a minimum of two extra files are used. If the RAM starts to fill up, then the COBOL system will open any number of files for areas that are temporarily swapped out of RAM.

- On DOS, the maximum number of open files is given by FILES in your CONFIG.SYS file. Note that five of these files are reserved for DOS.

- If a power outage or a system reboot occurs while an application is executing, the integrity of the file cannot be guaranteed.

Duplicate Keys

All alternate keys in indexed files can be duplicate keys.

To allow duplicate keys, you specify the phrase "WITH DUPLI-CATES" in the ALTERNATE RECORD section of the SELECT statement.

When you use duplicate keys, there are two limitations of which you should be aware:

- A maximum number of 65535 duplicate keys is allowed for every individual key in a standard file. Each time you specify a duplicate key, an increment of one is added to its occurrence number. However, because the occurrence number is used to ensure that duplicate key records are read in the order in which they were created, and any occurrence number whose record you have deleted cannot be reused, the duplicate key maximum may be reached.

- Primary keys should not allow duplicates. This is because, with duplicates allowed, it is not possible to uniquely identify records in a file.

Chapter 13

Compiler Directives

This chapter lists and describes the directives you can use to control the Personal COBOL compiler. Directives are used to specify options that affect the way the compiler behaves, what output it produces and how the compiled code behaves when run. All directives have a default built into the compiler; however, you can create your own defaults as described in *Setting Directives* below.

Setting Directives

Directives, which are specified prior to compiling, can be entered in a number of ways, and the order in which various options are passed to the compiler determines their precedence. At startup the compiler processes directives in the following sequence:

1. Directives are read from the file COBOL.DIR (if present), which is automatically processed every time you use the compiler.
2. Directives from the check menu **F9/F10=directives** option.
3. Directives from $SET statements in the program source code.

The setting of directives in COBOL.DIR, the check menu **F9/F10=directives** option, or $SET statements override their default settings. Additionally, later settings override earlier ones. So for example, specifying NOLIST in a $SET statement will override LIST() in COBOL.DIR.

The COBOL.DIR Directives File

COBOL.DIR is a directives file which is processed automatically by the compiler. Consequently, directives contained in COBOL.DIR override the defaults built into the compiler. The directives file is a standard ASCII text file containing any number of lines. Each line may contain one or more directives or comments. Directives in the directives file must be separated by a space and cannot be broken across two lines. Comment lines are indicated by an ampersand character (&) in column 1.

The compiler will look for a COBOL.DIR file first in the current directory. If it finds one there it will use it. Otherwise it will look in the COBOL system directories indicated by the environment variable COBDIR.

If the compiler rejects directives in the COBOL.DIR file compilation will continue. Therefore, if you create a COBOL.DIR file you should do a trial compilation and watch for "Rejected" messages at the beginning when the directives are being processed. If any occur, correct the COBOL.DIR file and retry until no errors are reported.

The $SET Statement

Many directives can be specified in the program source code in $SET statements. You specify the $SET statement in the following format with the $ character in column 7.

```
$set <directive> . . .
```

where <directive> is one or more of the compiler directives.

If more than one directive is specified, then they must be separated by spaces. A $SET statement cannot be continued onto a new line, but it can be followed by additional $SET statements.

An "initial" $SET statement is one that is not preceded in the source file by any other source statements except other $SET statements. When a directive is specified on a $SET other than an initial $SET, it affects compilation from the point the $SET is encountered onwards. The List of Directives below indicates which directives are allowed on $SET statements, distinguishing those only allowed on initial $SET statements.

List of Directives

COPYLIST	List COPY files
CURRENCY-SIGN	PIC currency sign
CURRENT-DATE	MMDDYY OR DDMMYY
DATE	Date for listings
ERRLIST	Print messages only
FORM	Page length
LIST	File for listing
LW	Page width
MF	Enable MF extensions
NESTCALL	Allow nested progs
OPTIONAL-FILE	All files optional
OVERRIDE	Change reserved word
REF	Addresses in listings
REMOVE	De-reserve a word
RESEQ	Generate line numbers
SEQCHK	Check line numbers
TIME	Put time on listings
WARNING	Message output level
XREF	Produce cross-ref

Descriptions of Directives

COPYLIST

Makes the compiler list the contents of files named in COPY statements.

Syntax:

Parameters:

integer   Must be between 0 and 99. The segment-
                       number

Default: COPYLIST

$SET: Any

The segment-number is the number of a COBOL segment. It must
be in the range 50 through 99. If it is not specified, the contents of
all COPY-files are listed. If it is specified, the contents of all COPY-
files in the first three divisions (that is, the Identification, Environment and Data Divisions), the root, and the given segment are
listed. An integer of 0 refers to the first three divisions and all root
segments.

NOCOPYLIST prevents the listing of the contents of any COPY-
files. If a segment-number is specified with NOCOPYLIST, only
COPY-files in that segment are listed. For example:

COPYLIST"53"   List all COPY-files in the first three divisions,
                      the root segment, and segment 53.

NO COPYLIST"53"   List only COPY-files that are in segment 53.

Whatever the state of this directive, the name of any COPY-file
open when a page heading is output is given in that heading.

CURRENCY-SIGN

Specifies the currency sign to be recognized in the PICTURE
clause.

Syntax:

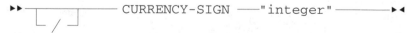

Parameters:

integer   ASCII code of the character, in decimal.

Default: CURRENCY-SIGN "36" (that is, "$")

$SET: Initial

You cannot specify a symbol which is also a valid PICTURE clause symbol.

CURRENT-DATE

Specifies the format of the date stored in the CURRENT-DATE special register.

Syntax:

```
>>──┬───┬── CURRENT-DATE ──"date-format"──────><
    └─/─┘
```

Parameters:

date-format Either DDMMYY or YYMMDD.

Default: CURRENT-DATE "MMDDYY"

$SET: Any

The DDMMYY parameter causes CURRENT-DATE to be stored in European format. The parameter can be specified in either upper-case or lower-case.

DATE

Puts the date in the DATE-COMPILED paragraph and at the top of each page of the listing.

Syntax:

```
>>──┬───┬──┬──────── DATE ──"string"──┬───><
    └─/─┘  │         DATE ─────────────┘
           └─NO─┘
```

Compiler Directives

Parameters:

string   An alphanumeric literal.

Default: DATE

$SET: No

Your personal computer keeps the date and time in the operating system. They are automatically inserted when you specify DATE. You can, however, enter the date yourself as the parameter. With NODATE, the paragraph is left unaltered.

With DATE, the system date or the string you enter appears at the top of each page of the listing. With NODATE, spaces are used instead.

ERRLIST

Specifies that the listing is to contain no source lines except those that have errors or flags.

Syntax:

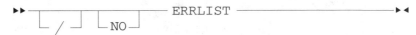

Parameters: None

Default: NOERRLIST

$SET: No

FORM

Specifies the number of lines on each page of the listing.

Syntax:

Parameters:

integer   Must be greater than 3.

Default: FORM"60"

$SET: Any

With FORM, a form-feed character is always produced at the head
of the listing file. With NOFORM, no form-feed characters or page
headings are produced anywhere in the listing.

LIST

Specifies the destination of the source listing file.

Syntax:

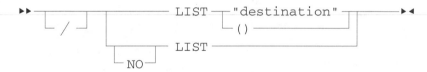

Parameters:

destination   A full file specification or a device-name.

Default: LIST

$SET: Any

If you specify an existing file, it is overwritten. When NOLIST is
specified, no source listing is produced. If you specify LIST with
no destination, the source listing is sent to the screen.

The device-name can be any suitable device, such as CON: for
the screen. LIST and NOLIST with no parameter may be used in
$SET statements within a program to list selected parts of the
program. The destination of the listing cannot be changed in this
way.

LIST() causes the source listing to be put in the file source-
filename.LST, where source-filename is the root of the name of the

program being compiled. Note that with this parameter you must use parentheses not quotes.

If you want to list the source to a file for every compilation you do, place the LIST() directive in the COBOL.DIR file. This will override the default LIST.

Alternatively, if you already have a LIST directive in your COBOL.DIR, making every listing go to the screen, you can override it by using LIST() on the command line.

LW

Sets the width of the listing.

Syntax:

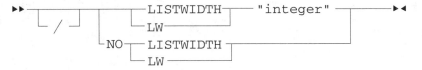

Parameters:

integer   Width in characters. It must be between 72 and 132.

Default: LISTWIDTH"72"

$SET: Any

LW"132" causes additional information to be displayed for each line listed. This includes the first eight characters of the current copy file name (spaces for the main file) together with the number of the line relative to the start of that file.

MF

Facilitates forward compatibility with Micro Focus products by selectively enabling Micro Focus-specific reserved words and changing the behavior of certain features to be compatible with particular versions.

Syntax:

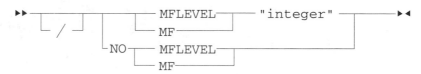

Parameters:

integer   The level of Micro Focus COBOL to be compatible with.

Default: MF"7"

$SET: Initial

The possible values of the parameter are:

7   COBOL/2 v2.5
        COBOL/2 Workbench v2.5
        Personal COBOL 2.0

If you specify MF without the parameter, all Micro Focus specific reserved words are treated as reserved words. It is equivalent to specifying MF"7". If you specify NOMF, none of the Micro Focus reserved words are treated as reserved words.

NESTCALL

Enables compilation of nested programs.

Syntax:

Parameters: None

Default: NONESTCALL

Compiler Directives

$SET: Initial

OPTIONAL-FILE

Makes the compiler treat all files opened for I-O or EXTEND as optional.

Syntax:

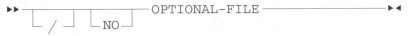

Parameters: None

Default: OPTIONAL-FILE

$SET: Initial

Under ANSI'85 Standard COBOL, a file is treated as optional only if it has the OPTIONAL phrase in its SELECT statement. For compatibility with the ANSI'85 Standard you must specify the NO OPTIONAL-FILE directive.

OVERRIDE

Replaces a reserved word by a new one.

Syntax:

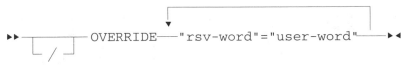

Parameters:

rsv-word	Existing reserved-word.
user-word	Any COBOL word not the same as an existing reserved word.

Default: No change of reserved words takes place.

$SET: Initial

This directive equates an existing reserved-word to the specified user-defined-word, so that, in the program, user-defined-word will be treated as a reserved word, and reserved-word will be treated as a user-defined word.

The equals sign must be surrounded by spaces. If the parameters are repeated they must be separated by spaces.

REF

Makes the compiler include in the source listing the intermediate code address of each data item or Procedure Division statement; and in the object code listing, the address of each Procedure Division statement.

Syntax:

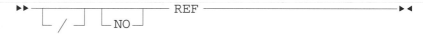

Parameters: None

Default: NOREF

$SET: Any

The address is 4 digits long and appears on the right-hand side.

This directive needs a line width setting of at least 90 (Specify the directive LW"90").

This directive can be useful in determining the locations reported in run-time error messages.

This directive can be enabled by the Personal COBOL check menu **F7=ref** switch. Press the **F7** key until the word REF appears on the information line. This automatically also enables LW(90).

Compiler Directives

REMOVE

Removes words from the reserved word list, so that they
can be used as user-defined words.

Syntax:

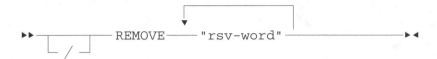

Parameters:

rsv-word   A reserved word.

Default: No reserved words are removed.

$SET: Initial

RESEQ

Makes the compiler produce line numbers.

Syntax:

Parameters: None

Default: RESEQ

$SET: Initial

These are COBOL line sequence numbers, starting at 1 and
increasing in increments of 1.

SEQCHK

Makes the compiler check the sequence numbers in columns 1 through 6 and identify source lines that are out of sequence.

Syntax:

```
►►─────┬───┬───┬─────┬──SEQCHK────────────────►◄
       └─/─┘   └─NO─┘
```

Parameters:	None
Default:	NOSEQCHK
$SET:	Any

TIME

Puts the time at the top of each page of the listing.

Syntax:

```
►►─────┬───┬───┬─────┬──TIME──────────────────►◄
       └─/─┘   └─NO─┘
```

Parameters:	None
Default:	TIME
$SET:	No

You can use this directive only with the DATE directive.

WARNING

Specifies the lowest severity level of errors to report.

Syntax:

```
►►─────┬───┬───┬──────────WARNING──"integer"──┬──►◄
       └─/─┘   └─ NO ── WARNING──────────────┘
```

Parameters:

integer   1, 2, or 3.

Default: WARNING "1"

$SET: Any

The possible values of the parameter are:

1 only those of level U, S, or E.

2 only those of level U, S, E, or W.

3 all - that is, levels U, S, E, W, and I.

With NOWARNING only those of level U or S are reported.

XREF

Makes the compiler produce a cross-reference listing.

Syntax:

Parameters: None

Default: NOXREF

$SET: No

The listing shows all data items and associated sequence numbers in alphabetical order. The sequence number shows the line where a data item is defined and is marked with a #. Further sequence numbers show where the item is used. The listing also shows what kind of data item it is, and its length in bytes if it is a group item. The listing continues with a similar description of the procedure names.

To produce the cross reference listing the compiler needs extra work space on the disk. The space needed depends on the number of data items and procedure-names and the number of times they are referenced.

Specifying XREF sets RESEQ.

This directive can be enabled by the Personal COBOL check menu **F7=ref** switch. Press the **F7** key until the word XREF appears on the information line.

Compiler Directives

Chapter 14

IBM Display Attributes

This chapter describes the attributes used when displaying data on the screen of an IBM PC.

Display Attributes

Your personal computer can display text on the screen in many ways. On a monochrome (two-color) display the text can be displayed at different intensities, underlined, in reverse video or blinking. On a color display, the text can be displayed in different colors on a colored background, and with text blinking.

Each text character displayed on the screen has an associated byte of information. This is the attribute. This attribute byte controls the way the character is displayed. The following sections describe the attribute bytes for monochrome and color displays.

You can change the value of the attribute byte and, therefore, change the way characters are displayed on the screen by using the Screen attribute and the User attribute.

The Screen attribute allows you to specify an attribute associated with each character position on the screen. You can define areas of the screen as having different attributes. Whenever a character is displayed on the screen, it has the attribute associated with that position on the screen.

The User attribute is associated with the whole screen. All of the characters that are displayed have the same attribute.

The User attribute overrides any Screen attributes that you may have already defined. Therefore, any text that is displayed while

the User attribute is enabled takes the User attribute rather than
any Screen attributes that are already defined. To use this feature,
a program must specifically enable the User attribute, and it must
also change the setting if anything other than the normal display
is required.

Display Attributes on a Monochrome Display

The following diagram shows the structure of the attribute byte
for a personal computer with a monochrome display. The effects
of setting (making equal to 1) and unsetting (making equal to 0)
these bits in the attribute byte are shown. You can set these attributes using COBOL system library routines described in the
section *Library Routines*.

Bit	Attribute
7	Blink
6-4	Turns off display or sets reverse video
3	Intensity
2-0	Normal or underline select

For example:

When bit 7 is set to 1, blinking is on.
When bit 3 is set to 1, text is displayed at high intensity.

Other bit combinations are:

	bits 6, 5, 4 all set	bits 6, 5, 4 all unset	bits 6, 5, 4 other settings
bits 2, 1, 0 unset	reverse video	no display	normal display
bits 2, 1 unset bit 0 set	underlined text	underlined text	underlined text
all other settings	normal text	normal text	normal text

Note that "normal" text on a monochrome display (non-high-lighted text on black background) can be obtained by a number of different bit settings, since several bits which are used to control color are ignored by the monochrome display. However, only one combination produces this "normal" text on both monochrome and color displays:

"Normal" setting= 0 0 0 0 0 1 1 1 (Decimal=007/Hex=07)

To ensure consistent results from programs that are used on both color and monochrome displays, you should make certain that you use this setting to achieve "normal" text.

Display Attributes on a Color Display

The following diagram shows the structure of the attribute byte for a personal computer with a color display. The effects of setting (making equal to 1) and unsetting (making equal to 0) these bits are shown. You can set these attributes using COBOL system library routines described in the chapter *Library Routines*.

Bit	Attribute
7	Blink
6-4	Background color
3	Intensity
2-0	Foreground (text) color

For example:

When bit 7 is set to 1, blinking is on.
Bits 6, 5, 4 control the background color as follows:

000	black
001	blue
010	green
011	cyan
100	red
101	magenta
110	brown
111	light grey

Display Attributes *(side tab)*

When bit 3 is set to 1, the intensity of the foreground color is changed (see below).

Bits 2, 1, and 0 control the foreground (text) color as follows:

	bit 3 unset	**bit 3 set**
000	black	dark grey
001	blue	light blue
010	green	light green
011	cyan	light cyan
100	red	light red
101	magenta	light magenta
110	brown	yellow
111	light grey	white

Chapter 15

Run-Time System Error Messages

Overview

Personal COBOL includes a sophisticated run-time system which executes both user programs and Personal COBOL itself. If the run-time system encounters an error it will output an error message. This will generally occur while you are running or animating your program, but could also occur while compiling.

Most error messages produced while compiling (checking) will be for syntax errors detected by the compiler. Syntax errors are documented in the On-line Reference, not in this manual. Syntax errors are displayed as an error number and by a line of asterisks that ends where the compiler detected the error, followed by a line of text briefly outlining the cause. Please refer to Chapter 5, *Checker (Compiling)* for instructions on how to reach the On-line Reference for syntax error information.

This chapter lists the text and severity of each run-time error, explains the error or problem that causes the message, and gives advice on how to prevent it. Some errors are environment dependent, so will not be issued by the Personal COBOL System.

There are two types of run-time errors:

Fatal   A message is sent to the screen and the
                        program terminates immediately.

Recoverable   The error is reported to the program. You can
                        trap these errors in your program, but often

they are the result of an error in your program's logic. If the program does not trap the error a message is sent to the screen and the program terminates immediately.

List of Run-Time Errors

RT001   Insufficient buffer space

Severity: Recoverable

Explanation: You have tried to OPEN a file directly or indirectly and, although you have not exceeded your system's file limit, something in your system is unable to allocate enough memory space for this operation.

Resolution: Although you can trap this error you must do STOP RUN as soon as it is reported.

RT002   File not open when access attempted

Severity: Recoverable

Explanation: You have tried to access a file without OPENing it first.

Resolution: OPEN the file with the open mode that you need and try the operation again. As this error implies there is an error in your program's logic you may want to terminate the run and correct your program.

RT003   Mode error

Severity: Recoverable

Explanation: You are trying to execute a device not a program.

Resolution: Open the device in the correct mode; or close any open files, do STOP RUN and correct your program.

RT004   Illegal file name

Severity: Recoverable

Explanation: A file-name contains an illegal character. This could be any character that is not part of the permitted character set or it could be the system-dependent delimiter, which on most systems is the space.

Resolution: Try the file operation again using the correct file-name.

RT005   Illegal device specification

Severity: Recoverable

Explanation: Devices to which your COBOL program can write are defined by the operating system. You have tried to write to a device that is not defined by your system.

Resolution: Try the operation again using a device name that your system recognizes.

RT006   Attempt to write to a file opened for INPUT

Severity: Recoverable

Explanation: You have tried to WRITE to a file that is open only for input.

Error Messages

Resolution: Close the file and open it with a mode such as I-O, which allows you to write to the file. As this error implies there is a mistake in your program's logic you may want to terminate the run and correct your program.

RT007   Disk space exhausted

Severity: Fatal

Explanation: The disk is full.

Resolution: This error can be trapped, but once it has been reported you must do a STOP RUN immediately to terminate your program's run. When your program has terminated, delete any files that you no longer need. Alternatively, if your operating system supports this, put a new disk in a floppy disk drive and redirect your program's file operations to this.

RT008   Attempt to input from a file opened for OUTPUT

Severity: Recoverable

Explanation: You have tried to read from a file that is open only for output.

Resolution: Close the file and open it with a mode such as I-O, which allows you to read from the file. As this error implies there is a mistake in your program's logic you may want to terminate the run and correct your program.

RT009   No room in directory

Severity: Recoverable

Explanation: The directory is full, or your program cannot find it.

Resolution: Delete any files that you no longer need. Alternatively, if your operating system supports this, put a new disk in a floppy disk drive and redirect your program's file operations to this. Alternatively, specify a different drive or directory for your file operations.

RT010   File name not supplied

Severity: Recoverable

Explanation: You have declared a file as an external file, but have not named it. This message occurs when you attempt to open that file.

Resolution: The only way you can continue at this point is if you are able to break out of your program, set up the external file name, then continue running your program. Otherwise, you should do STOP RUN, set up external file name, then run your program again.

RT012   Attempt to open a file which is already open

Severity: Recoverable

Explanation: You have tried to OPEN a file which is already OPEN and so cannot be OPENed again.

Resolution: Cancel your second attempt to OPEN the file. If the fact that the file is already OPEN is acceptable to you, continue to run your program.

RT013   File not found

Severity: Recoverable

Error Messages

Explanation: The operating system has been unable to find
                      a file which you have attempted to access in
                      your program.

Resolution: If your Operating System supports this, insert
                      the correct diskette, that is the one which
                      contains the required program, provided that
                      no files are currently OPEN on the present
                      diskette. If the error is the result of a spelling
                      mistake then ask for the correct file and
                      attempt the file operation again.

RT014   Too many files open simultaneously

Severity: Recoverable

Explanation: You have tried to exceed the maximum
                      number of files which you can have OPEN at
                      any one time. This may be a software or an
                      operating-system restraint, but you must not
                      violate it.

Resolution: CLOSE some of the OPEN files which you are
                      not currently accessing, and then try to OPEN
                      the relevant file again. You should then be
                      able to continue to run your program. De-
                      pending on your Operating System, you may
                      be able to increase the maximum number of
                      files you are allowed to have OPEN.

RT015   Too many indexed files open

Severity: Recoverable

Explanation: You have tried to exceed the maximum
                      number of ISAM files which you can have
                      OPEN at any one time. This may be a soft-
                      ware or an operating-system restraint, but
                      you must not violate it.

Resolution: CLOSE some of the OPEN ISAM files which you are not currently accessing, and then try to OPEN the relevant file again. You should then be able to continue to run your program. Note that ISAM files count as two files, one for data and one for the index.

RT016   Too many device files open

Severity: Recoverable

Explanation: You have tried to exceed the maximum number of device files which you can have OPEN at any one time. This may be a software or an operating-system restraint, but you must not violate it.

Resolution: CLOSE some of the OPEN device files which you are not currently accessing, and then try to OPEN the relevant file again. You should then be able to continue to run your program.

RT017   Record error: probably zero length

Severity: Recoverable

Explanation: You have probably tried to access a record that has had no value moved into it.

Resolution: Although this error is recoverable in the sense that it can be trapped, once it has been reported you must execute a STOP RUN statement immediately and then recode your program to ensure that the COBOL record length is not zero.

Error Messages

RT018   Read part record error: eof before eor or file open in wrong mode

Severity: Recoverable

Explanation: A part record has been found at the end of a file. Consequently your Run-Time System will treat the data file as a record and not finding a full record will report this error.

Resolution: Ensure that the record size you give when you READ from or WRITE to a file is consistent.

RT019   Rewrite error: open mode or access mode wrong

Severity: Recoverable

Explanation: You are attempting to do a REWRITE to a file that has not been opened with the correct access mode for this operation.

Resolution: CLOSE the file and reOPEN it in a mode such as the I-O mode, which allows you to do REWRITE operations on that file. As this error implies that there is a mistake in the logic of your code you may like to recode your program having first CLOSEd any OPEN files, and then execute a STOP RUN statement.

RT020   Device or resource busy

Severity: Recoverable

Explanation: You have attempted to OPEN a file that is assigned to a device or resource (for example, a line printer) that is not available at this time.

Resolution: You can trap the error status returned by OPEN and retry the OPEN at regular intervals until it succeeds.

RT021   File is a directory

Severity: Fatal

Explanation: You have tried to WRITE to a directory instead of to a file.

Resolution: You will have to recode your program so that it WRITEs to a file and not to a directory.

RT022   Illegal or impossible access mode for OPEN

Severity: Recoverable

Explanation: The mode in which you are attempting to OPEN a file violates the general rule of COBOL programming for that type of file, for example you may have OPENed a line-sequential file in the I-O mode.

Resolution: OPEN the file with a mode that is compatible with that type of file.

RT023   Illegal or impossible access mode for CLOSE

Severity: Recoverable

Explanation: The mode in which you are attempting to CLOSE a file is not possible for that type of file.

Resolution: CLOSE the file with a new access mode which is compatible with that type of file, or execute a STOP RUN statement and recode your program.

RT024   Disk input-output error

Severity: Recoverable

Explanation: This error could be given if you do a READ after a WRITE or if there is a verification failure or a parity error.

Resolution: In some circumstances this error will be fatal, but if it occurs during a READ you can trap it and then do a CLOSE on the file before executing a STOP RUN statement.

RT025   Operating system data error

Severity: Fatal

Explanation: You are trying to set up terminal characteristics for a device which is not a terminal.

Resolution: Recode your program.

RT026   Block I-O error

Severity: Fatal

Explanation: An error has occurred while you are attempting to access a disk. This could be the result of a corrupt disk.

Resolution: If you have a corrupt disk try to run your program again using your backup copy.

RT027   Device not available

Severity: Recoverable

Explanation: You are attempting to access a device which
                     is either not attached to your machine or if
                     attached is not online.

Resolution: Attach the device to your machine and ensure
                     that it is online. Repeat the file operation.

RT028   No space on device

Severity: Fatal

Explanation: You have attempted a file operation such as
                     WRITE for which there is not sufficient space
                     available on your disk.

Resolution: When your program has terminated you will
                     have to delete some of the files or directories
                     on your current logged in disk. Ensure that
                     you delete sufficient files on your disk so that
                     you have enough room to carry out successful
                     file operations.

RT029   Attempt to delete open file

Severity: Recoverable

Explanation: You have attempted to perform a DELETE FD
                     operation on an open file.

Resolution: Close the file before performing the DELETE
                     FD operation.

RT030   File system is read-only

Severity: Recoverable

Error Messages

Explanation: The file system which you are using is READ only, which effectively means that it is WRITE protected. You have tried to amend the information found within a file in some way, for example you may have tried to WRITE to a file or to DELETE information found within it. As the file system which you are using is READ only you can only READ the contents of its files, you cannot alter them in any way.

Resolution: You will have to abandon your attempt to alter the information within the file unless you can take your own personal copy of that file. You should then be able to alter the contents of your copy, but not of the original source.

RT031   Not owner of file

Severity: Recoverable

Explanation: You are attempting an operation on a file but the file's owner has not given you the necessary permission for that operation. You could for example be attempting to alter the access modes for a file, which only the file's owner can do.

Resolution: You will have to abandon your attempted file operation unless the file's owner gives you the permission necessary to do the operation you wish to carry out.

RT032   Too many indexed files, or no such process

Severity: Recoverable

Explanation: You have tried to OPEN an indexed file but the number of files that you currently have open is the system limit.

Resolution: You will have to CLOSE some of the indexed files which you are no longer accessing, and you should then be able to OPEN the file you require.

RT033   Physical I-O error

Severity: Fatal

Explanation: You have a hardware error of some type, perhaps you have failed to place a disk in the relevant drive or you may have tried to WRITE to a disk but the processor detected hardware interface has failed.

Resolution: You will have to try to correct the fault in your hardware, for example by placing a disk in the necessary drive.

RT034   Incorrect mode or file descriptor

Severity: Recoverable

Explanation: You are either trying to WRITE to a file which is open for READ purposes only, or READ a file which is open for WRITE purposes only.

Resolution: You will need to CLOSE the file and reopen using the correct access mode. As this error implies that there is a mistake in the logic of your program you may want to CLOSE any OPEN files, execute a STOP RUN statement and then recode your program to eliminate the logic error.Note:Sharable files opened INPUT (READ only) by the COBOL system will still require WRITE permission (from the operating system) to enable temporary locking to take place.

Error Messages

RT035   Attempt to access a file with incorrect permission

Severity: Recoverable

Explanation: You are attempting a file operation which you do not have sufficient permission to achieve. For example you could be trying to WRITE data to a file which has been set up with the READ attribute only.

Resolution: If you are the owner of the file you will be able to alter the attributes of the file so that you have the permission needed to effect the particular file operation you were attempting. If you are not the owner of the file you will not be able to carry out that operation successfully unless you copy the file and make the changes to the copy only. You will not be able to alter the source file.

RT036   File already exists

Severity: Recoverable

Explanation: You are attempting an inappropriate operation on an already existing file.

Resolution: As this error implies a fault in your program's logic you may like to recode your program to eliminate this mistake.

RT037   File access denied

Severity: Fatal

Explanation: Your attempt to access a file has been denied by the operating system. You may have tried to WRITE to a write-protected file or you could have attempted to READ from an OUTPUT device.

Resolution: Alter the access permission on the relevant file. Access can be READ only, if you just want to read the contents of the file without making any changes, or it can be READ and WRITE in which case you will be able to alter its contents.

RT038 Disk not compatible

Severity: Fatal

Explanation: You have tried to load a disk that is incompatible with the current version of your operating system. This could be because it was created under a previous version of the system or it could have been created under a completely different operating system. You would also receive this error if you tried to load a disk with a name that clashed with a disk that was already loaded.

Resolution: If the error is a result of a clash of names you can rename one of the disks and then you will be able to load both disks together if this is what you require.

RT039 File not compatible

Severity: Fatal

Explanation: You are trying to load a file that is not compatible with the structure of files under the current release of your software. This could be because the file was created either under a different operating system or under a previous version of your current system.

Resolution: You will need to create a new copy of the file which has the correct structure.

Error Messages

RT040 National Language Variants not set up correctly

Severity:	Fatal

Explanation: You have attempted to use the additional language variants at run-time, but the environment or side file that is required to set up the language either has not been set up correctly, or does not exist, or is invalid.

Resolution: Set up the required environment or side file before you attempt to run the program again.

RT041 Corrupt indexed file

Severity:	Recoverable

Explanation: Your Run-Time System does not recognize the control information for an indexed file and as the index has been corrupted in some way the data within the file is no longer accessible by your system. This error is recoverable in the sense that it can be trapped but should you receive it there is little you can do except to CLOSE any OPEN files and stop your program's run.

Resolution: You will have to rerun your program using the backup copy of that file.

RT042 Attempt to write on broken pipe

Severity:	Recoverable

Explanation: Your program has created a process as a result of a DD_logical filename mapping assignment (for example, the process may be a line printer spooler). The process was not created properly, or has died prematurely. This error occurs when your program attempts to write to the process.

Resolution:	You can trap the error status returned by the write operation, then open the file again.

RT043   File information missing for indexed file

Severity:	Fatal
Explanation:	You normally receive this error if the system crashed on the program's previous run, while the file was OPEN. Information was probably added to the end of the file, but the directory information was not updated and so that data cannot be accessed by your system. You can also receive this error if you copied the indexed file from one disk to another but only copied either the data part of the file or the index.
Resolution:	If the error is the result of a crash then whether you can access the necessary data or not is entirely system dependent. If however it is the result of a faulty copy you should be able to restore the missing part of the file from the .dat or .idx file.

RT047   Indexed structure overflow

Severity:	Fatal
Explanation:	There is some fault in the structure of your indexed file. You have probably tried to put another entry in the index when there is no room for it. This error could also be given if you have tried to access an old format indexed file, created perhaps using CIS COBOL.
Resolution:	If there is no room in your index for further entries you will have to reorganize your file.

Error Messages

RT065   File locked

Severity: Recoverable

Explanation: You have tried to OPEN a file which has
                      already been locked, or opened for output by
                      another user. Alternatively, you have tried to
                      lock or OPEN for output a file which another
                      user already has open.

Resolution: Your program can inform the system operator
                      (if there is one) that it is unable to access this
                      file and should wait until the other user has
                      finished using the file and closes it. You
                      should then be able to continue to run your
                      program.

RT066   Attempt to add duplicate record key to indexed file

Severity: Fatal

Explanation: You have tried to add a duplicate key for a
                      key which you have not defined as being able
                      to have duplicates.

Resolution: As this error implies that there is a fault in the
                      logic of your program you will probably
                      need to recode.

RT067   Indexed file not open

Severity: Recoverable

Explanation: You are attempting to access an indexed file
                      which you have not OPENed.

Resolution: OPEN the file in the relevant access mode and
                      then retry the unsuccessful file operation.

RT068   Record locked

Severity: Recoverable

Explanation: You have tried to access a record which is
                       currently locked by another user.

Resolution: Your program should inform the systems
                       operator (if one exists) that the record is
                       currently locked, and you should then wait
                       until the other user has released the lock on
                       that record. You should then be able to access
                       the relevant record. You should not
                       continually retry to gain access to the record
                       without operator intervention, as this could
                       result in your application hanging.

RT069   Illegal argument to ISAM module

Severity: Fatal

Explanation: This is the result of an internal system error.

Resolution: Contact Technical Support who will try to
                       help you discover the cause of your error and
                       how it can be rectified.

RT070   Too many indexed files open

Severity: Recoverable

Explanation: You are attempting to OPEN an indexed file
                       but you have already exhausted the system
                       limit which specifies how many of these files
                       can be OPENed at any one time.

Resolution: CLOSE some of the open indexed files which
                       you are not currently accessing. You should
                       then be able to OPEN the indexed file which
                       you require and to continue the program run.

Error Messages

RT071   Bad indexed file format

Severity: Fatal

Explanation: This error could be given if you are using a
                     file which has been corrupted, otherwise it is
                     the result of an internal system error.

Resolution: If the disk you are using is corrupt rerun your
                     program using your backup copy of the disk.
                     If this is not the cause of the error then you
                     should contact Technical Support who will
                     try to discover the cause of your error and
                     how it can be rectified.

RT072   End of indexed file

Severity: Fatal

Explanation: This is the result of an internal system error.

Resolution: Contact Technical Support who will try to
                     help you discover the cause of your error and
                     how it can be rectified.

RT073   No record found in indexed file

Severity: Fatal

Explanation: This is the result of an internal system error.

Resolution: Contact Technical Support who will try to
                     help you discover the cause of the error and
                     how it may be rectified.

RT074   No current record in indexed file

Severity: Fatal

Explanation: This is the result of an internal system error.

Resolution: Contact Technical Support who will try to
                     help you discover the cause of the error and
                     how it may be rectified.

RT075   Indexed data file name too long

Severity: Fatal

Explanation: The maximum number of characters that the
                     UNIX system allows a file name to have, is 14.
                     However when using ISAM, the extension
                     .IDX is added to the end of the user-defined
                     file name, and so your file name must not
                     exceed 10 characters in length, otherwise you
                     will receive this error.

Resolution: Rename the file with a shorter file name, that
                     is, one that is less than 10 characters in length.

RT076   Can't create lock file in /ISAM directory

Severity: Fatal

Explanation: For some reason your system is unable to
                     create a lock file in the ISAM directory. One
                     reason for this could be that in its previous
                     run your program terminated abnormally
                     (perhaps due to a power failure) leaving some
                     files locked. When you try to run this
                     program following its abnormal termination
                     you will receive this error.

Resolution: You will have to manually remove all of the
                     files that are still locked from the ISAM
                     directory before you can successfully run
                     your program.

Error Messages

RT077   Internal ISAM module error

Severity: Fatal

Explanation: This is the result of an internal system error.

Resolution: Contact Technical Support who will try to
                    help you discover the cause of your error and
                    how it can be rectified.

RT078   Illegal key description in indexed file

Severity: Fatal

Explanation: This is the result of an internal system error.

Resolution: Contact Technical Support who will try to
                    help you discover the cause of your error and
                    how it can be rectified.

RT081   Key already exists in indexed file

Severity: Fatal

Explanation: This is the result of an internal system error.

Resolution: Contact Technical Support who will try to
                    help you discover the cause of your error and
                    how it can be rectified.

RT100   Invalid file operation

Severity: Fatal

Explanation: You have attempted a file operation which
                    violates a general rule of COBOL in some
                    way. The most likely cause of this error is
                    that you have attempted a REWRITE on a
                    sequential file opened I-O, or on a relative file

with access mode sequential also opened I-O, without preceding it with a successful READ NEXT.

Resolution: Recode your program to ensure that the offending REWRITE statement is preceded by a READ NEXT.

RT101   Illegal operation on an indexed file

Severity: Fatal

Explanation: This is the result of an internal system error.

Resolution: Contact Technical Support who will try to help you discover the cause of your error and how it can be rectified.

RT102   Sequential file with non-integral number of records

Severity: Fatal

Explanation: This error could be given if:

- you have specified an incorrect record length for a sequential file

- the sequential file you are attempting to access is corrupt in some way

- the file which you have specified is not a sequential file.

Resolution: Recode your program so that it specifies the correct type of file, or if the error is the result of a corrupt file, attempt to run the program again using a backup copy of that file.

RT104   Null file name used in file operation

Severity: Fatal

Explanation: You have specified a variable name for a
                    filename instead of a literal, so on attempting
                    to OPEN that file only spaces are found.

Resolution: Recode your program specifying the correct
                    filename.

RT105   Memory allocation error

Severity: Fatal

Explanation: The Run-Time System is unable to allocate
                    sufficient memory space to successfully carry
                    out the attempted operation. This error
                    implies that there is no memory space left on
                    your system.

Resolution: You will have to obtain more memory in
                    which to run your program. Refer to your
                    Operating System documentation for details
                    of how you can obtain more memory, if this is
                    possible.

RT106   Dictionary error

Severity: Fatal

Explanation: This could be the result of a READ or WRITE
                    error to file or disk, but it is more likely to be
                    the result of an internal system error.

Resolution: Contact Technical Support who will try to
                    help you to discover the cause of your error
                    and how it may be rectified.

RT107   Operation not implemented on this Run-Time System

Severity: Fatal

Explanation: You are attempting to do a file operation which your Run-Time System does not support.

Resolution: You will have to recode your program so that it does not attempt such operations, or you will have to acquire a version of your system that does support this facility.

RT108   Failure to initialize data division

Severity: Fatal

Explanation: The Run-Time System cannot load your program properly because the data needed to correctly initialize the Data Divison has become corrupted.

Resolution: You should compile your program again to try to obtain good intermediate code.

RT109   Invalid checksum in Run-Time System

Severity: Recoverable

Explanation: The internal information within the Run-Time System has been altered. This error may be caused by a corrupted Run-Time System, or you may have illegally attempted to change the internal Run-Time System information.

Resolution: Contact Technical Support who will try to help you to discover the cause of the error and how it may be rectified.

Error Messages

RT116   Cannot allocate memory

Severity: Fatal

Explanation: For some reason a part of your Run-Time
                     System is unable to allocate you sufficient
                     memory to enable you to execute your code.

Resolution: You should try to reduce memory usage by
                     cancelling programs that are not in use, then
                     attempt the operation that caused this
                     message again.

RT117   Bad collating sequence

Severity: Fatal

Explanation: This is an internal system error.

Resolution: Please contact Technical Support who will try
                     to help you to discover the cause of the error
                     and how it may be rectified.

RT118   Symbol not found

Severity: Fatal

Explanation: You are unable to load your object file. You
                     could receive this error if you attempt to call a
                     program that has not been specified in the
                     COBPATH environment variable.

Resolution: Check to see that your COBPATH has been
                     set up correctly. If not, amend your
                     COBPATH to include the program being
                     called.

RT119   Symbol redefined

Severity: Fatal

Explanation: You are unable to load your object file
                   because it has an entry point with the same
                   name as a module already loaded.

Resolution: Once your program has terminated recode it
                   to remove the naming duplication. Resubmit
                   your program to your COBOL system.

RT120   Symbol string table of zero size

Severity: Fatal

Explanation: You probably have a malformed object file.

Resolution: Once the program has terminated you will
                   need to correct your object file. If this does
                   not work, contact Technical Support who will
                   try to help you to discover the specific cause
                   of the error.

RT121   Symbol is not in text section

Severity: Fatal

Explanation: You have attempted to CALL a subprogram
                   that is not an executable program.

Resolution: Check that the subprogram being CALLed is
                   an executable one. If required, correct the
                   subprogram's name in the CALLing program
                   and resubmit it to your COBOL system.
                   Alternatively, you have used the same name
                   for a called program as a previously defined
                   data-item. Once your program has termi-
                   nated, recode it to remove the naming
                   duplication. Resubmit your program to your
                   COBOL system.

Error Messages

RT122 Coblongjmp called below level of cobsetjmp

Severity: Fatal

Explanation: You may have returned control to a higher level in the CALL/PERFORM hierarchy than the level at which cobsetjmp was called. Coblongjmp must only be called from the same or from a lower level in the CALL/PERFORM hierarchy as cobsetjmp was. See your Operating Guide for details of cobsetjmp and coblongjmp.

Resolution: Check and correct the logic of your program, and then resubmit your program to your COBOL system.

RT123 Unknown relocation type

Severity: Fatal

Explanation: You are using incompatible versions of the object file and the COBOL run-time library.

Resolution: Once the program has terminated, you will need to resubmit your object file to your COBOL system with the current version of your COBOL run-time library. If this does not work, contact Technical Support who will try to help you to discover the specific cause of the error.

RT129 Attempt to access record zero of relative file

Severity: Recoverable

Explanation: The value specified in the RELATIVE KEY data-item contains the value zero.

Resolution: You should ensure that the value in the RELATIVE KEY data-item is greater than zero, then continue to run your program.

RT135   File not found

Severity: Recoverable

Explanation: The operating system has been unable to find a file which you have attempted to access in your program.

Resolution: If your operating system supports this, insert the correct diskette (that is the one which contains the required program) provided that no files are currently OPEN on the present diskette. If the error is the result of a spelling mistake then ask for the correct file and attempt the file operation again.

RT137   Open mode not supported for this file

Severity: Recoverable

Explanation: You are trying to open a device in an illegal mode; for example, opening a printer for input.

Resolution: Either the assignment of a file name is incorrrect, or your program needs to be changed.

RT138   File closed with lock - cannot be opened

Severity: Recoverable

Explanation: You are attempting to OPEN a file which you previously CLOSEd with lock, and because such an operation violates one of the general rules of COBOL programming you have been given this error.

Resolution: You will not be able to OPEN the relevant file. As this error implies that you have made a mistake in the logical structure of your program, you will probably want to CLOSE any remaining OPEN files, execute a STOP RUN statement and recode.

RT139   Record length or key data inconsistency

Severity: Recoverable

Explanation: There is a discrepancy between the length of a record, or the keys which you have specified, in your current program and its definition in the program in which it was first OPENed.

Resolution: This error implies that there is a fault in your program so you will probably need to edit your code, then resubmit it to your COBOL system before running it again.

RT141   File already open - cannot be opened

Severity: Recoverable

Explanation: You have tried to OPEN a file which is already OPEN and so cannot be OPENed again.

Resolution: Cancel your second attempt to OPEN the file and continue to run your program if the fact that the file is already OPEN is acceptable to you. However as this error implies that there is an error in the logic of your program you may wish to CLOSE any OPEN files, execute a STOP RUN statement and then edit your program to correct the fault in its logic.

RT142   File not open - cannot be closed

Severity: Recoverable

Explanation: You have tried to CLOSE a file which is not
                         OPEN which is impossible to achieve.

Resolution: You can abandon your attempt to CLOSE the
                         relevant file and continue to run your
                         program. However as this error implies that
                         there is a mistake in the logic of your program
                         you may wish to CLOSE any OPEN files,
                         execute a STOP RUN statement and then edit
                         your program to correct the fault in its logic.

RT143   Rewrite/delete in sequential mode not
              preceded by successful read

Severity: Recoverable

Explanation: You have violated one of the general rules of
                         COBOL programming as you have failed to
                         do a successful READ on a sequentially
                         accessed file prior to attempting a REWRITE
                         or DELETE on some of the information
                         contained within that file.

Resolution: If the previous READ was successful then
                         perform a READ on the relevant file before
                         you retry the unsuccessful REWRITE or
                         DELETE operation. If the previous READ
                         was also unsuccessful CLOSE the file execute
                         a STOP RUN statement and then recode your
                         program before you next run it.

RT144   Boundary Violation

Severity: Recoverable

Explanation: You have attempted to WRITE or REWRITE a
                         record which is larger than the largest, or

smaller than the smallest record allowed by
the RECORD IS VARYING clause of the
associated file.

Resolution: You should change the length of the record
you wish to write so that it fits within the
boundaries defined in the record description
entry of the associated file.

RT146   No current record defined for sequential read

Severity: Recoverable

Explanation: The file position indicator in your file is
undefined owing to a failed READ/START
or INVALID KEY condition. You have tried
to read another record in the file but as the
current record is undefined the system cannot
find the start of the record for which you
have asked.

Resolution: You should attempt a START op and continue
to do so until the file position indicator is
updated successfully.

RT147   Wrong open mode or access mode for read/start

Severity: Recoverable

Explanation: You have violated one of the general rules of
COBOL programming as you have tried to
carry out a READ or START opration on a file
which has not been OPENed for INPUT or
I-O, or is not OPEN at all.

Resolution: OPEN the file for I-O or for INPUT and you
should then be able to continue to run your
program. However, as this error implies that
there is a mistake in the logic of your program

you may want to CLOSE any files which are OPEN, execute a STOP RUN statement and then edit you code in order to rectify the fault in its logic.

RT148   Wrong open mode or access mode for write

Severity: Recoverable

Explanation: You have tried to WRITE to a file in sequential access mode that you have not OPENed for OUTPUT or EXTEND, or you have tried to WRITE to a file in random or dynamic access mode that has not been OPENed INPUT or I-O.

Resolution: CLOSE the file and re-OPEN it with the correct open mode for the file type. However, as this error implies that there is an error in the logic of your program you may want to CLOSE any files that are OPEN, execute a STOP RUN statement and then edit your code to rectify the fault in its logic.

RT149   Wrong open mode or access mode for rewrite/delete

Severity: Recoverable

Explanation: You have violated one of the general rules of COBOL syntax as you are trying to do a REWRITE or a DELETE on a file that you have not OPENed for I-O.

Resolution: CLOSE the file and reOPEN for I-O. However, as the implication of this error is that your program contains a logic error you may wish to CLOSE any OPEN files, execute a STOP RUN statement and then edit your code to eliminate the error in its logic.

Error Messages

RT150   Program abandoned at user request

Severity: Fatal

Explanation: You have interrupted the program by means
                          of a keyboard interrupt. The program is
                          closed down, and any open files closed
                          automatically by the Run-Time System.

RT151   Random read on sequential file

Severity: Recoverable

Explanation: You have violated one of the general rules of
                          COBOL syntax as you are trying to do a
                          random READ on a file which has sequential
                          organization.

Resolution: READ the file with the correct access mode.
                          As this error implies that there is an error in
                          your program's logic you may like to CLOSE
                          any files which are OPEN, execute a STOP
                          RUN statement and recode your program to
                          eliminate the mistakes in its logic.

RT152   REWRITE on file not open I-O

Severity: Recoverable

Explanation: You have violated one of the general rules of
                          COBOL syntax as you have attempted a
                          REWRITE on a file that is not OPEN I-O.

Resolution: CLOSE the relevant file and re-OPEN it for
                          I-O operations. You should then be able to
                          carry out the REWRITE operation
                          successfully. However, as this error implies
                          that there is a logic fault in the coding of your
                          program you may wish to CLOSE any OPEN
                          files, execute a STOP RUN statement and then
                          edit your code to eliminate the logic mistake.

RT153   Subscript out of range

Severity: Fatal

Explanation: A subscript which you have used in your
                        program is out of the defined range, that is, it
                        is either less than one or it is greater than the
                        number of occurrences of the item.

Resolution: You will need to recode your program.

RT154   PERFORM nested too deeply

Severity: Fatal

Explanation: This error usually results if you have used GO
                        TO to jump out of the range of a PERFORM
                        rather than to jump to an EXIT statement at
                        the end of its range.

Resolution: When your program has terminated you will
                        need to recode your program to ensure that
                        the GO TO in question jumps to an EXIT
                        statement at the end of the PERFORM's
                        range. You should then be able to
                        successfully run your program.

RT155   Illegal command line

Severity: Fatal

Explanation: The generic command line interpreter, which
                        must be present if your program is to be run
                        successfully, is not found on your system.

Resolution: Make sure that the interpreter is present to
                        enable your system to pick up the commands
                        correctly and then rerun your program.

Error Messages

RT156   Too many parentheses in a compute statement

Severity: Fatal

Explanation: You have coded a compute statement which is too complex for your system to handle successfully.

Resolution: You will have to recode your program. We strongly advise you to break the relevant compute statement into a number of simpler statements.

RT157   Not enough program memory: object file too large to load

Severity: Recoverable

Explanation: Either your program is too large for the available memory space, or the stack is full.

Resolution: If you have specified the ON OVERFLOW/ EXCEPTION clause in the relevant CALL statement the error is recoverable. Any associated imperative statement will be executed before the next instruction.

RT158   Attempt to REWRITE to a line-sequential file

Severity: Recoverable

Explanation: You have used the REWRITE statement in conjunction with a file whose organization is line sequential. The REWRITE statement cannot be used with line sequential files.

Resolution: Close the offending file before executing a STOP RUN statement to ensure that you do not lose any data from it. Recode your program to make the organization of the file to which you wish to do a REWRITE either sequential, indexed sequential, or relative.

RT159   Malformed line-sequential file

Severity: Recoverable

Explanation: A line-sequential file which you are trying to access is corrupt in some way.

Resolution: Rerun your program using the backup copy of that file.

RT160   Overlay loading error

Severity: Recoverable

Explanation: An error has occurred while trying to load the intermediate code for an independent segment. The segment is either missing or corrupted in some way.

Resolution: If the segment is missing, locate it. If you cannot find it, or if it is present and corrupt, resubmit your program to your COBOL system.

RT161   Illegal intermediate code

Severity: Fatal

Explanation: The intermediate code which is currently being processed is not valid code. You are probably trying to execute a corrupted file or one which has not been submitted to your COBOL system successfully.

Resolution: You will have to resubmit your source program to your COBOL system, to try to obtain uncorrupted intermediate code.

RT162   Arithmetic overflow or underflow

Severity: Fatal

Explanation: You have attempted to divide a data-item by zero.

Resolution: You will need to recode your program to avoid this illegal operation.

RT163   Illegal character in numeric field

Severity: Fatal

Explanation: By default the value which you enter into a numeric or numeric-edited field is checked to ensure that it is numeric. If any of the characters are found to be non- numeric then you will receive this error. The error can also be given if you have entered uninitialized numerics into numeric or numeric-edited fields, as these are automatically space filled and are thus classified as non-numeric items.

Resolution: If you unset the numeric field check switch on the run command line then the Run-Time System will not check that all values in a numeric or numeric-edited field are numeric and you should be able to run your program successfully. Alternatively, you can make sure that you initialize numeric and numeric-edited items with numeric values, which should enable your program to run successfully regardless of the setting of the numeric field check switch.

RT164   Run-time subprogram not found

Severity: Fatal

Explanation: You have attempted to call a subroutine
                   whose entry address has not been set up in
                   your Run-Time System.

Resolution: Check to see that you used a valid call
                   number in the unsuccessful subroutine call. If
                   not, amend your code to contain a call
                   number which your system recognizes. If you
                   did use a valid call number but still received
                   this error you should contact Technical
                   Support.

RT165   Version number incompatibility

Severity: Fatal

Explanation: You are using intermediate code which has
                   been produced on a version of your COBOL
                   system that is incompatible with the Run-
                   Time System you are currently using. Your
                   RTS, herefore, will not be able to execute
                   correctly any generated code you are
                   producing or have already produced from
                   this intermediate code. Alternatively, you
                   may have attempted to execute a file which is
                   not your COBOL system's intermediate or
                   generated code.

Resolution: Resubmit your source programs to your
                   COBOL system using the new version of your
                   software.

Error Messages

RT166   Recursive COBOL CALL is illegal

Severity: Fatal

Explanation: You have tried to CALL a COBOL module that is already active.

Resolution: You will need to recode your program.

RT167   Too many USING items

Severity: Fatal

Explanation: The list of items which you have supplied in a CALL....USING statement is longer than the Run-Time System can handle.

Resolution: Once your program has terminated recode it with group items rather than elementary items before rerunning it.

RT168   Stack overflow

Severity: Fatal

Explanation: You have nested a PERFORM statement or a series of CALL statements too deeply.

Resolution: Edit your program to reduce the number of levels within a nested PERFORM or CALL statement, then resubmit your source code to your COBOL system.

RT169   Illegal configuration information

Severity: Fatal

Explanation: You have attempted an operation for which your machine is not configured; the most likely cause of this is that ADIS is not configured correctly.

Resolution: Check that ADIS is configured correctly. See your Operating Guide for details of how you can reconfigure ADIS.

RT170   System program not found

Severity: Fatal

Explanation: A system program, for example ADIS or EXTFH, is not present on the current logged-in drive.

Resolution: Ensure that all the system programs are available on the logged-in drive and copy those which are not currently present using your backup system disk. Once all the necessary system programs are available you will be able to run your program.

RT171   Japanese operations illegal with this RTS

Severity: Fatal

Explanation: You are attempting to do Japanese operations with a non-Japanese Run-Time System, or you have used a Japanese version of your COBOL system to produce code which you are now trying to run using a non-Japanese Run-Time System.

Resolution: You will have to resubmit your program using a non-Japanese Run-Time System, or if you still want your program to perform Japanese operations then you will have to acquire a Japanese Run-Time system.

RT172   Recursive non-MF PERFORM is illegal

Severity: Fatal

Explanation: You have tried full recursion of a PERFORM
                   statement in a program that was submitted to
                   your COBOL system with the OSVS
                   parameter of the PERFORM-TYPE directive
                   specified. That is, you have attempted to end
                   two PERFORMs with the same return
                   address.

Resolution: You should either resubmit your program to
                   your COBOL system with a parameter other
                   than OSVS specified for the PERFORM-TYPE
                   directive, or recode your program so that each
                   PERFORM has its own unique return address
                   before you resubmit it to your COBOL system
                   with the MF parameter of the PERFORM-
                   TYPE directive specified.

RT173   Called program file not found in drive/ directory

Severity: Fatal

Explanation: You have attempted to call a file which is not
                   present on your current logged-in drive or
                   directory, or in a directory pointed to by the
                   COBDIR environment variable.

Resolution: Once your program has terminated you will
                   need to copy the relevant file into your
                   logged-in drive or directory. If there is not
                   sufficient space available to allow you to do
                   this, then you will have to set the COBDIR
                   environment variable to search the directory
                   or drive on which the file is present when
                   your program calls it. Refer to your
                   Operating Guide for details of the COBDIR
                   environment variable. Once you have taken
                   these steps, run your program again.

RT175   Attempt to run intermediate code program which had severe errors in it

Severity: Fatal

Explanation: You are attempting to run a program that produced severe faults when you submitted it to your COBOL system with the run-time switch E turned off.

Resolution: You should edit your source code to correct all the severe faults, resubmit to your COBOL system, then run the intermediate code that is produced. Note that when your program is being animated, ANIMATOR will report this error and will allow you to continue to run the program.

RT176   Illegal inter segment reference

Severity: Fatal

Explanation: You may have a corrupted file. Alternatively, your code contains a segment reference for the Forward Reference Table which is illegal.

Resolution: Resubmit your source code to your COBOL system. If you receive this error again, contact Technical Support who will try to help you to discover the specific cause of the error.

RT177   Attempt to cancel active program

Severity: Fatal

Explanation: You have tried to remove a currently executing program or its parents or grandparents, from memory.

Error Messages

Resolution: Once your program has terminated you will need to recode your program to ensure that you do not attempt to cancel a program (or its parents or grandparents) while it is still being executed.

RT178   Error during save

Severity: Fatal

Explanation: You cannot save the information which your program has generated. This can be caused by several different reasons but one of the most common causes is that you have attempted to BUILD a module that is too large for the available memory space.

Resolution: If the error is caused by a lack of space you can either delete some of the files which you no longer need on your current disk, or insert a new floppy disk to take the output from your program. You should then be able to rerun your program and save the information given by it.

RT179   Error during chain

Severity: Program not found

Explanation: You have tried to chain to another program which your system is unable to find.

Resolution: Once your program has terminated you will need to copy the relevant file into your logged-in drive or directory. If there is not sufficient space available to allow you to do this, then you will have to set the COBDIR environment variable to search the directory or drive on which the file is present when your program calls it. Refer to your Operating Guide for details of the COBDIR

environment variable. Once you have taken
these steps, run your program again.

RT180   End-of-file marker error

Severity: Fatal

Explanation: A file-marker used to indicate that the end-of-
                     file has been reached is missing from one of
                     your files.

Resolution: You will need to resubmit your code to your
                     COBOL system, or use a debugger to place
                     the end-of-file marker at the end of the file.
                     You can then rerun your program.

RT181   Invalid parameter error

Severity: Fatal

Explanation: A parameter which you have used is not one
                     which is recognized by your system. You
                     have probably used a parameter for a Run-
                     Time System subprogram which is not within
                     the first 64K of the Data Division.

Resolution: Amend your code to contain a parameter
                     which is known by your system. That is,
                     ensure that the parameter is within the first
                     64K of the Data Division.

RT182   Console Input or Console Output open in wrong direction

Severity: Fatal

Explanation: You are either trying to READ input from the
                     screen or WRITE to the keyboard.

Resolution: You will have to recode your program.

Error Messages

RT183   Attempt to open line-sequential file for I-O

Severity: Fatal

Explanation: You have tried to open a line-sequential file in the input-output open mode, but this mode is not supported for files with this organization.

Resolution: When your program has terminated you will have to recode your program to ensure that the file with organization line sequential is opened for input, output, or extend. You will then be able to rerun your code.

RT184   ACCEPT/DISPLAY I-O error

Severity: Fatal

Explanation: You have either tried to READ input from the screen or WRITE to the keyboard, or the ADIS module has not been able to open your terminal's channels for I-O.

Resolution: Your program contains an error in its logic so you will need to recode.

RT187   Run-Time System not found on $COBDIR path

Severity: Fatal

Explanation: The Run-Time System cannot be found on the path you have set up in the COBDIR environment variable. Alternatively, you may not have installed your COBOL system correctly.

Resolution: Ensure that the Run-Time System is on the path you have set up in the COBDIR environment variable. Alternatively, ensure that your COBOL system has been installed correctly. If it has not, you must reinstall your COBOL system, using the information given on installing your software in your Release Notes.

RT188   File name too large

Severity: Fatal

Explanation: A file name which you have used has more characters than the maximum number allowed by your operating system.

Resolution: Once your program has terminated you will need to recode your program, renaming the offending file with a shorter file name. You will then be able to run your program again.

RT189   Intermediate code load error

Severity: Fatal

Explanation: You are unable to load your intermediate code. You could receive this error if you attempt to load intermediate code that either has not been successfully produced, or has been corrupted in some way.

Resolution: Try to obtain good intermediate code, for example, by resubmitting (or submitting) your source code to your COBOL system. You should then be able to load your code and run the program successfully.

RT190   Too many arguments to CALL

Severity: Fatal

Explanation: A CALL within your program cannot be
                       successfully executed because of the number
                       of arguments which you have used with it.

Resolution: When your program has terminated you can
                       recode it using group items rather than
                       elementary ones. You should then be able to
                       run your program successfully.

RT191   Terminal type not defined

Severity: Fatal

Explanation: Your terminal is not defined in: the termcap
                       file in COBDIR, or the terminfo database, or
                       the cobcap file(depending on your
                       environment). Your operating system is
                       therefore unable to drive your terminal as it
                       has no environment specification for it.

Resolution: Set up the necessary environment for your
                       terminal.

RT192   Required terminal capability description
            missing

Severity: Fatal

Explanation: A compulsory entry, for example cursor
                       movement or clear screen, is missing from
                       your terminal configuration database
                       ("termdesc" or "termcap").

Resolution: Add the missing entry to your terminal
                       configuration database ("termdesc" or
                       "termcap").

RT193   Error in variable length count

Severity:	Fatal
Explanation:	The intermediate code which is currently being processed is not a valid operation. You are probably trying to execute a corrupt file or one which has not been produced.
Resolution:	You will have to resubmit your source code to your COBOL system.

RT194   File size too large

Severity:	Fatal
Explanation:	A file which your program is accessing is too large for successful execution to continue.
Resolution:	When your program has terminated you should recode your program spreading the data over more than one file to ensure that no file becomes too large for your operating system to handle. Having recoded your program you can then rerun it.

RT195   DELETE/REWRITE not preceded by a read

Severity:	Fatal
Explanation:	Before a DELETE or a REWRITE statement can be successfully executed in sequential access mode the last input-output statement executed for the associated file must have been a successful READ. In your code no READ statement precedes your attempted DELETE or REWRITE.

Error Messages

Resolution: When your program has terminated recode your program making sure that the last input-output statement to be executed before the DELETE or REWRITE is a READ statement.

RT196   Record number too large in relative or indexed file

Severity: Fatal

Explanation: The relative record key has exceeded the system limit, that is, the file is too large for the system to handle.

Resolution: Alternatively, the record key which you have specified is too large for the system to deal with successfully, or the pointer to the record has been corrupted in some way so that it is either too large or it is not a multiple of the record length.

RT197   Screen handling system initialization error

Severity: Fatal

Explanation: This error may be caused by one of the following:

- your display adapter is in the wrong mode

- your screen handling interface has not been correctly initialized because your terminal does not have the required capabilities

- memory has been incorrectly allocated.

Resolution: If you are using a DOS or OS/2 system, the monitor must be in alphanumeric display mode rather than graphics display mode. You can set the display mode to a valid alphanumeric mode by using the DOS MODE utility and then rerunning your program. If your memory has been incorrectly allocated, you must rerun your program.

RT198   Load failure

Severity: Fatal

Explanation: The system cannot load a program, usually because there is insufficient memory.

Resolution: Rerun your program having made more memory available.

RT199   Operating system error out of defined range

Severity: Fatal

Explanation: A system call has returned an unexpected error number which is not documented.

Resolution: Contact Technical Support who will try to help you to discover the specific cause of this error.

RT200   Run-Time system internal logic error

Severity: Fatal

Explanation: You can receive this error if the amount of memory available on your machine is so low that not even the Run-Time System can be fully loaded properly. In this case you will have to free some memory and then you should be able to run your program successfully.

Resolution: However, the most common cause of this error is that your Run-Time System has halted as a result of an internal logic error from which you cannot recover. If this is the case, you will need to contact Technical Support who will try to help you to discover the cause of the error.

RT201   I-O error in paging system

Severity: Fatal

Explanation: There is no room available in your current directory or on the floppy disk which you are using, for the paging file.

Resolution: When your program has terminated, delete some files which you no longer need in your directory to make room for the paging file or insert a new floppy disk.

RT202   Exported functionality error

Severity: Fatal

Explanation: You have either caused an internal Run-Time System error by invalid use of an exported function, or the code produced by a preprocessor within your COBOL system contains errors.

Resolution: Ensure that all of your external assembler applications call and use Run-Time System functions correctly before you attempt to run your program again. If you are using a preprocessor as part of your COBOL system, you should use the software as a standalone preprocessor to isolate the problem areas.

RT203   CALL parameter not supplied

Severity: Fatal

Explanation: You have not supplied your currently
                     executing program with all of the parameters
                     mentioned in the linkage section of your main
                     program.

Resolution: Recode your program to ensure that it
                     contains all of the necessary parameters, or
                     check that it is a valid caller.

RT206   Reading unwritten data from memory file

Severity: Fatal

Explanation: You are attempting to read data which has
                     not been written, from the core file.

RT207   Machine does not exist

Severity: Recoverable

Explanation: You have tried to access a machine that is not
                     connected to your network, or if the machine
                     is part of your network, it is not online.

Resolution: Make sure the machine is connected to the
                     network and online, then attempt to access it
                     again.

RT208   Error in multi-user system

Severity: Recoverable

Explanation: This is normally caused by an unexpected
                     error occurring within the network or file-
                     sharing facilities. A corrupted network
                     message will also return this error.

Error Messages

Resolution: You may be able to recover from this error by
                   executing a COMMIT statement.

RT209   Network communication error

Severity: Recoverable

Explanation: This is normally given if an incorrect
                   checksum has been received in a
                   communications packet.

Resolution: Your program should continue to execute
                   after you have received this error but the
                   effect of the error is undefined.

RT210   File is closed with lock

Severity: Fatal

Explanation: You have tried to open a file which you have
                   previously closed with lock.

Resolution: Recode your program to avoid opening a file
                   which has previously been closed with lock.

RT211   Program linked with wrong library

Severity: Fatal

Explanation: You have tried to link a program that is
                   incompatible with the current version of
                   either your Run-Time System, your object file
                   or your COBOL run-time library. For
                   example, your Run-Time System will not run
                   a program linked using a different object file
                   format or COBOL run-time library.

Resolution: If your object file is incompatible with the
                   current version of either your COBOL run-
                   time library or your Run-Time System, you

will need to resubmit your object file to your COBOL system, and then relink with the current version of your COBOL run-time library. Otherwise, you will just need to relink your program.

RT212   Malformed assembler subroutine file

Severity: Fatal

Explanation: You are attempting to access an assembler routine that is not in the specific format for such a file.

Resolution: Examine the example assembler routine which was supplied to you with your system and alter the structure of your routine to be the same as this. Ensure that it is linked properly, it has the correct structure, and you used the right assembler. You should then be able to run your code successfully.

RT213   Too many locks

Severity: Recoverable

Explanation: You have either tried to exceed the maximum number of simultaneous record locks per file you can have, or you have exhausted an operating system or network resource, for example dynamic memory.

Resolution: Execute a COMMIT or an UNLOCK operation on the relevant file and you should then be able to continue to run your program. You should not try to retain a record lock for longer than it is necessary, and this should help to prevent the occurrence of this error.

Error Messages

RT214   GO TO has not been ALTERed

Severity: Fatal

Explanation: You have violated one of the general rules of
                     COBOL programming.

Resolution: CLOSE any files which may be OPEN,
                     execute a STOP RUN statement and then edit
                     your program to avoid such illegal
                     operations.

RT218   Malformed MULTIPLE REEL/UNIT file

Severity: Fatal

Explanation: Your file header is not correctly formatted, or
                     you are not using a MULTIPLE REEL/UNIT
                     file.

Resolution: You will have to attempt to run your program
                     again using a backup copy of the relevant file.

RT219   Operating system shared file limit
            exceeded

Severity: Recoverable

Explanation: You have tried to exceed your operating
                     system's limit on the number of shared files
                     that you can have OPEN simultaneously. As
                     this figure is operating system dependent,
                     you will need to consult your Release Notes
                     for details of how many shared files your
                     system permits to be OPEN at any one time.

Resolution: CLOSE some of the open shared files you are
                     no longer accessing and retry the file
                     operation.

RT220   Attempt to execute more than one SORT or MERGE simultaneously

Severity:	Fatal
Explanation:	You have coded your program in such a way that it is attempting to execute more than one SORT or MERGE operation at the same time. For example, you may have coded a SORT statement in the input or output procedure of another SORT statement, an operation that is specifically prohibited under the rules of ANSI COBOL.
Resolution:	You will have to recode your program to ensure that it does not execute more than one SORT at any one time.

RT221   SORT/MERGE error: see status key

Severity:	Fatal
Explanation:	You receive one of these three errors if you attempt a SORT/MERGE operation which is unsuccessful for some reason. These errors can result from a variety of causes; for example, you may have too many files OPEN when you attempt a SORT/MERGE operation, or the file which you are trying to access may be locked.
Resolution:	The action you should take if you receive one of these errors depends on the situation in which it occurs.

RT222   SORT/MERGE error: see status key

Severity:	Fatal
Explanation:	You receive one of these three errors if you attempt a SORT/MEGE operation which is unsuccessful for some reason. These errors can result from a variety of causes; for

example, you may have too many files OPEN when you attempt a SORT/MERGE operation, or the file which you are trying to access may be locked.

Resolution: The action you should take if you receive one of these errors depends on the situation in which it occurs.

RT223   SORT/MEGE error: see status key

Severity: Fatal

Explanation: You receive one of these three errors if you attempt a SORT/MEGE operation which is unsuccessful for some reason. These errors can result from a variety of causes; for example, you may have too many files OPEN when you attempt a SORT/MERGE operation, or the file which you are trying to access may be locked.

Resolution: The action you should take if you receive one of these errors depends on the situation in which it occurs.

RT225   Program Component not found

Severity: Fatal

Explanation: You are attempting to load a program overlay which is not present in the expected directory. Alternatively, a program component which was previously located can no longer be found because it has been deleted or the application has changed to a different directory.

Resolution: Ensure that the program files are always readily available.

RT226   EXTERNAL file definition inconsistent

Severity: Fatal

Explanation: The definition of an EXTERNAL file
                contained in the program being loaded is
                inconsistent with its definition in a previously
                loaded program.

RT254   Keyboard interrupt to ANIMATOR during ACCEPT

Severity: Fatal

Explanation: While using ANIMATOR you have
                terminated your program with a keyboard
                interrupt.

Error Messages

For Further Reference

The COBOL 85 Example Book by Jerome Garfunkle, (Micro Focus Publishing, 1994). Available early 1994.

Micro Focus COBOL Language Reference Manual by Micro Focus Products Group (Micro Focus Publishing, Palo Alto, 1993).

Using Micro Focus Personal COBOL by Dr. Mark W. Smith and Doug Coker (Business and Educational Technologies, William C. Brown Company, Dubuque, 1994).

Getting Started with Micro Focus COBOL by Dr. John Crawford (John Wiley & Sons, New York, 1994).

Programming Language - COBOL (FIPS 21-3), American National Standards Institute, 1985.
May be obtained under reference number X3.23-1985, from ANSI Sales, 11 West 42nd St., New York, NY 10036.
(212) 642-4900

Index

Index

Index

MICRO FOCUS PERSONAL COBOL
END USER SOFTWARE LICENSE AGREEMENT

IMPORTANT: YOU SHOULD CAREFULLY READ THIS LEGAL AGREEMENT. BY INSTALLING AND USING THE SOFTWARE, YOU ACCEPT ALL THE TERMS AND CONDITIONS OF THIS AGREEMENT AND AGREE TO ABIDE BY THEM. IF THESE TERMS AND CONDITIONS ARE NOT ACCEPTABLE TO YOU, DO NOT INSTALL OR USE THE SOFTWARE, BUT RETURN IT UNUSED TO MICRO FOCUS OR YOUR VENDOR AND YOUR MONEY WILL BE REFUNDED.

Scope of Agreement. This Agreement covers, and the "Software" includes, the computer programs enclosed in this package, their accompanying user documentation, and any related computer programs, documentation and information provided by Micro Focus Incorporated ("Micro Focus") as part of the Micro Focus Personal COBOL package.

License. Micro Focus grants to you a nonexclusive, nontransferable license to use the Software in object code form on one "Computer System". The Computer System must be a single user computer. Any shared use of the Software on a local area network or multi-user system is not permitted under this License. Please contact a Micro Focus Publishing representative for information on alternative forms of licensing. You agree not to attempt to modify, reverse engineer, reverse compile, or disassemble the object code for the Software.

Warranty for Recording Medium. Micro Focus will repair or replace free of charge any defective recording medium on which the Software is recorded if the medium is returned to Micro Focus by you within ninety (90) days after purchase. This warranty does not cover defects due to accident, abuse, service or modification by any unauthorized person, or any cause occurring after initial delivery of the medium to you. ALL IMPLIED WARRANTIES WITH RESPECT TO THE RECORDING MEDIUM, INCLUDING THE IMPLIED WARRANTIES OF MERCHANTABILITY AND FITNESS FOR A PARTICULAR PURPOSE, ARE LIMITED IN DURATION TO NINETY (90) DAYS FROM THE DATE OF RETAIL PURCHASE.

Procedure for Returning Media. Defective media may be mailed to Micro Focus Publishing, ATTN: Media Returns, 2465 East Bayshore Road, Palo Alto, CA, 94303, U.S.A. Postage must be prepaid.

Warranty for Software. MICRO FOCUS SOFTWARE IS LICENSED ON AN "AS IS" BASIS. MICRO FOCUS DISCLAIMS ALL IMPLIED WARRANTIES, INCLUDING WARRANTIES OF MERCHANTABILITY AND FITNESS FOR A PARTICULAR PURPOSE. MICRO FOCUS MAKES NO REPRESENTATIONS CONCERNING THE QUALITY OF THE SOFTWARE AND DOES NOT PROMISE THAT THE SOFTWARE WILL BE ERROR FREE OR WILL OPERATE WITHOUT INTERRUPTION.

Limitation of Liability. IN NO EVENT WILL MICRO FOCUS BE LIABLE FOR ANY INDIRECT, INCIDENTAL, SPECIAL, CONSEQUENTIAL OR OTHER DAMAGES ARISING OUT OF THE USE OF THE RECORDING MEDIUM OR THE SOFTWARE BY ANY PERSON, WHETHER OR NOT INFORMED OF THE POSSIBILITIES OF DAMAGES IN ADVANCE. MICRO FOCUS' TOTAL LIABILITY WITH RESPECT TO ALL CAUSES OF ACTION TOGETHER WILL NOT EXCEED AMOUNTS PAID BY YOU FOR THE SOFTWARE. THESE LIMITATIONS APPLY TO ALL CAUSES OF ACTION, INCLUDING BREACH OF CONTRACT, BREACH OF WARRANTY, NEGLIGENCE, STRICT LIABILITY, MISREPRESENTATION AND OTHER TORTS. SOME JURISDICTIONS DO NOT ALLOW THE EXCLUSION OR LIMITATION OF INCIDENTAL OR CONSEQUENTIAL DAMAGES SO THE ABOVE LIMITATION OR EXCLUSION MAY NOT APPLY TO YOU.

Ownership of Software. Micro Focus and its suppliers have and will retain all ownership rights to the Software, including all patent rights, copyrights, trademarks, service marks, related goodwill and confidential and proprietary information. You have no rights in the Software except as explicitly stated in this Agreement.

Use by Government. Use, duplication, or disclosure by the Government is subject to restrictions as set forth in subparagraph (c)(1)(ii) of the Rights in Technical Data and Computer Software clause at DFARS 252.227-7013 or subparagraph (c)(1) and (2) of the Commercial Computer Software-Restricted Rights at 48 CFR 52.227-19 as applicable. Contact Micro Focus, 2465 E. Bayshore Road, Palo Alto, California 94303.

Assignment and Delegation. You may not assign this Agreement or any rights under it and may not delegate any duties under this Agreement without Micro Focus' prior written consent. Any attempt to assign or delegate without that consent will be void.

Exclusive Agreement. THIS AGREEMENT IS THE COMPLETE AND EXCLUSIVE STATEMENT OF AGREEMENT BETWEEN THE PARTIES AND SUPERSEDES ALL PROPOSALS, COMMUNICATIONS, PURCHASE ORDERS AND PRIOR AGREEMENTS, VERBAL OR WRITTEN, BETWEEN THE PARTIES. THIS AGREEMENT IS GOVERNED BY THE LAWS OF THE STATE OF CALIFORNIA.

Create Powerful Commercial Applications with these Micro Focus Products

Micro Focus COBOL

A complete compiler product for developers. Micro Focus COBOL is IBM's AD/Cycle™ COBOL for the workstation platform and is available on DOS, OS/2 and major UNIX environments. It supports the highest level of ANSI standard COBOL, with many other syntax variants, including those of IBM's mainframe COBOL compilers.

Micro Focus COBOL has the power to create new applications in a PC/network environment, with Graphical User Interface (GUI) and file handling options, including the use of SQL, to downsize applications from PC-based mainframes and to develop applications which are portable across many platforms.

Product Highlights

- Animator -- visual debugging tool
- Source and object portability for DOS, OS/2, UNIX and AIX
- ANSI, SAA™, X/Open™ COBOL and more
- Mainframe power on the workstation
- 32-bit architecture and performance
- Programming for GUIs -- Windows, PM
- SQL and file handling support
- Application distribution for DOS, Windows and OS/2

Micro Focus Toolset

Micro Focus Toolset™ is a collection of programmer productivity aids and utilities distributed as an add-on product to Micro Focus COBOL. It provides programmers with the tools necessary to develop industrial strength COBOL applications quickly and efficiently.

Product Highlights

- Dynamic loading and memory management
- Portable code generation
- Program and text editor
- Mixed language debugging utility
- Report design and generation utility
- Many other tools and technologies
- Bundled copy of Micro Focus OSX

Contact your Micro Focus office or Authorized Micro Focus Distributor for more information on these products.

Micro Focus Professional COBOL

Combines the facilities of Toolset and OSX with the power of Micro Focus COBOL in a single, function key driven, integrated environment. It provides programmers with the tools necessary to develop industrial-strength COBOL applications quickly and easily. Professional COBOL is especially useful for developing portable applications and applications designed for use on a network.

Product Highlights

- Micro Focus COBOL, Toolset and OSX in one package
- Integrated development environment
- Program and text editor
- Run Time Environment
- Network file sharing
- Portable GUI support
- Common communications Interface
- Application installation and integration tools

Micro Focus COBOL Workbench

Micro Focus COBOL Workbench® is an integrated collection of programming productivity tools containing and extending all elements of Micro Focus COBOL, Toolset and OSX. Workbench binds these tools together in an Advanced Integrated Environment to support the development of applications for multiple target platforms including MVS, VM, DOS/VS(E), DOS, Windows, OS/2 and UNIX.

Workbench logically groups components for PC and mainframe development. Separate menu systems, designed for the different requirements of PC and mainframe programming, present the components to the programmer in an organized manner.

Workbench provides the tools necessary for offloading mainframe development in the form of EBCDIC support, file transfer support, and mainframe to PC file conversion. Workbench can be combined with other Micro Focus products to address CICS, IMS, 370 Assembler and DB2 development.

Product Highlights

- Mainframe development support
- PC development support
- Advanced visual productivity tools
- Structure analysis
- Change/impact analysis
- File maintenance, conversion and transfer
- Regression testing
- Performance tuning
- CUA style graphical interface
- AD/Cycle Level/2 integration

Contact your Micro Focus office or Authorized Micro Focus Distributor for more information on these products.

Use These Workbench Add-On Products to Tailor Your Development Environment

Micro Focus ADMVS

Micro Focus ADMVS™ is a quick start development environment for developing applications that are targeted for execution under MVS, and provides a set of tools and facilities under OS/2 and DOS that are familiar to MVSA developers. Panels that resemble TSO/ISPF/PDF panels seamlessly integrate the Micro Focus COBOL compiler and Advanced Animator® with an SPF-like source editor, MVS JCL and PROC execution facilities, commonly used MVS utilities, and an ISPF Dialog Manager.™

Product Highlights

- TSO/ISPF/PDF for OS/2 and DOS
- COBOL and Animator Integration
- Integrate Add-on Products -- DB2, IMS, CICS, Assembler
- File Management using MVS DSNs
- MVS JCL Execution and PROCs
- MVS Utilities, SORT and IDCAMS
- Panel Definition Facilities
- Dialog Manager Emulation

Micro Focus CICS Option

The Micro Focus CICS Option™ is a complete PC-based CICS emulation, load and go, user-friendly system for DOS and OS/2. It has a high level of support for the CICS API (Application Programming Interface), an integrated menu driven development environment, easy to update resource tables and support for a variety of database access methods including DL/I, IBM Database Manager and XDB™ for DB2 emulation. 3270 screen emulation is complete with full BMS support and screen painters to automatically generate the required BMS macros for use in PC or host environments. Micro Focus CICS Option requires Micro Focus COBOL Workbench v2.5 or later.

Product Highlights

- Complete CICS emulation system for DOS and OS/2, with ASCII and EBCDIC options
- Integration with Workbench development tool
- Fully Integrated CICS BMS screen painting
- Full data support including VSAM, DB2 (XDB), DLI - IMS/DB (Micro Focus IMS Option), OS/2 DBM, Micro Focus Host Compatibility Option (HCO) and Fileshare

Contact your Micro Focus office or Authorized Micro Focus Distributor for more information on these products.

Micro Focus CICS OS/2 Option

The Micro Focus CICS OS/2 Option is a complete PC-based CICS development and production system for OS/2. It has a high level of support for the CICS API (Application Programming Interface) and provides communication facilities for connecting to other CICS systems either on the host or on a network supporting a distributed CICS architecture. With CICS OS/2, mainframe based CICS applications can be downloaded to a workstation or network for production, while maintaining a link to the host if required. Micro Focus COBOL is a prerequisite product for the Micro Focus CICS OS/2 Option.

Product Highlights

- Complete CICS system for OS/2 with ASCII support
- Integration with Workbench development tools
- BMS screen painting facilities
- Full data support including VSAM, DB2, DLE - IMS/DB, and OS/2 DBM
- Built-in cooperative processing capabilities
- Download mainframe CICS applications

Micro Focus IMS Option

The IMS Option™ for Micro Focus COBOL Workbench is an implementation of mainframe IMS for the workstation. It enables developers to make dramatic improvements in programming productivity by allowing IMS application development to be performed away from the mainframe system within a dedicated environment.

Product Highlights

- Compatibility with mainframe IMS
- Rapid system generation - DBD, PSB, MFS, ACB Gens
- IMS DB compatibility
- Multi-user sharing of IMS databases
- MFS screen definition and generation
- Integration with Micro Focus Workbench

Contact your Micro Focus office or Authorized Micro Focus Distributor for more information on these products.

Enjoy "A Better Way of Programming" with these Micro Focus Tools

Micro Focus Dialog System

Micro Focus Dialog System™ enables developers to prototype and create graphical and character oriented user interfaces that can be portable across many environments. It separates details of the user interface from the underlying business application logic. The user interface is able to grow and evolve without requiring changes to the program. Dialog System is designed to be used by developers and designers with minimal or no prior knowledge of Graphical User Interface programming APIs. Dialog System is designed for applications that have been created with Micro Focus COBOL or Microsoft COBOL v4.0 or later. Developers need Micro Focus COBOL in order to build and link the complete application together with the Dialog System run time library.

Product Highlights

- User interface independent of business logic
- WYSIWYG development facilities
- Graphical and character modes
- Client/server applications architecture
- IBM AD/Cycle product - supports CUA
- Supports DOS, OS/2, Windows UNIX, and AIX
- Graphical emulation under DOS, OS/2 character mode

Micro Focus 370 Assembler with ANIMATOR/370

Micro Focus 370 Assembler with ANIMATOR/370™ provides the mainframe programmer with the ability to support COBOL programs containing dynamic calls to Assembler subroutines on a PC. 370 Assembler programs can be compiled, linked and tested completely independent of the mainframe. Micro Focus 370 Assembler with ANIMATOR/370 offers a new full-screen, source oriented analysis tool and interactive debugging facility that will make the development and maintenance of 370 Assembler applications on PCs more productive than ever.

Product Highlights

- Full BAL compatibility and support
- ANIMATOR/370 - source oriented analysis tool and interactive debugging facility
- Probe utility
- On-screen DUMP Facility
- Pop-up Hex Adder/Converter
- 370 production only environment

Contact your Micr Focus office or Authorized Micro Focus Distributor for more information on these products.

For more information on these Micro Focus products...

contact the Micro Focus office or Authorized Micro Focus Distributor in your area.

Micro Focus Offices

Micro Focus Inc.
United States
Tel: (800) 872-6265

Two locations:
2465 East Bayshore Road
Palo Alto, CA 94303
Tel: (415) 856- 4161
Fax: (415) 856-6134
Telex: 278704 MFCIS UR

1000 First Ave., 3rd Floor
King of Prussia, PA 19406-1310
Tel: (215) 992-3400
Fax: (215) 992-3700

Micro Focus Limited
26 West Street
Newbury
Berkshire RG13 1JT
United Kingdom
Tel: (635) 32646
Fax: (635) 33966
Telex: 848046 MICROF G

Micro Focus GmbH
Am Moosfeld 11
D-81829 München 82
Germany
Tel: (89) 42094-0
Fax: (89) 42094-211

Micro Focus Japan (KK)
Mitsui Nishi Azabu Bldg. 4F
Nishi Azabu 4-17-30
Minato-ku, Tokyo 106
Japan
Tel: (3) 3486-7791
Fax: (3) 3486-5055

Micro Focus SARL (Paris)
Les Algorithmes
Batiment Epicure, St. Aubin
91194 Gif-Sur-Yvette Cedex
France
Tel: (1) 6941-3362
Fax: (1) 6941-2787

Micro Focus Barcelona
Josep Tarradellas, 15 E-1
08029 Barcelona
Spain
Tel: (34) 3-410-0405
Fax: (34) 3-410-0518

■ ■

For the number of your nearest Micro Focus Authorized Distributor, contact Micro Focus Publishing. Tel: 1-800-551-5269 or 1-415-856-4161. FAX 1-415-496-7188.